BORDERLANDS OF THEOLOGY
AND OTHER ESSAYS

BORDERLANDS OF THEOLOGY
AND OTHER ESSAYS

by
DONALD M. MACKINNON
*Norris-Hulse Professor of Divinity in the University of Cambridge
and Fellow of Corpus Christi College*

Edited and Introduced by
GEORGE W. ROBERTS
Associate Professor of Philosophy in the University of Kansas
and
DONOVAN E. SMUCKER
President of Mary Holmes College, Mississippi

*Bob Havenlick
New York*

J. B. LIPPINCOTT COMPANY
Philadelphia and New York

*1/4/74
Strand
28 Broadway Ave*

Library of Congress Catalog Card No : 68-24741

Printed in Great Britain

CONTENTS

CONTENTS

PART III

METAPHYSICS AND EPISTEMOLOGY

EDITORS' INTRODUCTION

IN THE ESSAYS collected in this volume Professor MacKinnon discusses a great variety of theological, philosophical, moral and political topics. It is part of his accomplishment that he is able to deal with such a remarkable range of topics in a first-hand and authoritative way. But if these diverse efforts, however remarkable, were not connected there would perhaps be little justification for presenting them in a single volume. The fact is, however, that they are connected. Professor Mac-Kinnon does something to bring out their connections with one another in his introductory essay. Indeed it will be obvious that despite their diverse topics they are connected, both in content and in manner, to a very considerable degree. In this introduction we wish mainly to underline some features of the *manner* of Professor MacKinnon's thought, which he does not adumbrate in his introductory essay, but which seem to us to connect his efforts in different fields and to endow those efforts with some of their characteristic opportunities and dangers. But we will also make some remarks on the continuing relevance of Professor MacKinnon's essays to the fields he discusses, and on the problems that underlie the further development of his thought.

Professor MacKinnon's thought is in many ways, in several senses reflective, meditative, dialectical, concrete. We do not mean that he does not often concern himself with very general, very abstract questions. On the contrary, some of his most characteristic efforts have been made in connection with questions that are, on the face of it at least, of an extremely remote, abstract, philosophical character. He has, moreover, never been averse to the consideration and use of the technical terminologies devised by philosophers and theologians for the

7

discussion of these very general questions in very general terms. At any rate he is far more inclined to use these terminologies, far more convinced that their use will help us make further advances in our philosophical or theological efforts than is, for instance, Professor John Wisdom, to whose work he often alludes and of whom he writes *in extenso* in the review-article on Professor Wisdom's *Paradox and Discovery* we have here reprinted.

In this connection we may remark the profound historical learning Professor MacKinnon brings to bear on all the fields he considers. We may also remark the extent of his indebtedness to traditional philosophers and modes of philosophizing. This indebtedness is selective and critical; he is quick to condemn irrelevance and anachronism. But he clearly owes much to Kant in epistemology and metaphysics and in moral philosophy; in moral philosophy he is also heavily indebted to Butler.

Nevertheless, Professor MacKinnon's thought embodies a movement to the concrete in some respects comparable to, and influenced by, the diverse movements to the concrete found in, and characteristic of, philosophers of the linguistic or analytic school in Great Britain and philosophers of the existential and phenomenological schools on the European continent. This is true despite the fact that the linguistic and existential movements are so often set in polemical opposition. Indeed their several proponents sometimes regard their cross-channel counterparts as hopelessly removed from the sorts of concrete reflection that would alone enable them to deal properly with philosophical difficulties. No doubt the movement to the concrete that is so characteristic of twentieth century thought is at times an extremely equivocal commonplace.

The fact remains that Professor MacKinnon, almost alone in the English-speaking world, indeed almost alone, has tried with considerable success to think in ways that approximate, and that enable him to assimilate and to react to, some of the characteristic concerns, emphases and insights of these opposed movements. But while he has been engaged with these contemporary developments he has also been concerned to assess and to utilize the inheritance of philosophy from, for instance,

Plato and Aristotle, the scholastics, the British empiricists and the idealists. These endeavours have given him some quite considerable advantages as a moral philosopher; he is able, for instance, to bring to bear the insights of Kierkegaard, Buber and Marcel upon the claims of the utilitarians with devastating effect. They have also given him advantages in metaphysics and philosophy of religion. One of these advantages lies in his acquaintance with and profound concern for the positivistic and linguistic critique of speculative metaphysics and theology, which enable him to write on the problem of metaphysics with a wariness and sophistication whose absence in continental authors frequently makes them appear merely dogmatic or naïve.

Yet in neither case is Professor MacKinnon unbalanced by his advantages. If he criticizes utilitarian moral theorists for their disregard of, *inter alia*, the limits set by justice and veracity, he nevertheless recognizes the extent to which, within those limits, we should today all be utilitarians in our social and political calculations. When he expounds the existentialists he does not indulge in facile invidious comparisons of their metaphilosophical sophistication with that found in analytic circles. He concerns himself instead with effecting a proper appreciation of their substantive philosophical accomplishments.

Analagous remarks can be made about Professor MacKinnon's relations to historical and contemporary developments in theology. It is not perhaps so unusual for a theologian to plumb at once the depths of continental theologians like Barth and von Balthasar, and at the same time to continue the reflections of Forsyth, Scott Holland, or Dodd. Still it seems to us that the degree of Professor MacKinnon's combined involvement with these theological traditions is unique. Certainly he is uniquely well placed to consider the relations of these developments in theology to speculative philosophy, epistemology, and the philosophy of religion.

These considerations are far from irrelevant to the ways in which Professor MacKinnon carries us to the concrete. But they do not sufficiently illuminate one way he does so, which gives rise to some of the most distinctive features of his thought.

It is characteristic of analytic philosophy to lay great stress on the distinctions between the different levels and types of thought that pertain to any given subject-matter or set of problems. It is, for instance, now usual for analytic moral philosophers to distinguish sharply between substantive ethical questions and meta-ethical questions, that is questions about the nature of ethical questions of the first order. Sometimes it is allowed that perfectly general and fundamental ethical questions, questions of ethical principle, are of a peculiarly reflective character as contrasted with other substantive ethical questions. It may then be allowed that such questions of principle are, as other first-order ethical questions are not, in a certain sense philosophical questions. But questions of ethical principle are still sharply distinguished from questions addressed to the general nature of ethical discourse. It is also usual for analytic moral philosophers to distinguish, though often with less certainty, ethical and even meta-ethical questions from questions in moral psychology and in metaphysics. It is usual for these philosophers to insist that questions of these different sorts should be treated separately or at least in such a way that they do not become confused, in such a way that we do not begin to suppose that answers to questions of one of these types will include answers to questions of another.

Professor MacKinnon does not write without attention to such distinctions, whether in moral philosophy or elsewhere. In the essays collected here, and in other places, for instance in his *A Study in Ethical Theory*,[1] he gives distinctions of the sort mentioned careful, if not always conventional, consideration. But he does not treat questions of these different sorts in isolation, nor does he regard them as mutually irrelevant to the degree that they are widely thought to be by analytic moral philosophers.

He has noticed and he seeks further to explore the extent to, and the ways in which discussions of these quite different types sometimes overlap and inter-penetrate, echo and influence one another. It has struck him how even such an abstract, purely analytic, doctrine as Moore's view that good is a simple,

[1] A. and C. Black, 1957.

indefinable, non-natural quality, may lend a certain colour to consideration of the most particular ethical questions, and by affecting the aspect of those questions for those who reflect on them may alter the outcome of their reflections and influence the actions based on them.[1] It has also struck him that the declarations of inevitability with which men's responses to the realities of the nuclear age are studded, have an affinity with those philosophical arguments about freewill and determinism by which, in a sphere remote from practice, attempts are made to undermine our notions of the responsibility we have for our actions.

These and similar observations have, we believe, in part been made possible for Professor MacKinnon by his concrete approach to moral philosophy. Undoubtedly we all begin *in media res*, confronted by and engaged on a vast variety of particular first-order ethical questions, and sometimes meet with or arrive at questions that pertain to ethics in other ways, all too confusingly related to the particular ethical questions with which we began. The impulse to distinguish the different sorts of questions that mingle in and intersect with our practical deliberations is a natural one. The difficulty is that we hardly begin to make the necessary distinctions, when we begin to feel we may be left, having made them, with the *disjecta membra* of the moral life. It is easy to be overcome by this feeling and to turn back, with little but scorn for our efforts at distinction, to the realities of practical life. It is also easy to ignore it, or to flout it, and to press on to the extreme reached by those moral philosophers who forever proudly proclaim the purity of their analytic efforts, unrelated altogether to questions of concrete ethical concern. It is easy, too, to pretend to meet this difficulty by an account of the different sorts of ethical question that does little but present vulgar confusions in fancy dress. Alternatively, the meta-ethicist may take to serving an exceedingly thin gruel in the philosophical soup-kitchens.

[1] Professor MacKinnon has discussed Moore's doctrines and their practical influence in this and in other respects in his *A Study in Ethical Theory*, largely in relation to the reflections of J. M. Keynes on Moore's influence in "My Early Beliefs" (in *Two Memoirs*, Rupert Hart-Davis, 1949).

Professor MacKinnon avoids these unfortunate reactions to philosophical reflection on moral and political matters. He continues to press on our attention the differences of level that emerge in ethical reflection, even while he works to improve our grasp and deepen our understanding of the sorts of connection that exist between types of ethical reflection in some ways extremely remote from one another. He finds himself reflecting on questions of direct practical importance, and as he continues his reflections he finds himself naturally led on to levels of thought quite different from, though still related to those with which he began. He delineates with great sensitivity the affinities and conflicts that arise within and between these different levels of thought. Among the conflicts he considers is that between his own style of deepened reflection on concrete ethical questions, and the thought of those whose concern for the distinctions of type within ethical reflection has led them to deny or neglect some of the connections and resonances of the different types. Professor MacKinnon would allow that the distinctions as well as the affinities among particular ethical questions, questions of general ethical principle, meta-ethical questions, questions in moral psychology, and questions in metaphysics should be brought out as fully as possible. But he would insist that even these efforts might serve to improve the quality of our reflections on all levels, including the most concrete, and not only on the level of meta-ethical philosophy.

The same mode of consideration in the concrete, in the sense that the affinities and relevance to first-order, particular questions are continually sought, even while we pursue the more general and the higher-order questions to which we are naturally led in the development of our reflections on them, characterizes Professor MacKinnon's thought on non-ethical subjects as well.

It is part of the business of any philosopher to compare and to contrast, to show the connections and want of connections between different types of problem and subject-matter. Accordingly, if a philosopher is to do all that he might, he will have to consider the relations and the differences between those subjects and problems that are most remote from one another, as well as those that are most closely connected. It is partly for these reasons that Professor MacKinnon's essays on almost any topic are full of references to other topics, even some quite different topics.

But this is not, by itself, a sufficient explanation of the degree to which this is true of Professor MacKinnon's thought. Again we submit that his concern to reflect the full range of considerations to which our efforts to meet problems will on occasion naturally lead us, affords part of the explanation of this feature of his thought. The same habit of consideration *in concreto* encourages him to relate discussions of problems in theology, for instance, to the circumstances in which those discussions took place and by which their forms and development were influenced. He carries this line of thought further by suggesting that it also applies to those who make use of it. In this way he at once takes to the limit and indicates the limitations of such circumstantial considerations.

As for the relevance of these essays to present-day thought and problems in the fields discussed, we think enough is said in the essays themselves and in Professor MacKinnon's introductory essay to make that relevance plain enough in most cases. But there is at least one matter on which something more might be said. That matter is raised by the essay on "Verifiability", which was the first paper in a symposium whose other participants were the late Dr F. Waismann and Professor William Kneale.[1] It is also involved in the other essays in this volume in which Professor MacKinnon discusses Kantian epistemological themes, most notably in his essay on Professor P. F. Strawson's *The Bounds of Sense*.

Waismann's symposium paper has received much attention and acclaim, and it is one of the merits of Professor Mac-Kinnon's paper to have provoked it. In it Waismann introduced the notion of *open texture* as a characteristic of some concepts, and used it to argue that material-thing propositions could not be reduced to propositions about sense-impressions. It is not

[1] The symposium on "Verifiability" was presented at the Joint Session of the Aristotelian Society and Mind Association in 1945. The papers may be found in *Proceedings of the Aristotelian Society*, Supplementary Volume XIX (1945), at pp. 101–164.

our intention here to explain or explore further these moves by Waismann, which have been given close scrutiny by many philosophers. What we wish to remark is the way Waismann brushed aside Professor MacKinnon's description of the verificationist doctrine as *evidentialism*, the idea that the meaning of a statement is simply the evidence that could conceivably be produced for it, as irrelevant to the most recent developments of empiricism. Also we should remark how Waismann argued against Professor MacKinnon's suggestion that the notion of causal relatedness is essentially involved in our notion of objective reality.

Waismann was right to think that the conception of levels of language, each distinguished by its own irreducible logic but nevertheless related by meaning to other levels, did represent a novel development in empiricism to which he himself contributed. But Waismann was wrong if he expected that ideas of the sort he thought had been superseded would have no further role in the development of analytic philosophy. In fact the reductive verificationist dogma still has a widespread deep influence on philosophers.

He was also wrong to pay no more attention than he did to Professor MacKinnon's suggestion that certain special concepts, categorial concepts, play a central role both in effecting the evidential relations, and in establishing the logical differences, between different levels of language. In so far as Professor MacKinnon's words might be taken to imply that the concepts of quantum mechanics could be rejected on *a priori* grounds, no doubt Waismann was right to protest at them. All the same he did not give an adequate account of the uses of the notion of cause in discussions of reality. Waismann at times gave the impression that causal notions have a merely historical relation to our notion of reality. But this was surely a mistake; surely causal notions, whether or not they are to be analysed in terms of regular sequence, belong to the central core of notions involved in thought about what is the case.

We believe that Professor MacKinnon's reflections on these topics deserve to be taken seriously, and carried further. One way in which they could be taken further is by consideration of the way causal ideas may crop up in extremely simple cases of reflection on philosophical theories. For instance, when plain men are presented with the idea that nothing, at least no material thing, exists unperceived, they may respond with the lie direct, "How absurd! How can anyone think that the table doesn't exist when no one's in the dining room?" In a word they may respond merely by referring to counter-examples. But they may respond in another way as well. They may say, "You see the porch-roof out the window. But you don't see the pillars that support it. Now if things don't exist unperceived, what's holding the porch-roof up?"[1]

We do not wish to suggest that the idealist philosophers who fathered this preposterous theory would have no "answer"; philosophers always do. But the plain man's response to the idealist doctrine with a causal argument shows nevertheless that causal notions are very closely and fundamentally related to our notion of reality, and are required for any adequate account of the way we distinguish external realities from our perceptions of them. This is a matter that deserves further study by philosophers.

But it is not along these lines, at least not merely along these lines, that Professor MacKinnon would have us consider philosophical difficulties about theology and speculative metaphysics. The verificationist difficulties here do not vanish, though they are transformed, when we have eliminated the reductionist preconceptions that play havoc with the epistemology of common sense. As the debate about these difficulties has advanced, it has become increasingly clear how closely they are related to the older difficulties for religious belief, comprised under the title "the problem of evil". Despite some strictures on this problem, Professor MacKinnon does not deny but acknowledges the relevance of its elements to theology and the philosophy of religion. He does not deny or minimize the reality of evils, physical and moral. He will have no truck with those who do so by declaring these evils to be illusory, by scholastic re-description of them as privations, or by alleging

---

[1] Perhaps it is worth while recording that we have here given a slightly stylized version of an actual conversation between a philosopher and a plain man.

that they are incorporated in some optimistic scheme of development. On the contrary, he is aware that the most sophisticated modern-day philosophies of religion and theologies may incorporate subtle forms of these old evasions. He is also aware of the ways in which first-order religious and theological evasions of these difficulties may find their way on to other levels of discussion. It does not escape him, for instance, that meta-religious studies such as Mr D. Z. Phillip's *The Concept of Prayer* may provide a refuge in which religious beliefs avoid confrontation with reality.

Professor MacKinnon recognizes the difficulty of relating the characteristic language of Christianity (and of other religions) to reality. He sees that when language is used to refer to the transcendent, the concepts and categories it expresses are strained to breaking point, however much our language in religion and theology, in speculative metaphysics, and in morality presses us towards these limits. This is one reason he concerns himself with paradoxical styles of thought, and problems as to their status.

But he has not neglected how many of the doctrines of Christianity are, in part at least, tied to reality by claims of simple fact. Professor MacKinnon detects evasion in the theological doctrines of the demythologizers who, under the pressure of historical and even epistemological difficulties, have tried to evacuate Christianity of its contingent historical contents by reinterpretation. We may also remark parallel evasions on the level of meta-religious thought. Some recent linguistic accounts of religious belief have tried to take a short way with verificationist difficulties through disclaiming any sort of relation to reality, in or beyond experience, for references to the transcendent. Some of these accounts have gone so far as to interpret even the simplest matter-of-fact beliefs in religion away from any requirement of correspondence to reality.[1]

Professor MacKinnon sees how the claims of Christianity involve both references to the transcendent and statements of

[1] See, for instance, Ludwig Wittgenstein, *Lectures on Aesthetics, Psychology and Religious Belief*, ed. by Father C. Barrett, Blackwell, 1966.

simple fact. He sees indeed how both these elements are combined, above all in its Christology, in ways that are profoundly perplexing, but still essential to its teaching. No doubt the peculiar combination of these different sorts of claim in Christianity adds to the difficulties associated with belief in it. It may nevertheless be true that the most favourable *locus* for a clarification of these difficulties, including difficulties about the status of reference to the transcendent, lies in the distinctive complexities of Christian doctrine.

But the enterprise upon which Professor MacKinnon is engaged is not yet complete; we shall perhaps be better able to judge it when we have before us his Gifford lectures, *The Problem of Metaphysics*. It is already clear, however, that his approach to the problems of philosophy of religion combines an unusual openness to secular and even anti-religious perspectives with a highly original effort to treat these problems in a Christological light.

GEORGE W. ROBERTS
DONOVAN E. SMUCKER

ACKNOWLEDGMENTS

WE ARE VERY grateful to Professor MacKinnon for the opportunity to assemble and to present this collection of his essays, and we wish to thank him not only for this privilege, but also for his generous contribution of time and effort in the preparation of it. We doubt that in his position we could have mustered a like grace in dealing with the importunities to which we have subjected him.

We wish also to extend our thanks to Dr Cecil Northcott of the Lutterworth Press who has performed his part in this endeavour with commendable understanding, patience, and efficiency.

For the publishers, Professor MacKinnon and ourselves we wish to acknowledge permission to reprint materials included in this volume received from the following editors and publishers:

The Syndics of the Cambridge University Press for the title essay, *The Borderlands of Theology* (1961), Professor MacKinnon's inaugural lecture at Cambridge; the Editor of *Essays in Christology in Honour of Karl Barth* (1956) for "Philosophy and Christology"; the British Broadcasting Corporation for "Our Contemporary Christ" (1962), "Order and Evil in the Gospel" (1963), "Where the Report Fails" (1948) (printed here under the title "An Approach to the Moral and Spiritual Problems of the Nuclear Age"), and "Reflections on the Hydrogen Bomb" (1954), from *The Listener*, and for "P. F. Strawson's *The Bounds of Sense*", delivered in the Third Programme in 1966; the Editor of *Theology* for "Scott Holland and Contemporary Needs" (1952); the Editors of *The Cambridge Review* and W. Heffer & Sons Ltd. for "Some Notes on Kierkegaard" (1956); the Editor of the Aristotelian Society for "Metaphysical and Religious Language" (1954) from its *Proceedings*, and for

"Things and Persons" (1948) and "Verifiability" (1945) from Supplementary Volumes to its *Proceedings*; the Editor of *Theology* and the Society for the Promotion of Christian Knowledge, publishers of *Traditional Virtues Reassessed* (1964), for "Justice" (1962); the London School of Economics and Political Science for "On the Notion of a Philosophy of History" (first published by the Oxford University Press, 1954); the Editor of the *New Statesman* for "R. G. Collingwood as a Philosopher" (1954), which first appeared under the review-head "Books in General"; Messrs William Collins, Sons & Co., Ltd., for "Ethical Problems of Nuclear Warfare" from *God, Sex, and War* (1963); the Editor of *The Church Quarterly Review* for "John Wisdom's *Paradox and Discovery*" (1967); and the Editor of *The Observer*, London, for the use of the picture on the cover.

Corrections and additions have been made in the essays where it seemed necessary or appropriate.

AUTHOR'S INTRODUCTORY ESSAY

THIS COLLECTION OF papers has been made possible by the initiative, kindness and hard work of Professor George Roberts and Professor Smucker. At their suggestion I have added this introductory essay, indicating the sort of unity that binds together the items of this collection. Inevitably such an essay has grown in the course of preparation: for it has become not simply a partial description of what is contained in the papers which follow, and the different *foci* of interest to which they bear witness, but an interpretation of past work in the light of present preoccupations and indeed of intention for publication of much more extended and sustained work, now almost ready to appear. So I do not simply describe or characterize; I try to show where the thought here embodied has led and is leading me. Especially in the concluding section I have argued for a viewpoint to which increasingly I would commit myself publicly, namely that if we live in an age in which we must acknowledge faith to be precarious, we also live in an age in which our perception of the objects of faith may be renewed.

The papers which this volume contains bear witness to three related preoccupations; the first is philosophical, the second theological and the third ethical. But the three are in fact related. Thus, if I say that in philosophy my chief concern has been with the question of the limits of experience, of intelligible, descriptive discourse, with the kind of questions discussed by Kant as that philosopher is presented in Mr P. F. Strawson's recent book *The Bounds of Sense* and by Professor Wisdom in some of the papers contained in *Paradox and Discovery*, I know that this preoccupation has deeply affected and been affected by my besetting theological concern with issues of Christology. Again, where ethics are concerned, it is with the group of issues that certainly raise very sharply the adequacy of utilitarian norms of judgment, which very soon remind the reflective student of the tragic elements in human life, of the sorts of deeply personal dialectical self-interrogation in which, in the concrete, the issue discussed in traditional moral philosophy under the rubric "conflict of duties" is sometimes worked out that I have largely occupied myself. In Plato's highly significant quarrel with the tragedians we find the birth of a kind of ethical reflection which deliberately eschews the method of description and re-description and substitutes the quest for an authoritative transcendent norm which at once supplies a standard of judgment and a resting place for the interrogative spirit. More than perhaps we realize we are in bondage to the consequences of that revolution. And it is at least arguable that when the tumult and the shouting dies it will be seen that the role of the existentialists has been to set a question-mark against it, and to raise (as of course Hegel in his *Jugendschriften* may be said to have raised) the question of the ontological import of the tragic dialectic. I say that this issue has been raised; it has been raised but not resolved. For even if we substitute a quite different system of projection for the expression of our discontent with ethical naturalism, we shall still have to face the question of truth and falsity, the question whether what we represent in any sense corresponds with what is.

So the three issues to which I have continually returned are mutually involved one with the other.

Take first, however, the philosophical questions which have chiefly engaged me. In a sentence, what has concerned me is the question of the experiential significance of factual concepts. It is undoubtedly one of the central themes of Kant's *Critique of Pure Reason*, and one with which he is able to deal with particular acuteness by means of his rigorous demarcation of categories from other concepts. There is no doubt whatever that he assigns a special role, a role that he characterizes as necessary in the sense of indispensable, to certain notions and concepts, for instance the notion of spatio-temporal unity and the concepts of substantial permanence and causality. For him we know *a priori* (in a sense he tries painfully and not always unsuccessfully to define) that whatever enters our experience as a physical event, however remote in time or distant in space, must find its date and place in the same time order as the writing of this essay. Again he agrees we know apart from the detailed and various deliverances of our experience that whatever is to qualify as an objective constituent of that experience must manifest certain pervasive factors; and the necessity of their presence he is at pains to make a matter of proof. If we do not know *a priori* what the world is like in its rich variety and its complex and vastly detailed history, we know the forms to which that detail must conform; we know what conditions must be satisfied if anything is to be treated as a constituent of the world to which we belong. Yet he insists that even where these structural notions are concerned, it must be possible to qualify the conditions of their use in relation to our experience. Without the notion of the conformity of events to law, we cannot spell out the order of our world; we cannot even through our senses have commerce with anything worthy to be called a world. Yet the significance of the notion is exhausted by the continuity it enables us to introduce into that with which our senses make it possible for us to have commerce, a continuity without which what the senses disclose would be empty of objective significance for us.

I mention Kant here although I do not ignore the extent to which his Analytic of Principles has been criticized by modern logical empiricists technically competent in respect of the tremendous transformations effected in our understanding of the natural world since his day. One cannot work and teach in Cambridge without being made continually aware that it is in the laboratories of the molecular biological research unit and in the Mullard Radio astronomical observatory rather than in the libraries and lecture rooms of the Divinity School that the frontiers of human knowledge are being pushed back! But even as these frontiers are extended, so men still find themselves, if they are technically competent, able to assimilate and make their own what is learnt; assimilate and assess, distinguishing the merely speculative from the partially confirmed, the tentative from the relatively certain, the kind of reorganization of theoretical concepts demanded by increase of understanding over against the system supposedly to be replaced.

The modern logical empiricist, however deeply he may quarrel, e.g. with Kant's adherence to the authority of Euclidean geometry, must admire his sharp perception of the special status and role of structural concepts or categories. For this perception enabled Kant to pioneer a kind of empiricism that was not in bondage to the illusion of supposing the complexities of the actual public world to be constructible out of the short-lived, fragmentary, private simplicities of individual sense-experience. It was a part of his achievement to enable the empiricist principle of the necessarily experiential import of factual concepts to be stated without any suggestion of the falsehood that conceptual activity is a sort of ghostly surrogate for the vivid actuality of sense awareness.

It is for these reasons as well as for others that his criticism of the possibility of transcendent metaphysics remains classical. I say "as well as others"; for it was a sample of his great insight that he recognized how much metaphysics was bound up with a nisus from the relative to the unconditioned, an urge that sought satisfaction by a delineation in theoretically satisfying terms of the ultimate order of being, of things as they are. And it was the intellectual illusion on which this aspiration depended that he sought to uncover, but to uncover with a profound sympathy for the dimensions of the human spirit evidenced by this preoccupation with the unattainable.

It is with the range of philosophical problems to which Kant's view supplies one way of entry that I have been chiefly concerned. If the canon of experiential significance obtains, what claim can we make for what we say, however subtle, even idiosyncratic our manner of expression, concerning the unconditional and the transcendent? Certainly we must press through à l'outrance our sense of the sort of indirection that we must anticipate in any suggested system of projection we may adopt or seek to develop. There is no substitute here for sheer hard work, for the kind of hard work that is involved in tracing precisely what it is that metaphysicians are about with the concepts they frame, and the uses to which they put them.

"Every sort of statement has its own sort of logic"! It was a weakness on Kant's part to be so deeply in bondage to generalized forms of expression, whether his field was theory of knowledge or ethics. His work is suffused by a hostility to the particular, even though, of course, we must allow that in his ethics he cultivated so extreme a formalism in order to capture in the most diverse types of human action what was present in all of them as source of sovereign moral authority throughout all the changes and chances of concrete individual life. Yet if we concede that the serious moral philosopher must be prepared to listen to those who describe, and himself to describe and redescribe in detail, we must also insist that he has to guard against the illusion of supposing that mere subtlety and elaboration in description somehow of themselves confer validity. The question remains of the frontiers of intelligibility; if we find, for instance, a point of departure for metaphysics in discontent with the ethical naturalist models of the human situation, if we go on to clothe that discontent in expression as rich and effective as the first part of the second book of Plato's *Republic*, we still have to ask, concerning the claims of truth and falsity, what we thus convey to ourselves. A mere appropriateness of linguistic form is not itself a guarantee of factual import.

We do well never to forget that in this respect, if in none other, the work of those philosophers, mainly to be found more in central Europe before its subjection to Nazi domination and in the U.S.A. than in the United Kingdom, who are properly called "logical positivists", was of great value. For all the carelessness of which they have been proved guilty in their philosophical pamphleteering, their most serious work was informed by a profound insistence that philosophers should take seriously the canons of verification recognized where the admissibility or the inadmissibility of scientific hypotheses was under discussion. In Popper's *Logik der Forschung* and in the many papers in which his fundamental thesis has been developed and refined by himself, by his pupils and associates, the demand has been converted into a general recognition of the supreme importance to be attached to a proposition or hypothesis or suggested natural law being regarded as vulnerable to falsification. It is, of course, no accident that Popper (not only in his quarrel with those who emphasize, as he does not, the roles of induction and confirmation in scientific discovery) admits a deep indebtedness to Kant in his clear recognition of the interplay of spontaneous intellectual and imaginative construction, and empirical observation in the advance of our knowledge of the world. And if I mention Kant's name before that of any other philosopher in this section of my essay, I do so because a critical study of his work, among many other fruits, alerts the student continually to the depth of the need that what we claim to be the case shall somehow be vulnerable to specifiable methods of proof or disproof. Whether we can to any extent succeed in indicating what form such methods may properly be expected to take is a supremely exacting problem; but there is no flight possible from the logical empiricist's insistence that what the metaphysician or religious believer is concerned with lies beyond the fields in which true can be distinguished from false. Admittedly there is a paradox in asking the question how statements relating to that which transcends the frontiers of intelligible factual discourse may be verified; but it is a paradox that we have to employ in order to fasten our attention on the fact that if there is no sense whatsoever in which in a metaphysical statement we are concerned with what is, or is not, the case, the whole enterprise is vacuous and without significance.

There is no substitute here for hard work; and the same obtains when we come to the related topic of Christology. I say related, and this may seem a mistake. Yet if I ask myself why I remain in some sense a Christian, it is because of the questions set to me by the person of Christ. Of course these are theological, not metaphysical, questions; yet in framing them the problem of metaphysics is immediately raised again. For instance, if a man asks what Jesus means when in the words of the Fourth Gospel he says that "he and the Father are one" (*hen*), he is immediately involved in questions touching the content and limitations in significance of the concept of substance or entity. The part of philosophy called ontology, according to Professor P. T. Geach, is concerned to give as satisfactory and complete an account as possible of our ultimate conceptual scheme; in the working out of the doctrine of the person of Christ, such an ultimate conceptual scheme has been taken for granted, and the legitimacy of its use in principle in respect of the transcendent has not been queried. It has been bent to new purposes; the concept of substance has been enlarged and stretched in its use in the representation of Christ's relation to the Father. But that which it has been used to convey in outline is regarded as transcendent of the order of the world, as belonging indeed to the very arcana of the transcendent in itself.

Yet even before the movement of Christological thought involved the theologian in the inescapable subtleties of the passage beyond an economic to an essential Trinity, we are by contemplation of the person of Christ involved in perplexing questions of significance. If we say that in the Gospels we are confronted with a figure whose ground and source is not in himself, who continually points beyond himself, who confronts men with the paradoxical claim, conveyed brilliantly in a phrase of the late Dr W. R. Inge, of an "infinite self-abnegation", we are gripped fast by the issue of the significance of what we say. We refer, of course, to a concrete historical individual, with an identifiable *Sitz im Leben*, on whose mission critical historical analysis and advancing archaeological exploration may throw new light, as they have done and may continue to do on Solon and Pericles, on Sulla and Julius Caesar, on Hannibal and Cleopatra. There are whole sections of the life and teaching of Jesus that are, however we conceive the source material, matter for the professional historian; for instance, the relation of the judicial processes by which he was tried, the relative responsibility of Pharisees, of priests, of Roman officials for his execution. But when we ask what, if anything, is meant by speaking of him in the concreteness of his human existence as the Truth, we face not only paradoxical innovation in the use of the notion of truth: we face the question of the sense in which a concrete individual may not simply teach or reveal what is true, as Jesus did to the Samaritan woman and to others, but *be* the Truth. And if this is not the same question as reflection on transcendent metaphysical speculation raises, it has analogies thereto.

27

It is, of course, tempting to say that a study of Christological language forms an important chapter in a general investigation of ways in which the frontiers of factually significant discourse have been transcended. Such an investigation would of course also include detailed treatment of Kant's claim that where the moral universe was concerned we were free to use concepts in expounding the "postulates of pure practical reason" in ways free of the restrictions laid down in his first critique. We may well conclude that his account of the morality that elicited the laying down of these postulates must be judged at once too formal and too narrowly conceived to do justice to the complexities of human existence. Yet we can reject this aspect of Kant's moral theory, while still taking most seriously his insistence that it is in the moral life that we enjoy commerce with the transcendent. We have to reckon with a whole range of different styles of thrust beyond the limits of experience, which have their sources in the actual lives of men and women: the kind of thrust of which Professor Wisdom[1] has well remarked we find expressed in great literature, in Sophocles and Shakespeare, in Conrad and Flaubert, in Racine and Lawrence rather than in the speculative writings of professional philosophers. In such a liberalized inventory of essays in the transcending of the frontiers of empirical significance, Christology has its place. Yet it is not in any of the forms in which it is expressed, whether the quasi-narrative descriptions of the Synoptic Gospels, suggesting an origin for their central figure resistant to the kind of location proper to the place of his human birth and nurture, and the kind of dating which in principle we must be able to assign to his birth and to the precise identification which again in principle we must suppose possible, where his parentage is concerned, or the relatively precise ontological formula of the Nicene definition of his relation to the Father, to be regarded as a kind of imaginative enlargement of human material. Dr

---

[1] I should like here to acknowledge how great my debt is to Professor Wisdom, both in respect of what I have learnt from his writing and of what I have learnt from him in discussion. Although he is a philosopher and not a theologian, I am deeply aware of the extent to which this section of my essay has been affected by his teaching and I should like to acknowledge a debt that extends a long way beyond the actual references to his published writings.

28

Norman Sherry[1] has given us, where a number of Conrad's novels are concerned, including not only *Almayer's Folly* and *Outcast of the Islands* but also *Lord Jim* and *The Shadow Line*, a fascinating account of the material that the novelist organized to such remarkable effect. His *Conrad's Eastern World* is valuable to any student of the working of the creative imagination. We could indeed say the same of the late Dr Ernest Jones' study of Shakespeare's writing of Hamlet in Freudian terms in his well-known book *Hamlet and Oedipus*. If it is not literary criticism it is a valuable suggestion of the role fulfilled in the writer's biography by the writing of one of the most elusive of his tragedies, advancing unquestionably understanding of the work, even if Jones fails in the end to reckon with it as an achieved whole. Both Sherry and Jones in their different ways direct their readers' attention to the labours of composition (in Shakespeare's case, as Jones understands him, one could say the spiritual travail) out of which their respective subjects' work was born. In each case one could say that it was from their power of reflective assimilation of their material that their work sprung; they both enlarged our understanding of the human scene by way of their imaginative re-ordering of that which they received; in the case of Conrad the life he met and read about in his Eastern world, in Shakespeare's case a tradition of tragic drama on which he set the seal of his own experience and through which, by deep reflection, he was enabled to come to terms with himself.

There is a very influential current in contemporary theological thinking which emphasizes the extent to which in the figure of Jesus the Christ, of whose historical existence it is alleged that we know next to nothing, we have to reckon with a series of essays in spiritual experience wherein the Church, whether collectively or in the persons of individual members of a genuine creative originality, has sought to come to terms with itself, with its life and the questions an inherited tradition of faith and practice thrust upon it, in its own particular environment, often (in the case of the evangelists and the sources of the material they used) projecting this self-interrogation in the

---

[1] *Conrad's Eastern World*, C.U.P., 1966.

form of a narrative concerning the life and death of Jesus. Fundamentally such a narrative is not to be understood referentially, that is by the effort to make what sense one can of it as a description of what took place and its significance, but rather through some sort of *Nacherlebnis* of the experience out of which it sprang. Such tendencies are congruous with emphases in the philosophy of religion which deliberately avert from questions concerning the truth and falsity of what men and women believe (supposing that their beliefs can be rendered intelligible), but concentrate entirely on resolving the question of intelligibility by assigning to religious expressions their role in prayer and public worship, in rituals, in promoting and furthering a way of life, and argue that when such roles have been set forth, all that requires to be done has been done.

For better or worse I am deeply convinced that tempting though such an escape route may seem to be, both to those perplexed by the historical problems raised by Christian origins, and to those at a loss to know how sense is to be assigned to expressions which combine a definitely referential intention with supposition of the transcendent as an element in that to which reference is made, it is one doomed in the end to evacuate Christian faith of any serious intellectual content. Further, if we allow any note of the principle *lex orandi, lex credendi* as advertising those credenda which must merit the labours of the theologian working under the imperative—*let faith seek understanding*—we have to allow that it is the supposed presence of the divine in the concrete historical actuality of Jesus of Nazareth ("God's presence, and his very self and essence all divine"—to use the traditional language in the form of Newman's great hymn) which has provided Christian faith with its differentia and indeed its most characteristic problematic. If in the one, of whom in the Fourth Gospel John the Baptist says that "there stands one among you whom you know not", we have to reckon with one who is substantially one with the Father (*homoousios*, not a mere simulacrum of the divine, but its actual *parousia*), we are certainly faced with an almost overwhelmingly difficult problem in establishing the proper "system of projection" for the representation of that with which we have to do. But here is the point, or rather the person, to whom in the end our statements refer. They are measured not by their adequacy to deepen our experience of the world around us, to advance our spiritual self-comprehension, but by the extent to which they designate and characterize, however ineffectually, however we must hedge their competence by agnostic caveats, the one with whom they deal.

There is a sense in which anyone who is a philosopher must regret the intrusive preoccupation of the question of faith, regret it lest such preoccupation deflect the energies of his thinking from its proper concerns and infect his disinterestedness with the *parti pris* attitudes of apologetics. Yet it is the case that while increasingly both this self-knowledge and a deepening distrust of the ecclesiastical *Apparat* lead me to be mistrustful of a very great deal I have enjoyed, yes enjoyed, in the world of the Christian religion and be aware that I must surely come equally to mistrust a great deal more, the domination of the *mysterium Christi* deepens its almost obsessive sovereignty over my mind. Here is a point at which a whole number of enquiries fuse and are in fact brought to a near explosive flash-point. Indeed I find myself mistrustful of much that calls itself radical theology because it seems to me to fail (as *malgré tout* the massive *oeuvre* of Karl Barth does not fail) to allow these question to be put with sufficient sharpness. A comforting sense of the authority supposedly resident in the experience of the Church provides an anaesthetic, or at least a tranquillizer, against allowing ourselves to be bothered by the impact of the problem of metaphysics upon Christology; as if we were enabled to avoid the sharp needle of enquiry concerning how best to represent the one with whom we have to do by suggesting that in the end even as the proper study of mankind is man, so Christian man finds his appropriate study in himself.

There are indeed related questions here touching the nature of Christ's work, the sense to be given to his teaching, to his words, above all to his death, and there is the problem of the resurrection, a problem crucially one for historian and metaphysician at the same moment. In a way it is abstraction to speak of Jesus Christ apart from his description as the one who died, and who was raised again. As a matter of historical fact, belief that he was raised was the sufficient, necessary condition, of the early Christian mission. But who was it who was thus believed to have been raised? And what of the relation of his rising to what he was and to what he is? It is here we come to rest, not in any way belittling the significance of questions of contingent fact answered by empirical observation, but bringing out the extent to which in Christology such questions are found inextricably woven together with the facing of issues touching the relation of the temporal to the eternal. "Of that of which we cannot speak: of that we must be silent." So Wittgenstein towards the end of the *Tractatus*. A year or two ago there was an outburst of feverish clerical protest against the way a London vicar was treated on one of the B.B.C.'s satirical television programmes, against the way in which this vicar's words were drowned by a clamour of loud anti-Christian protest on the part of the other participants in the show. Inevitably every effort was made to ensure that such ill-mannered silencing of the Christian view should not occur again; I say "inevitably". For it is a mark of the pathetic intellectual (and spiritual) naïvety of the clerical mind not to see that it may be that in the present situation such enforced and publicly demonstrated aphasia is one of the only methods of effective communication open to Christians. I do not mean that in such circumstances a dignified silence has its own impressive quality; I mean more profoundly that we must recognize our inability significantly in speech to transcend the frontiers of intelligible discourse, and that in this present, a certain sort of silence may be a means of communication, may indeed be the "system of projection" that we need. For a Christian the memory of Christ's reported silence before his accusers and judges is and must be a paradigm of authentic *marturia tei aletheiai*. "Answerest thou nothing?" Whatever other comment the episode mentioned invites, it can hardly be denied that it provided a most telling illustration of the theological shallowness of the official Christian mind, preoccupied always with the needs to make parrot-like repetition of its sterile *Credo*, and hardly ever with the deeper questions of the manner of Christian presence to the world.

And so I come to the third group of essays, those concerned with questions relating to the limits of obedience to the civil power. No one who recalls the history of the years between 1933 and 1939 can fail to realize the extent to which readiness to resist Hitler, while there was opportunity to do so without world war and with a minimum use of force, was inhibited by the wide influence of pacifist opinion and sentiment in the United Kingdom. There were, of course, other factors; thus when Hitler re-occupied the Rhineland in March 1936, thereby nullifying the strategic import of France's Eastern European commitments and rendering it impossible for her effectively to spring to the aid of Czecho-Slovakia, when that country was threatened by the advance of the relentless *Drang nach Osten*, he chose to do so at a moment when public opinion in Britain was markedly more hostile to Italy, by then almost completely victorious in Abyssinia, than to a Germany, concerning whose treatment under the Treaty of Versailles and subsequently there obtained a vague but persistent sense of guilt. Again, we must not forget the extent to which public opinion on the Right was rendered, if not favourable to Hitler, at least in a measure tolerant of his enormities by fear of Bolshevism, cunningly exploited by Nazi propaganda and especially after the outbreak of the Spanish Civil War in July 1936. But no one who recalls, for instance, the kind of argument that went on ceaselessly in the weeks before Munich concerning the formal justice or injustice of a war undertaken to thwart Hitler's designs against Czecho-Slovakia, and who sets these private scruples in the objective context of a grand strategy of aggression laid down in the conference in the Chancellery in Berlin on November 5, 1937, and summarized in the "Hossbach Minute", can fail to realize that his own hesitations helped to make straight the highway of Hitler's conquering power, and worse still, established even for a short time in Europe that "neue Ordnung", whose unspeakable monument remains in the fate of the Jewish people.

Yet while those memories remind one of the tragic follies of which the scrupulous are guilty, they also serve to show the sharp relevance to the world in which we have lived and in which we live today of the question of the limits of obedience. The true heroes of Hitler's wars are not those who died in his service in the holocausts of "Operation Barbarossa"; they are such men and women as the Austrian peasant Franz Jägerstätter, and the defiant university students of Munich, who gave their name to the Munich students' revolt of 1942. We are not likely to find the survivors of their fellowship high in the councils of NATO; yet they are assuredly those whom the International Military Tribunal at Nuremberg in 1945–6 proclaimed to all the world as the true heroes of war-time Germany, the men and women who said an immensely personal and an intensely costing "no" to evil-doing, commended to them (from pulpits and by weight of theological argument) as their patriotic duty pleasing in the sight of God.

In a recent T.V. interview, Professor Ritchie Calder spoke of the younger generation of today as differentiated from its parents' generation by the presence of Strontium 90 in its bones; and inevitably even a writer of an earlier generation, who deals with these topics in the post-war world, must deal with them against the background of that new situation which came into being on August 6, 1945, at Hiroshima, followed a few days later by the similar destruction of Nagasaki. A great deal of attention has inevitably been paid by the Christian churches to the moral problems raised by the use of nuclear weapons, by their development (and we live in the age of the H-bomb and the I.C.B.M., not of the A-bombs which were used in the closing stages of the war against Japan); and the number of reports prepared under the auspices of e.g. the World Council of Churches, the British Council of Churches, the Church Assembly of the Church of England, etc. bears witness to the depth and seriousness with which the problems have been faced. In including in this volume papers of my own relating to these issues, I have done so because I honestly believe that a good deal of this literature, especially that produced on the initiative of the British Council of Churches is reflective of a fundamental intellectual failure, not only to measure up to the ethical realities of the issues raised by modern weaponry, but more widely to the significance of Christian presence in the post-

Constantinian world. I say this freely in as much as I was myself a very active member of the first Commission of the British Council of Churches on these topics, that which produced in 1946 the report *The Era of Atomic Power*. I should say now without much hesitation that I regard the time I put in helping to prepare this report as almost entirely wasted. True: it bequeathed to Christian posterity the phrase: "We must learn to live with this dilemma", even as the subsequent Commission, which reported in 1959, enlightened the world with the solemn injunction, "We must learn to live with the Bomb". But we left altogether on one side the challenge conveyed in Oppenheimer's haunting observation, "the scientists have known sin". In an outstanding article published in *Theology* for September 1966, Dr. Margaret Thrall, a lecturer in Hebrew in the University College of Bangor, has offered what in my view must be regarded as a definitive judgment on the painstaking and painful efforts of those who have followed the paths laid down by the successive commissions set up by the British Council of Churches; it is very significant that at the time of writing (late March 1967), no reply to her article has appeared. It is not for me to summarize her argument, only to commend her achievement in writing one of the most acute papers in the field of Christian ethics that has come my way for a long time, and to express the hope that my own undertaking is congruous with hers. What I would further plead, however, is the overt recognition by Christians that where questions of conscientious objection are concerned (if we except the Society of Friends) they must realize their duty almost to start again from scratch. It was the late Father R. M. Benson of Cowley, the founder of the Society of St John the Evangelist, whom few would call a "radical theologian" who spoke of the conversion of Constantine as the greatest single disaster which ever overtook the Christian Church. We have come surely in this century to realize that he spoke the simple truth; it is indeed the fast-growing recognition of the deep insight expressed in these words by Benson that in part underlies and is expressed in the present, richly creative ferment in the Church of Rome. (Perhaps we may hope soon to experience the explosive force of a comparable upheaval even in the stagnant backwater of the Church of England "as by law established".) It is only when we come to acknowledge the truth of Benson's judgment that we can receive as a profound liberation the disintegration of what we still inaccurately call our "Christian culture", and welcome, in the first instance, the sort of aphasia I illustrated towards the end of the last section of this essay, as a moment in the only possible renewal of faith presently open to us. Of course, that is no guarantee that it is such a moment, no assurance that our speechlessness will issue in the rebirth of faith; here as always recollection of the mystery of the Incarnation should bid us expect uncertainty rather than security, the *status viatoris* rather than the *status comprehensoris*.

It is not irrelevant here to recall that we are already experiencing something of the grand emancipation which this *Überwindung* brings in, for instance, the central field of Christology. Thus historians of Christian doctrine have long paid lip service to the extent to which Anselm's soteriology takes for granted and extrapolates in his theology the characteristic forms of feudal social order. Yet in their own constructive work these theologians have often been much slower to see the extent to which profound understanding of divine self-emptying (and indeed the light its confession throws on the nature of God-in-himself) has been impeded by the imagining of God's supremacy after the image of the sovereignty exercised by an absolute ruler and the acclaim he demands as his due, after the image of the salutation accorded a newly-crowned monarch, rather than the response proper to the *Ecce Homo* of the moment of faith. It is not irrelevant to recall these matters here because if we cannot subscribe without reservation to the thesis *lex orandi, lex credendi*, it is still true that the objectives of Christian confession are inevitably suffused by the styles of Christian life: if Christian life is identified with the continuance of a particular cultural complex, of which Christian faith is judged a constituent part, then what we believe inevitably reflects the involvement of the *fides qua credimus* in a total way of life, acknowledged more precious and more stable than faith itself and the *fides quae creditur* diminished to the level of that

36

which can be conceived as supporting and underwriting the culture we supposedly cherish. But these things have passed away, and with them comes at once the chance radically to rethink Christian attitudes to the moral questions raised by the obligation "to wear weapons and to serve in the wars", and in particular by modern weapon systems.

It is a commonplace to point out that among the many historical failures of the Christian churches, that where the ethics of war and peace are concerned is among the most flagrant. But the present situation provides those of us who are not bemused by devotion, e.g. to the State establishment of the Church of England (a singularly unattractive "sacred cow", though the animal still has her devotees) and who have not put our consciences into pawn to the allegedly better informed sources of information which the British Council of Churches is able to recruit to man its many commissions, with a tremendous opportunity to "start again from the beginning". We need not neglect the insights that have undoubtedly been achieved in the past; indeed, in political theory ancient, medieval and modern, there is vast wealth of insight concerning the uses and effective control of political power, of which ecclesiastics have shown themselves in all ages of all men often the most unwilling to avail themselves. But we are able (in a situation which is extreme in that it is one in which the life of faith must be experienced as something precarious and threatened from every quarter) at least to admit the renewal at least of the foundations of our belief and of our understanding of its focus and centre, and also of the kind of living which is properly expressive of that belief. And here it is my conviction that the issue of conscientious objection, indeed the issue of the duty of such objection in the face of such expressions of public policy as the Anglo-French Suez adventure in 1956, or the American war in Vietnam today, is an issue which enables us to see as raised in the same context problems concerning the ontological import of human behaviour, the inwardness of the *mysterium Christi* and the manner of Christian presence in the world.

To my mind there is no single Christian utterance more

deeply expressive of conventional piety and more deeply hostile to the demand for the renewal of Christian understanding than the plea contained in the report on the moral problems raised by nuclear warfare in the report of the committee set up by the British Council of Churches, which reported in 1959: "We must learn to live with the bomb". As I review the papers assembled in this volume, and seek to interpret them by this essay, I know that I cannot claim for them that they do more than indicate the sort of problems to be dealt with more extensively in my forthcoming Gifford lectures on the problem of metaphysics, and in the Prideaux Lectures given in 1966 at Exeter University on the divinity of Christ, and in a long manuscript on faith which I hope eventually to publish; yet I would hope that they might provide encouragement for those who like myself would see in the present opportunity to break asunder the fetters of the past and not, in the false humility so often today characteristic of the professional Christian layman, to embrace a kind of acquiescent determinism, dignifying our conformism with the title of "responsible behaviour". There is little to edify in Christ's parable of the unjust steward; there is nothing at all to edify in Lenin's actions in Russia in the autumn of 1917, yet as our pictures of those actions gradually emerge, even if we remain shocked by Lenin's opportunism, his ruthlessness, his inflexible determination to achieve supreme power at any cost, he does at least set a question-mark (and after all he is most certainly one of the architects of our world) against the sort of facile historical determinism fashionable among those Christian conservatives who often, oddly enough, are eager to claim the radical name. Of course freedom in all its forms remains a very frightening thing, and the enemy of the security we all of us too often in one way or another identify with faith.

To reject the determinism implicit in the plea quoted from the Committee's report is in its way an expression of metaphysical belief and of metaphysical belief closely related to Christological conviction. It is with the validity both in practice and in theory of such belief that these papers reveal me as continually concerned, and it is as advertisement of the unity of these concerns that their collection is perhaps justified.

Part I

THEOLOGY AND
PHILOSOPHY OF RELIGION

BORDERLANDS OF THEOLOGY

THE PHILOSOPHER of religion today knows that his task is primarily critical. He may well be led to suppose that his first task is that of elaborately and exhaustively describing the various forms of religious discourse so as to bring out their likeness to, and their difference from, other forms of discourse. He must not shirk the detailed exploration of the most varied manifestations of religion. Thus if one confines one's view to Christianity, the language of the pulpit and the prie-dieu, the formal utterance of liturgical prayer, the descriptive prose of the Gospel narrative, the parabolic in careful distinction from the allegorical, the dogmatic theologian's borrowings from the stock-in-trade of the traditional metaphysician, the language which seems to hesitate between the frankly meta-physical and the factually descriptive (one thinks of some of the language of the Fourth Gospel)—all these and other forms of Christian discourse will call for examination. The philosopher may indeed hope that if he pursues his work with sufficient thoroughness and patience, with sufficient flexibility of cross-reference and example, the nature of religious discourse will begin to emerge. Description and redescription will (he may hope) almost imperceptibly pass into vindication; we will begin (again he may hope) to feel ourselves at home in the sense of knowing what we can and what we cannot do, with the language whose logic we are exploring.

On the other hand, such hope may remain unfulfilled. The philosopher may find that the work of description and redescription leaves him with a further task which, borrowing a useful expression from Jeremy Bentham, I will call "censorial". The philosopher *may* well find that very much that belongs to the most deeply ingrained and most pervasive styles of traditional

41

religious discourse cannot possibly be accepted without gross violation of principles which in the investigation of natural, and indeed of historical fact, we all of us take for granted, whether or not we possess the technical expertise, or the training in the philosophy of logic, required to formulate them explicitly. No serious philosopher can hope to dodge the questions involved in the claim of religious credenda to *truth*.

I shall mention only one among the various suggested contemporary devices for avoiding these questions; the suggestion that they can be evaded by an analysis of faith in terms of self-commitment to a person leaves unanswered (or even deliberately seeks to evade) the distinction between such commitment and that involved in a *Führerprinzip*. Self-commitment is made validly to this person rather than to that because *this* person said and did certain things, thereby at once defining and authenticating, or at least effectively suggesting, certain claims. To take the simplest and most familiar example, when Peter at Caesarea Philippi is recorded to have said in answer to Jesus' question: "Thou art the Christ", his words had a definitive sense. They were not a mere acclamation; Peter believed that what he said was true, even though it is certain (if we may trust the historical narrative to be in any sense an account of what actually happened) that he had very much, almost all, to learn of the analysis of what he affirmed to be the case. But what is crucial is that he was affirming something to be the case, on the basis of evidence, which he could have given if pressed, even if what he affirmed outran the evidence at his disposal. "Flesh and blood have not revealed the secret to you, Simon, son of John", says Jesus at once to Peter, according to the elaborated version of the incident given by St Matthew. Thereby Jesus seems clearly to suggest that what Peter affirmed was something beyond the reach of human ratiocination, although it in no sense implied that Peter could not have formulated the premises on which his affirmation rested. What account can be given of the status of such supposed facts, and of the evidence which warrants our affirming or denying this or that proposition concerning them? To some more familiar than myself with the experimental methods of the exact and natural sciences the very notion of such a fact as the one affirmed by Peter will seem something unintelligible and as such inadmissible as a subject of discussion. It falls under the same censorship that Bentham in his ethical writings rigorously applied to the seemingly sterile preoccupation with their supposed inner life which he judged characteristic of those who found the moral value of actions in the motives from which they were done. Yet it is with the status of *such* facts as that affirmed by Peter that the philosopher of religion is professionally concerned.

Already I may have succeeded in indicating to my audience some of the grounds which led me to choose for this inaugural lecture the subject of the "borderlands of theology". It is with the pressures coming from the other side of the theologian's supposed frontiers that the philosopher of religion is concerned. But that philosopher would make a great mistake if he failed to take account of the fact that the Christian religion itself is subject today (as indeed constantly in the past) to its own special sorts of discontent experienced both by those who profess it, and by those who look at it from without in a mood of mingled irritation and sympathy, and by those who reject its claims outright for other motives than a repudiation of its credenda as unintelligible. We can, and must, predicate "critical" of these discontents; a glance at some of them may reveal something of their relation to the kind of difficulties the philosopher is primarily concerned to articulate, *with which in certain places they overlap*. It *may* be that this brief study will serve further to illustrate some of the characteristic tasks of the philosopher of religion.

The phrase "Your God is too small" has obtained currency primarily through its use as the title of a popular book. But it is a phrase which, for all its crudity, evokes a quick response from many who will never read the volume to which it gives a name. "Your God is too small": here we note that the fact of something answering to the description "divine being" is not called in question; rather there is implicit a challenge to worshippers of such a being of having made him too exclusively after the image of their own parochial requirements.

43

In one sense there is nothing altogether unfamiliar in this. The charge the words convey in the contemporary idiom is the old one of anthropomorphism. And here the professional student of the history of philosophical theology is bound to remember that if according to the venerable tradition of the "way of analogy", a middle road must be sought between agnosticism and anthropomorphism, it is the latter which is the worse offence against the metaphysical and indeed the religious light. If we can predicate analogically of God (and I am not concerned this afternoon to argue for or against the possibility of such predication), we do so by a method wherein we dare follow the "way of eminence" only after we have evacuated the attributes we predicate of God of any hint of the anthropomorphic by a radical following of the "way of negation"; so too according to one possible interpretation of the opening sections of his work, the *Parmenides*, Plato is concerned to bring out how transformed out of all recognition our notions of participation and copying (*methexis* and *mimēsis*) must be if we are to employ them of the relation of particulars to Forms. One might point to an even more obvious example of the presence of self-criticism as an essential element in religious life, to the witness of the prophets, whether one thinks of the eighth-century Hebrew prophets, or of those who in other ages have by their activity earned more or less deservedly the title. A philosopher might even wish to label the sort of criticism of which I am now speaking "same level" criticism, to distinguish it from his own "other level" criticism which must include "same level" criticism among its objects. Only there is (as perhaps my reference to the issue of analogical predication will have indicated) an important overlap between the two.

In one sense then we are simply concerned with a new set of variations on a familiar theme. But we do ourselves ill-service if we fail to observe the novelty. For what we have to reckon with is a criticism of our habitual religious idiom and imagery which is the more searching for being diffuse and hardly assimilated, more easily described and illustrated than set out in a few neat formulae.

Now one distinguished Cambridge theologian has expressed

in some of his writings one most important aspect of the sort of discontent which I am trying to capture. I refer to Dr C. E. Raven, and to a warning that one can find very frequently repeated in his writings from popular, occasional addresses to the sustained argument of his Gifford lectures. I refer to his insistence that theologians and indeed religious teachers cease from treating the created universe as if it were no more than the stage for the drama of redemption. The image is surely worth comment. Its inspiration, of course, lies deep in Dr Raven's long pondered efforts to assimilate with an evolutionary model of the universe, one might say a particular empirically based cosmology, the supposed finalities of Christian faith. These efforts have made him the sustained opponent of any presentation of the person and work of Christ which presents him simply as a divine intruder. He pinpoints the frequency with which in popular apologetic, and indeed in the writings of sophisticated theologians, Christ is portrayed as a strange invader from another world, whose brief and sudden appearance in this world confers upon it what little significance its history may have; and this significance is only that of the stage, or setting, of his life.

We are familiar with the experience of seeing (to take one example) *Hamlet* played now against one carefully designed background, now against another. May be on occasion we are moved seriously to criticize the sets, the *décor*, the costumes of this production or that; but the substance of the play is relatively unaffected.

To make this point clearer (using the technical language of the philosophy of logic) I might say that Sir Michael Redgrave's or Sir Laurence Olivier's realization of the character and history of the prince is in external relation to the background, and to the peculiar conceits of those concerned with the stage-management of the production in which one or other plays the part of Hamlet. (To explain by illustration how I use here the term "external relations", I might say, for example, that the geometrical truth that the angles of a Euclidean triangle are equal to two right angles is in external relation to the fact that Octavius defeated Marcus Antonius at Actium; the geometrical truth would still obtain as a geometrical truth, however the truth of such truths be understood, if Antonius and not Octavius had been victorious.)

If this explanation of my use of the term "external relation" is plain, you will understand what I mean when I speak of Redgrave's or Olivier's conception of the Prince being in external relation to the settings of the production, and what therefore I think Dr Raven wishes to formulate when he suggests a tendency on the part of theologians and religious teachers to treat the universe simply as the stage-setting for the drama of redemption. Dr Raven argues rightly that a Christian has only to bring together his understanding (however half-formed and ill-digested) of the origins of the world to which men and women and their history belong, to see how utterly unacceptable the implied suggestion of much popular Christian teaching that the world in its prolonged and perhaps now faintly decipherable history is to be regarded simply as a setting for something frequently described as the "drama of redemption". The phrase "the drama of redemption" itself may have a partial legitimacy as underlining the fact that we are here dealing with a thing done as well as a word spoken, with drama as well as *rhēma*, with something, moreover, which in its detail manifests suggestive and important likenesses to (as well as differences from) the tragedies achieved by ancient and by modern dramatists; yet in itself it has the inevitable effect of detaching altogether the events of the life and death of Jesus and their *sequelae* from the setting to which they belong, that is, from the history of the universe as a whole. They are rendered powerless to illuminate their context, and moreover, in spite of the crucially significant fact of the readiness of Jesus to speak to the generality of men and women in parables, that context is rendered powerless to illuminate the supposed mysteries of faith.

We can surely discover in the kind of thinking and speaking which aroused Dr Raven's protest a half-deliberate, half-unrecognized diminution of the stature of the Christian revelation to something which traditionally religious men find manageable and familiar. In a work written in 1927 but published only a few years ago in France, and now about to appear in English, *Le Milieu Divin* (Collins, 1960), Père Teilhard de Chardin (for whose work Dr Raven publicly expressed his admiration) has voiced these discontents with hardly exampled force and insight.

"Where are the roots of our being?" he asks. "In the first place", he replies, "they plunge back and down into the unfathomable past. How great is the mystery of the first cells which were one day animated by the breath of our souls! How impossible to decipher the welding of successive influences in which we are forever incorporated!—however autonomous our soul, it is indebted to an inheritance worked upon from all sides—before ever it came into being—by the totality of the energies of the earth" (p. 30).

No English translation can do justice to the subtle French prose in which the author pursues to its end this self-interrogation. The student of French literature will at once recognize in Teilhard a kinship with Descartes and Pascal, contrasted fellow-students of the writings of Montaigne. "What am I?" he asks, putting the question as a man aware of the hardly limitable vastnesses of the universe to which he belongs. And although he wrote this work more than thirty years ago, his meditation, at once intellectually informed and spiritually mature, is singularly enlightening for men and women today.

When I speak of men and women today I would insist that I am not thinking simply of those with the technical training necessary to judge between competing empirical cosmologies; I am thinking also of those quite ordinary men and women who are filled with an understandable, and indeed entirely proper, *awe* as they stand or believe themselves standing on the threshold of the space-age. To such men and women it seems that human beings are beginning to emancipate themselves from the bonds of their earthly parish and they await the changes in perspective which such emancipation must bring, as if they were altogether unafraid of any altered view of their own status which such changes must bring. Their awe before the space-age includes among its ingredients an element of sheer exhilaration as well as alert curiosity. It is hard altogether to acquit professional theologians, and indeed religious teachers generally, of ignoring the events which have aroused these emotions as if nothing very remarkable had happened, or were going to happen. Teilhard's book is an instance of a genre of religious writing, achieved at a deep level of combined spiritual and intellectual self-consciousness, of which in this age of new-style Copernican revolution we stand in urgent need.

To speak in these terms is not for a moment to ignore the critical problem of which I spoke at the outset of this lecture; the language of such an essay as the one by Teilhard which I have mentioned raises its special problems of validity, intelligibility, etc. But the critical philosopher who takes religious discourse as his province must not leave out of account the impulse represented and expressed by such essays towards the reconciliation of opposed elements in our spiritual and intellectual inheritance as the one I have mentioned and others whose need I have advertised.

Again the same philosopher equally cannot afford to neglect the protest which any manifestation of the synthetic impulse comparable to that displayed by Teilhard, and indeed by Dr Raven, immediately elicits from those who without failing to appreciate the validity and the importance of Dr Raven's protest, yet distrust any doctrine, any image of the relation of the world to God which blurs the reality of evil, both physical and moral (both in the sense of *Übel* and of *Böse*). Whatever else we may question, we may not question the reality of the pain from which sufferers from various forms of cancer are suffering even as this lecture is delivered. If the "world is a vale of soul-making", it shows many signs of being a badly botched job (if I may echo a familiar comment on the so-called "argument from design", most empirically vulnerable of all traditional forms of theistic proof).

It is perhaps worth recalling at this juncture that the atheist, who in his argument emphasizes such points, by his emphasis makes it clear that his temper is closer to that of the believer than that of the agnostic; his criticisms are in a profound sense "same level criticisms" (to revert to the phrase I used earlier), whether directed at the premise of some version of the "argument from design" or invoked to impugn some image of the unity of creation. Moreover, the language in which he speaks sometimes has unmistakably, even passionately, religious overtones and undertones.

Passing however from the sphere of physical evil (of *Übel*) to that of moral (of *Böse*), we have to acknowledge that the New Testament itself leaves altogether unresolved the questions inevitably raised by the action and the role of Iscariot. The Son of Man goes indeed the way prescribed for him in the scriptures he is concerned to fulfil; but woe to that man by whom he is handed over to his foes. "It were good for that man that he had not been born." It would be hard to find anywhere a sharper enunciation of the existence of sheer discontinuity in a world in the same utterance represented as providentially ordered.

The critical and historically informed student of these opposed styles of argument and feeling may well trace in them transcripts into the idiom of religious belief and aspiration of some of the essential impulses underlying the opposition of monist and pluralist in the domain of traditional metaphysics. An inquiry into the extent to which this is so might throw some light on the vexed and many-sided question of the relation of religion and metaphysics in some of its forms; but for the present enough has been said to show the importance of allowing our conception of what religious discourse is to include within its concept some sense of its vitally self-critical character, a self-critical character of which perhaps I have said enough to bring out its complexity and many-sidedness.

"Your God is too small." As a second illustration of this diminution of God's stature to the dimensions (shall I say?) of the ecclesiastically manageable, I should like to refer to the subject of literature, of the religious person's attitude to literature. "The poets knew it all already." So Sigmund Freud, referring perhaps to the striking fact that Sophocles fashioned out of the Oedipus story a drama of the slow process whereby a man achieved self-knowledge, a self-knowledge that he sought at the outset with complete self-confidence and determination to know the truth, but which when he attained it, was more than he could bear. When he sees his little world and his role in it for what they really are, he blinds himself, as if to see no more with his eyes what he cannot bear to perceive.

But the humility displayed by Freud is often absent from the devotedly religious man, who tends to speak and act as if there were no *revelations* (I have chosen that word deliberately) concerning the human situation to be obtained from writers of the stature of Sophocles and of Shakespeare. We are many of us familiar with the frequently reiterated falsehood "The Church has known it all along"; but sometimes one is forced to wonder whether those who are wont to accompany such words with a sad, rather weary smile, intended to convey their own participation in this alleged inheritance of traditional wisdom, stop to consider the arrogance of their remark. Did not Shakespeare *reveal* something new in his achievement of *Hamlet*? Perhaps the word "reveal" is ill-chosen in view of the ceaseless study and reflection the figure of the Prince has provoked; maybe I should have said "left to those who came after, a source of revelation". It can hardly be denied that our understanding of such notions as responsibility, free-will, decision are enlarged, even transformed (or should be enlarged and transformed) by the dramatist's most subtle exploration of the Prince's personal history. And this enlargement the dramatist achieves not by the enunciation of some general principle, but by laying bare, in the subject of his hero, the deepest recesses of the human spirit, the half-acknowledged emotional overtones and undertones which belong to any process of decision, and which can so easily be overlooked.

"What is man that Thou art mindful of him?" Dr Raven has well pin-pointed the destructive habit of the devout of representing the created universe as the setting of the "drama of redemption". Such an attitude diminishes the stature of the Creator. But we can detect an analogous diminution when devout men show themselves unwilling to allow their insight into human beings to be enlarged in ways at once unexpected and unfamiliar through great literature. I say analogous diminution; for if one's image of the creature is contracted, that contraction reacts inevitably upon one's image, however fragmentary and uncertain it may be, of the creator.

As a final illustration of this point, I would just mention how often men speak and act as if for the adult novels were only properly read for relaxation, unsuitable reading for the serious hours of the morning. "I am afraid I just haven't time for novels, nowadays." Do we, I wonder, reach for such works as *Anna Karenina, Middlemarch, Nostromo, The Wings of the Dove, The Rainbow* for relaxation? Or if we do treat them simply as light reading, have we not already resolved in advance that we will not learn from them or take them seriously? In such an attitude of mind there surely lies a most certain source of the most deadly spiritual philistinism.

This kind of criticism as much as that to which Dr Raven and Teilhard give expression is, I repeat, "same-level criticism"; both alike can be grouped together as parallel manifestations of the protest "Your God is too small"; both alike in their working-out must form material for the "other level" criticism characteristic of the philosopher; both alike overlap with the philosopher's distinctive work. Did not the late Dr Friedrich Waismann, who wrote illuminatingly of Kafka's *Trial* as well as of the formalist interpretation of mathematics, speak often of the need of a "logic of poetry"?

The last manifestation of "same level" criticism which I wish to mention is somewhat different; but it is almost as important as the other two assaults upon the theologian's territory, as he tends to define it, of which I have spoken. The philosopher of religion easily tends to think that the greatest obstacles today in the way of religious belief are to be found in the unintelligibility and inadmissibility of such fundamental concepts as that of a creator God, an immaterial soul, etc. But it may be that as a matter of empirical fact, the most deep-seated unwillingness to take seriously the claims of the Christian religion has its roots in a sharp criticism of Christian ethics, of the Christian image of the good life. This criticism may take the shape of an unwillingness to call good One represented as behaving towards his creatures in respect, for instance, of the demands he makes upon them, as the Christian God is very frequently represented. Or it may simply call attention to features of the Christian image of the good life which are open to serious criticism, or are even found repulsive. Thus it is beyond question that the proper Christian attitude to suffering is regularly presented as something that many must judge unmanly (in the deepest sense), and not infrequently as unconsciously masochistic. In Germany, Dr Rudolf Bultmann, the distinguished New Testament scholar, has concerned himself for many years with the attempt to make Christian truth, purged of its supposedly mythological elements, capable of assimilation by men and women of the twentieth century. But in so far as he *sometimes* does this, mainly by carrying out ingenious translations of clauses of the creed into the characteristic idioms of Martin Heidegger, one is tempted to say that *on those occasions*, if he makes what he is translating intelligible, he does so at the cost of making it repellent.

Christians need to reckon very seriously with the authority and influence exerted today by a set of moral beliefs which I will describe as a purified and profoundly self-critical utilitarianism. This is a utilitarianism purged of the self-confidently philistine attitudes of Bentham and James Mill, against which the latter's son reacted so sharply. But it still shares with a considerable part of the utilitarian tradition a sense of the importance of those human experiences men judge worth having for their own sake and would have as widely diffused as possible, and also of the power of scientific methods at once to yield men knowledge of what is, and to bring an undeniable richness of life within their grasp. To dismiss the attitude I have very briefly and inaccurately characterized as a "secular morality" is simply to use in its respect first a seven- and then an eight-letter word! If our appraisal of contemporary religious practice is to be accurate (and it is with religious practice in its vast complexity articulated in language that the philosopher is concerned), we must reckon with this kind of discontent, even as we must reckon with those who, without committing themselves to explicit religious beliefs, point to flaws and inadequacies in the ethical attitude I have just sketched.

One could wish, however, that one saw more awareness of

the kind of dissatisfaction I have sketched among the devout, a sharper sense of the questions which are certainly being put to them by those who see the Christian image of the good life as at once distorted and ambiguous, an image which seems seriously to deflect men and women from securing and even enjoying the richness of experience with which the future may even now furnish themselves and their descendants.

To return for a moment to the so-called "Christian attitude of suffering". Those of you who are familiar with the writings of the great eighteenth-century Christian moral philosopher, Bishop Butler, will remember the care with which he traces the necessary role of what he calls resentment in our proper human nature. I wonder if any of my hearers recalled Butler's careful analysis of that propension and his recognition of its indispensability when they read Edith Bone's account of her seven years solitary confinement in Hungarian Communist prisons. Her occasional spirited displays of fierce anger at those who were inflicting intolerable indignities upon her, were among the means whereby she believes herself to have retained her sanity during her "seven years' solitary".

Christian moral teachers should surely, as they survey much conventional religious language concerning the *acceptance* of suffering, acknowledge the importance of distinguishing between an acceptance which is positive, active and spirited (in the Greek sense), and one which can only be dismissed as negative, passive and acquiescent. The notion of *acceptance* is viciously ambiguous, and can be invoked in defence of attitudes to evil, both moral and physical alike, which very little reflection reveals as at once sterile and humanly unworthy, as indeed sometimes suggesting that Christian faith has a kind of vested interest in human failure and disaster.

I have dared in this last section only to touch on matters of such complexity and importance that my whole lecture might well have been devoted to them. But in conclusion I should venture to remind my hearers of the purposes I have sought to fulfil by my whole lecture. If the philosopher of religion who devotes his attention in the first instance to the Christian religion, is to treat of the field with which he is concerned

53

concretely, attending, as far as he can, to the actualities of that which he is exploring, he must (in my view) be particularly alert to the sort of "same-level" criticisms I have mentioned, and indeed to others which I have not had time to indicate. The philosopher is *not* an apologist; apologetic concern, as Karl Barth (the one living theologian of unquestionable genius) has rightly insisted, is the death of serious theologizing, and I would add, equally of serious work in the philosophy of religion. But because the philosopher must always be a man of the borderlands, he may perhaps feel a peculiar kinship with those who, from similarly situated territory, make protesting raids upon the theologians' cherished homeland.

PHILOSOPHY AND CHRISTOLOGY

This rehabilitation of the Christology is, however, not merely a piece of New Testament exegesis which challenges the adequacy of the ruling reconstruction of the development of primitive Christianity, and sets St. Paul and the author of the Fourth Gospel far nearer to the Jesus of History than is normally allowed; it has implications for Christian Theology and for philosophy which vitally affect the doctrine of the Incarnation. The New Testament scholar, who is also a Christian, cannot patiently permit the dogmatist or the philosopher to expound the doctrine of the Incarnation on the basis of an analysis of human nature illustrated by the humanity of Jesus. He was unique; and this particularly rivets the Christian doctrine of the Incarnation to the Christology and to the soteriology involved in the Christology, and presents an awkward material to the philosopher who is operating with a rigid doctrine of evolution. There are metaphysical implications in the Christology; and the New Testament scholar, who is compelled to adopt a rather crude conception of revelation, precisely because he is a historian and has to interpret documents recording a movement of God to man and not of man to God, has nevertheless the right to demand that the Christian dogmatist should start from this particular revelation, and that the philospher should at some point or other in his philosophy make sense of it by some other means than by obscuring the particularity of the Old Testament and by refusing to recognize that in the end the particularity of the Old Testament is only intelligible in the light of its narrowed fulfilment in Jesus, the Messiah, and of its expanded fulfilment in the Church.[1]

WITH THESE words the late Sir Edwyn Hoskyns, at the conclusion of an essay which was, in the main, a piece of New Testament scholarship, indicated certain wider issues concerning the nature of theology which had been

[1] *Mysterium Christi*, ed Deissmann and Bell, 1930.

raised for him by his work on the New Testament. What he seems to be saying amounts to something like this. There are three distinguishable intellectual enterprises, named severally philosophy, Christian theology and Christology; they are distinguishable formally by the degree of abstractness and generality which they display, and it is Hoskyns' contention that, ordered as they have been in the first part of this sentence, they form a series constituted by a movement from the absolutely general to the rigorously particular. Further, it is his intention to assert without equivocation that, for the Christian, the Christology of which he speaks is sovereign both over philosophy and over Christian theology. It is with the grounds of that claim, and with the consequences that follow from admitting it, that this essay is concerned.

Much has been written concerning the relationship of faith and reason, even concerning the relationship of philosophy and theology; but there is much less material on the more crucial and more searching issues raised by the relationship of the Christological heart of the Christian mystery to philosophical analysis. To introduce this topic it may be worth while to look for a moment at one of the more shocking implications of the passage quoted from Hoskyns. Some readers of his words may have been startled by the fact that he seems to contrast something which he calls Christology with something else which he calls Christian theology; surely it may be asked: "Is not Christology a part of Christian theology?" Certainly the student of the history of Christian doctrine in the University of Oxford will be tempted to think of the development of the doctrine of the Incarnation as simply one chapter among others, of the narrative he has somehow to memorize. But Hoskyns is saying something of the greatest importance in insisting that the reality of the matter is not like this at all; Christology is rather the name of something that sets in motion, and keeps in restless activity, the whole work of the characteristically Christian theologian. The question that sets him going, and that indeed underlies and controls his every task, is the besetting riddle: "What think ye of Christ?"; this is not one question among many, any more than in the heyday of the classical physics the so-called "law of causality" was properly regarded as one law among many; rather, just as the "law of causality" was the form of all laws by which the workings of physical nature were thought to be set out, so the question concerning the Christ insinuates itself into every theological discussion and debate, transforming them and twisting them often in directions otherwise unthought and unforeseen.[1]

It is clearly Hoskyns' fear in this passage that the Christian theologian will resist the acknowledgment of this supremacy over his enterprise of the Christology. On this score it must be said that he wrote at a time when in Great Britain, and indeed in other countries, theologians were showing themselves unwilling to acknowledge the unique status of the thing called Christology; it was the age of such notorious *mots* as the saying of the late Archbishop William Temple that the language of the Council of Chalcedon revealed the "bankruptcy of patristic thought"; it was a time when there was very great confusion concerning the proper frontiers of philosophy, and theology, and when indeed this blurring of frontiers was continually praised as something at once intellectually valid, and apologetically and pastorally desirable. Even today those who are concerned with philosophical studies in British universities, and who also profess and call themselves Christians, are reproached by the *bien-pensants* if they do not present to their students an unhealthy hybrid called a "philosophy of life", something which is neither philosophy nor theology but a violation of the integrity of both disciplines, and indeed a standing menace to the spiritual health both of the man who purveys it and of those condemned to listen to him. If the present writer may be permitted a personal comment at this point, he might observe that for him to suppose that what he could offer the students in his ordinary class at nine in his lecture room could be in any sense whatever an adequate substitute for the mysteries of the Eucharist at which he may have assisted at seven-thirty the same day, would be a treason alike to his faith and to his philosophical conscience.

[1] Cf. the impressive introductory sections of Heinrich Vogel, *Christologie*, Vol. 1, where he insists that we always remember that it is always Christ who puts this question to us.

It should perhaps be remarked that, in the paragraph under discussion, Hoskyns had particularly in mind a person whom he called "the philosopher who is operating with a rigid doctrine of evolution". That is to say, just as he saw in the theologian a man continually tempted to escape from admitting the sovereignty of the Christology, so he saw in the philosopher someone tempted to borrow from the biologist the category of evolution, and with its help impose on all things in heaven and earth a particular image and shape; those indeed who knew something of the theological state of Cambridge at the time at which he wrote, would also realize that he had in mind some of the unhappier excursions into philosophy of the late Professor J. F. Bethune-Baker. He might indeed have defined the confusions he feared as a blurring of the proper task of philosophy itself; for the philosopher is concerned not to use categories such as evolution in order with their aid to build a speculatively satisfying picture of what is, but primarily in order to understand their force and function, what has been called their peculiar logic.

It is of course no accident that Hoskyns' unequivocal avowal of the sovereignty of Christology comes at the end of a piece of New Testament work;[1] in other places he repeatedly insisted that for the Christian there was no escape from the hard discipline imposed on him by the necessity of continual, critical study of the New Testament. Indeed, the acceptance of this discipline was part and parcel of the acknowledgment of the sovereignty of Christology; if one consequence of its acceptance was to make serious theological work a less delicately and closely woven unity than the theologian might desire, that untidiness was itself an expression of his fidelity to the underlying demands of his enterprise. To acknowledge the supremacy of the Christology is to confess that finality belongs somehow to that which is particular and contingent, to that which has definite date and place, to that which is described by statements that are not "truths of reason", or, in more modern language, "necessary propositions". Further, it is to involve the confession of faith inextricably with the deliverances of flickering human percep-

[1] E.g. in *The Riddle of the New Testament*.

58

tion and observation; indeed, the paradoxical and bewildering character of this involvement is clearly recognized in the New Testament itself, where, for instance, in the Fourth Gospel, the reader meets highly sophisticated discussion of the relations of seeing and believing. If he is a philosopher, as perhaps some of those for whom the author intended his book may have been, he will recognize a certain familiarity in the often tense and emotionally charged dialogue; he may even find in it, not simply echoes of the Platonists, but curious anticipations of what men of profoundly sceptical and critical intellect like Kant and Hume were later to write on the limitations of human sensibility, imagination and understanding.

It was from his New Testament work that Hoskyns came to avow the sovereignty of the Christology; and this fact sharply differentiates the manner in which he avowed it from that in which it was confessed by another of the great British theologians of this century, the late P. T. Forsyth. It also enabled him to raise, both in the passage we are considering and in other places,[1] some of the consequences of thus exalting the contingent and particular over the necessary and universal, which received less overt attention in Forsyth's work. To exalt the Christology above theology and philosophy is not to dispense with the work either of the theologian or of the philosopher; nor is it in any sense whatsoever to deny the relevance of the work of the philosopher to the work of Christology, nor to escape the inevitable difficulties of their overlap and interplay. The very language of particularity and contingency is language which is part of the stock-in-trade of technical philosophy; to say that the proposition "Christ was crucified under Pontius Pilate" is not a necessary proposition, is to draw on the resources of an entire philosophy of logic; to suggest that in the writing of the fourth evangelist we find suggestions of the idiom of Kant and Hume is not to call attention to a superficial resemblance of outward style, but to suggest a similarity at the very heart of their several intellectual concerns. Moreover, the critical philosopher is inevitably aware of the special problems

[1] In the introductory material to his great unfinished commentary on the Fourth Gospel (1940).

of historical knowledge; and he cannot throw over his sense of their difficulty when he comes to scrutinize the peculiar claim of Christ. Indeed, it is of the very nature of that claim to press upon him these problems more sharply, even to the point of intellectual agony, if he takes them seriously. The admission of the sovereignty of the Christology is not, for the philosopher, any sort of escape from his own special problems; still less is it a device whereby he is able to say that theology has its own place, its statements their own special logic, and that it is enough for him to point out this uniqueness and to defend it against those who would impugn or criticize it. Of course, Christology is what it is and not something different, even as much as poetry and pure mathematics are what they are, and neither of them to be confused with everyday description, or theoretical physics. But poetry does overlap with conversation, and there is a most difficult problem sometimes in distinguishing the pure from the applied in the field of mathematics; and when we come to Christology the interplay is more devastating, the overlap is more bewildering. For when we say that *for us* Christ died and was buried, we speak of what men certainly saw and touched; at least we so engage ourselves that if they did not touch and see, then the whole enterprise comes to an end and there is nothing more to be said. And yet we do not stop simply at recording what men saw and touched; with our *pro nobis* we go beyond seeing and touching, and therefore are immediately faced with questions of validity that seem familiar, very like questions we have faced before in other places, and yet strangely and frighteningly outrunning them and bearing us we know not where.

We can make this clearer, if we retrace our steps. Readers may have noticed a certain ambiguity in the use of the word "Christology" in the preceding pages. Sometimes it has been used as the name of a set of propositions, sometimes with a more psychological nuance, for the intellectual processes involved in their formulation. It will be impossible to keep the two altogether distinct; but for the moment it may be wise to concentrate on the latter. What is it for men, what has it been for them to be faced with the intellectual task of hammering out a

Christology, of acknowledging its peculiar sovereignty over the movements of their minds? How indeed is Christology itself related to the Christologies that men have fashioned, even to such hard-won, authoritative insights as the Homo-ousion?

Certainly Christology is like nothing else; it is unique; and yet it overlaps here, there and everywhere; and where philosophy in particular is concerned, the overlap presents inescapable problems. These arise in many places; we have already noticed how the fourth evangelist displays a sense of the issues defined by the great eighteenth-century writers on the theory of knowledge. But also it cannot be too often recalled that, to get its own problems stated, Christology must borrow from the jargons of logic and ontology; we need, for instance, the category of radical contingency in order that the shock of the claim which Christ makes shall not be blunted.

Here I hope I shall be forgiven if I venture a brief piece of intellectual autobiography. After I had been reading philosophy at Oxford for five terms, in the long vacation of 1934, I began to move on from the study of the text of Kant to the writings of the British idealists of the nineteenth and early twentieth centuries. Almost suddenly, as it seemed, I found myself faced with a problem; why need God have created a world? Was there not in the notion of a *creatio de nihilo* something which violated any conceivable "principle of sufficient reason"? If the question of the why of creation were unanswerable, were we not committed to a blind irrationality at the heart, and at the foundation, of being? Of course I need not have gone further than Leibniz' famous correspondence with Clarke on Newton's views of space and time to find an earlier, classical statement of very much the same difficulty; only, in this correspondence the range of the discussion is restricted to the compatibility of a particular view of space and time (one which admittedly lay at the basis of Newtonian physics), with the "principle of sufficient reason", whereas the idealists seemed, by their use of it, to put a question mark against the opening clauses of the Nicene creed.

But even before I thus allowed the teachings of the absolute idealists to affect the fabric of my faith, I became aware that

61

philosophically some of their most characteristic doctrines had not gone unchallenged. Green, I knew, had written much in criticism of Mill's logic; but I was dimly aware that others like the Austrian Gottlob Frege and the Englishman Bertrand Russell had shared Green's profound dissatisfaction with Mill, but had not found in Green's intellectual masters the answers they sought to such questions as the nature of arithmetic. In the winter I passed on to the study of Russell and Moore and found, in their logical pluralism, something which was at once more profoundly disturbing intellectually, and yet in certain ways oddly reassuring. It is of this ambivalence that I would like to speak.

Both Russell and Moore seemed, in different ways, conclusively to refute any sort of ontological argument; here indeed they seemed to resume the accents of the authentic Kant, the Kant of the Dialectic, and to speak his meaning with an inescapable rigour and clarity. There was no road from essence to existence, from concept to reality; no sleight of hand could make of existence a predicate or attribute. Between truths of reason and truths of fact there was a great gulf fixed; by no *a priori* reasoning was it possible to establish the nature of what is. To know whether or not something existed, appeal must be made to observation; it was impossible from attention to any description we might entertain to decide whether or not it applied in reality.

Of course there was something very disturbing about such a doctrine, and the further exploration of its consequences was not initially reassuring; it seemed as if the universe were falling apart; the acceptance of some relations at least as genuinely external to their terms seemed to take any sort of deep-level connectedness out of things. This impression was deepened by the strength of the case made out by philosophers of this school, for treating causality as a sort of "regularity of sequence", even for identifying it more simply with the possibility of establishing functional correlations in the world of experience. There seemed in the world of the atomist no pathway towards God, no means even of seeing the world as a whole as something setting a problem by its existence; the very notion of the world as a whole seemed logically suspect. Perhaps, from time to time, one looked back wistfully at the confused profundities of the idealists from which one had been emancipated.

And yet there was gain as well as loss. For one thing, Moore made it possible for me to be a realist; his laborious arguments concerning the status and nature of objects of perception made it clear that, whatever perceiving was, it was a finding rather than a fashioning. Further, truth was not to be identified with an internally coherent whole of judgments; it resided in the correspondence of proposition and fact. Thinking had a reference beyond itself; even if it was hard to speak of any sort of "sufficient reason" in things, yet things were somehow there to come to terms with. They might lack any sort of connectedness; it might even be possible to speak of being *per se* as intelligible. Yet for the logical atomist, there *were* things with which men were coming to terms; the world was not simply an expression of their immanent rationality, but something given.

Looking back now I can see that what I welcomed was in the end some sort of rehabilitation of the notion of the transcendent. Whatever else they did, the philosophers of the Cambridge school seemed to me the settled foes of metaphysical immanentism; it was this which attracted me *religiously* towards them, even while I knew that they were, some of them at least, avowed atheists. Somehow, although this atheism challenged and unsettled me, it seemed a more honest and somehow less corrupting thing than the monistic insistence on, for instance, the rational necessity of evil to the articulation of the good.[1]

If I may comment on this fragment of autobiography, I must say three things. Presumably there is something here which can fall under the rubric *fides quaerens intellectum*; I came to philosophy as one already committed to Catholic Christianity, and I suppose that in philosophy I sought at once confirmation of my beliefs, and an apologetic instrument whereby I might make those beliefs more congenial to other minds. But I found neither of these; rather, first, the demands of rationality in the sense of the absolute idealists seemed to impugn the first article of the creed, seemed to make irrational the very notion

---

[1] I am referring to evil both in the sense of *Übel* and of *Böse*.

of a creator God; then the rigorous criticism of their doctrines seemed to push me further away from any sort of ease in respect of the language of faith, even while at the same time it did become a little less impossible to admit the transcendent as something sheerly given, although the manner of its givenness seemed utterly obscure. Thus the quest of faith for understanding seemed to end, if not in a cul-de-sac, at least in a maze.

Yet faith survived; or rather I suppose that I should say it did not let me go; and the study of the New Testament gradually awoke in me the realization of something which I later found expressed in the passage from Hoskyns quoted at the outset of this essay. There was something called Christology which was unique, a kind of human intellectual response to the overwhelming fact of the ministry, crucifixion and resurrection of Jesus. The four books of theological history, which we call the Gospels, were examples of this sort of response; they were compact of factual record and interpretation, and the effort to disentangle the two moments seemed sometimes hardly worth making. But even if the facts to which they were a response seemed to elude articulation in detail, the Gospels remained a vital testament to something altogether incommensurable with ordinary human experience, yet at the same time organically one with the particularities of an individual stretch of human history. And to this the Church's Liturgy also bore witness in the effectual remembrancing of the Christ.

But if faith was autonomous, its autonomy was not the bare independence of something which could exist altogether unaffected by the questionings of philosophy. Thus it could be said that the logical atomists had restored a clear perception of the irreducible difference between existential and attributive propositions; to say that tame tigers existed was to assert a fact of a wholly different logical order from that conveyed by the statement that tame tigers growled. Essence certainly did not entail existence; the principle of the ontological argument was logically invalid. Looked at from one point of view this movement of thought could be regarded as a preamble of faith, a sort of catharsis of the mind whereby it was made ready to admit that the sheerly particular could be "the place where it is demanded of men that they should believe". But, of course, neither Moore nor Russell saw their logical work like that; and the believer who finds their arguments seem to make the way of faith more accessible to him, must remember and take seriously the context to which those arguments belong. They are not offered in any sense as a preamble of faith; they belong to philosophical thinking which frankly is atheistic in bias, and the believer who finds them enlightening must acknowledge the setting in which they occur and treat it with a proper seriousness.

It may be that this seriousness will take the form of saying that, in the last resort, atheism may be less hardly reconcilable with faith than certain sorts of idealism, even that atheism is a dialectical moment, for some at least, in the argument of faith. That is a bold step of which more will be said later in this essay; but now it must be clearly insisted that if the Christian believer flirts with atheism, he is transforming, by his very flirtation, the object of his attention. There is something opaque to him in the atheist's position, as the atheist himself accepts it, whether the atheist be a logical pluralist or a Marxist. This may be, of course, because the Christian has moved on to a place, or towards a place, where the atheist's repudiation of God has become almost trivial in comparison with his own sense of the sheer Godlessness of being; it may be because he has a little approached, as the saints have undoubtedly done, towards the place and the hour wherein Christ cried: "My God, my God, why hast thou forsaken me?" Or it may be because he is intellectually slothful, and prefers to cheat. But the fact remains that faith cannot somehow swallow up the philosopher's atheism; the latter has to be acknowledged as something which has its own laws, even its own dignity; and if the believer is at the same time technically competent in philosophy, he will be conscious of himself as arguing about the issues this atheism raises in two ways at the same time. He will certainly see the thing *sub specie aeterni*, even *sub specie crucis*, which is perhaps the same perspective; and yet he will also know that for instance the arguments of the logical atomist raise questions which must be faced at their own level. Thus it is by no means clear that the treatment of inference by Russell and Wittgenstein[1] altogether dispenses with the need of invoking some sort of "synthetic *a priori*" truth. But this is a technical question which can be discussed only by those who are professionally competent to undertake its discussion.

So the movement between Christology and philosophy seems, if our illustrations are in any way representative, not to conform to any pre-conceived pattern; certainly the two enterprises have a genuine autonomy. And yet at the same time the gulf between them is crossed, now in one way, now in another. The man of faith will be aware of his faith as something which may work as an unconscious, even an unacknowledged, motive in his intellectual picking and choosing; he will even have to be on guard against a certain sort of intellectual masochism, whereby he shows himself ready to assent to arguments simply because they seem to make faith harder for him. But all the time, if he is a philosopher, he will see a kind of intellectual attraction and repulsion at work between the concepts and categories whereby he secures to himself Christ's very grasp upon him, and those by which he shows forth to himself the stuff of the world about him in all its familiarity and diverse richness.

Yet it will be remembered that in the passage with which this essay began Hoskyns asserted the sovereignty of Christology not only over philosophy, but over theology. He was writing in 1930; and since then, in the growing fullness of Karl Barth's dogmatic exposition, we have a working out of the consequences of such an acknowledgment of the sovereignty of Christology by a theologian which is truly classical alike in comprehensive range and detailed thoroughness. For Barth there are no problems in theology which are not in the end Christocentric; whether it be the relation of time to eternity, the predestination of men to heaven or to hell, the besetting facts of sin and evil, the flickering impulses of love and of an unattainable, unimaginable beauty in the human heart, the political obligations of men in organized society—all must be seen

---

[1] In the latter's *Tractatus Logico-Philosophicus*, and in the former's lectures on "The Philosophy of Logical Atomism", published in *The Monist*.

in terms of Christ, who in his very concreteness is God's dealing with men. His method can be illustrated in every sort of way; but perhaps a reference to a part of his attack on the problem of the evil will throw into clear light its utter concreteness. In the end, for Barth, the problem of the evil will *is* the problem of Judas Iscariot; the theologian must not speculate in the sense of asking how evil can be somehow the occasion of good. He must allow his thinking on this subject to be riveted to what he knows of God's actual engagement with the issue, an engagement of which in a sense the whole Bible speaks, but which reaches its sharpest point in the upper room, when Jesus bids Judas go forth into the night to do what he has purposed to do, and when in the garden his receiving of the kiss of betrayal precipitates the traitor upon the road which leads him to "his own place". This concentration on Iscariot is in no sense an illustrative device; it is justified because he is in the place where the problem is raised with archetypal and definitive seriousness. Every detail of the relations of Christ with Judas demands the closest possible scrutiny, and no hermeneutic effort can be spared to lay bare the very depth of their controversy; for *there* is the problem of evil, seen not apart from, but in terms of, the betrayal and rejection of Christ.

In the end the traditional distinction between particular and universal disappears; we cannot speak of the crucifixion of Jesus, and the events which led up to and achieved it, as an instance of human evil-doing. In one sense, of course, it most certainly is that; the language of Caiaphas, for instance, is that of "ecclesiastical statesmen" all down the ages; we can catch the hints of a similar accent in Archbishop Geoffrey Fisher's hesitancy to give full support in unequivocal terms to men like Father Trevor Huddleston in their struggle against the morally and theologically intolerable policies and actions of the South African nationalists *vis-à-vis* the Bantu. But because Jesus is who he is, his rejection and crucifixion can only be—evil itself.

Jesus is sheerly concrete, sheerly particular; he is "man for man" only through having a place in history, through belonging to a particular time, and through being exposed to its peculiar needs and tensions. But the self-giving which makes him thus "man for man" and "man for God" belongs to eternity; this life, so ordinary in so many ways, so cribbed and cabined, so pitifully incomplete, has its ultimate ground and setting in the love of God, which indeed it makes concrete in the depth of human history. We could dare to say, we would be justified in saying, that the ministry of Jesus is not an instance or an example of the love of God, but rather its very substance; a point of which in the New Testament itself the epistle to the Ephesians offered a classical exposition.

There is in Barth's thought a note of positivism. He is always the champion of the concrete against, for instance, the abstract or merely possible. In his discussion of the meaning of pre-destination, he will have nothing to do with any theorizing which averts attention from Christ. The mysteries of election can only be approached across, through, and in the One whom God has chosen, in whom his choice of men is concrete. If we are to speak of "double predestination", we should perhaps begin by recalling the Lucan dialogue between the thieves crucified with Jesus, and even in our beginning remember that, in those three hours, the very sense of hell itself is being trans-formed by the One who has entered the darkness of human condemnation. Abstract theorizing and preaching concerning the final destiny of men which averts from the manner in which the very foundations of their destiny are laid, namely the ministry, death and resurrection of Jesus, is worse than sterile.

There is certainly a note of positivism here, something analogous to that sounded by Bertrand Russell when he said, suggesting the application of the methods of mathematical logic to the solution of classical philosophical problems: "When-ever possible, let us substitute logical constructions out of the observable for inferred, unobserved entities." There is in Barth something analogous to this recommended logical economy. We must, he insists, substitute for abstract, general statements concerning the being and purposes of God, and of men, state-ments that show them in terms of, or set them in relation to, Jesus Christ. We cannot speak of something called the "Chris-tian doctrine of man" without mention of the prayer of Jesus in the wilderness, on the hillside, and in the garden, of his compassion for leper and for blind, for tax-gatherer and for prostitute, his inexorable sternness towards scribe and pharisee (the self-righteous heart turned in upon itself); we certainly cannot write of that doctrine without, as it were, setting at the head of our page the laconic, cynical *double entendre* of Pilate: "*Ecce Homo.*" The impossibility here is a logical impossibility; its disregard is sheer self-contradiction.

Barth's standpoint, then, has a positivist quality; and it is also strongly ontological. If his quarrel with the *analogia entis* of Erich Pryzwara and other Catholic theologians is a decisive, even a fundamental moment in his thought, we did not need to wait for the publication of his pamphlet on Rudolf Bultmann[1] to see that his thinking throughout the *Dogmatik* is ruled by a sense of the primacy of what is over our thought of it. Thinking for him does not "make it so"; it can only, if it is valid, achieve for the thinker some sort of correspondence between his thinking and what is, a being which at its very foundation, i.e. its relation to God, is pivoted upon Jesus Christ, true man and true God. In a way Barth's very quarrel with the *analogia entis* is rooted in his conviction that it seems to assign to an abstract, or at best to an analogically participated transcendental, the role that belongs to Christ alone.

His thought is positivistic *and* ontological; and as von Balthasar has pointed out so clearly,[2] he displays a remarkable kinship with some of the great masters of the spiritual life in the Catholic tradition. For if in Catholic theology the "five ways" are often presented as a kind of rational "preamble of faith", Catholic ascetic theologians have never forgotten (with all their quite proper regards for the rights of human reason), that Christ is *the* way to God, and that men by baptism are set upon that way, and none other; the way which leads from Galilee to Jerusalem, from life to death; the way which reaches its term, and receives its definition, in the creative and inclusive mystery of the Paschal night, of whose abysses it would seem that those

---

[1] *Rudolf Bultmann, Ein Versuch ihn zu verstehen* (1953).

[2] In his *Karl Barth: Darstellung und Deutung seiner Theologie* (1951). In this most valuable book the cruciality of Barth's study of Anselm for his development is stressed.

who wrote, for instance, of the "dark night of the soul" were also speaking.[1] Barth's Christocentrism is passionately evangelical; but it is also something which enables those who are rooted in the great traditions of Catholic spirituality to understand anew the inwardness of their inheritance. In his theology there is no element of philistinism, only the intellectual achievement of a profound Christocentric self-discipline.

To a large extent the same was true of Forsyth; even if his writings were not given, by reason of their circumstances, the sort of direction and unity which Barth has achieved for his. But with Forsyth too there is the same patient, yet inexorable, insistence that the centre of the Christian mystery shall not be obscured by any speculative dialectic; such concepts as reconciliation, and the overcoming of evil by good, are to be interpreted in terms of the *opus operatum* of the ministry of Jesus, and not vice versa. Forsyth had read widely in philosophy, and he shared with Sören Kierkegaard the sense that the Hegelian outlook trivialized the tragic depth of human existence, making even of Gethsemane itself a charade. For those who are concerned with the interplay of philosophy and theology, it is always interesting to remark how Forsyth invoked against the Hegelians the Kantian doctrine of the primacy of the practical reason. He found Kant's metaphysical agnosticism congenial, and like him, used it as a means of bringing out the supreme importance of the moral order, even the unscaled and unplumbed heights and depths of the world of freedom. He was on edge in the presence of ontological divinity, coining the word "Chalcedonism" to express his (certainly unfair) impatience with all its forms. Although he does not use the concept of "myth", nor show any sense of its logical complexity, there is no doubt that he would have claimed for the "mythological", properly understood, a place near the heart of any human understanding of the *mysterium Christi*, or at least of any understanding of that understanding; for he made a use of the notions of *Kenosis* and *Plerosis* to give a defence of that mystery from the unskilled and irreverent probing of the un-

---

[1] Cf. here Père Yves Congar, O.P., on *Le Purgatoire* in the volume *Le Mystère de la Mort et sa célébration chrétienne* (1951).

disciplined intellect, almost classic in its profundity, and in these notions there is certainly (in their fusion of the metaphysical and the factually descriptive), an element of the "mythical". But of this Forsyth was unafraid, only insisting that if we were serious in finding our way to the Father in the Son's glorification of him upon earth, and in the Father's glorification of the Son in the raising him from the dead, we must be content to let our representations of the Absolute experience the full weight of a Christocentric transformation.

Perhaps enough has now been said to bring out something of what a subordination of theology to Christology must involve; and, as the examples of both Barth and Forsyth have illustrated, this subordination does not involve any indifference to philosophy. Rather it was possible to remark in Barth's case a certain analogy between his procedure and that recommended by Lord Russell in his well-known "method of logical constructions"; even to speak of his method as positivist is to say something about it which it would be, perhaps, possible only for a philosopher to say. Further, in Forsyth's case we have noticed his appeal to Kant; there is no doubt that he called Kant his philosophical master and that he accepted this allegiance partly because such a philosophical method as Kant's seemed to him to secure the proper autonomy of the Gospel, the possibility of being engaged by the self-revelation of God on its own terms. It is almost certainly no accident that the philosophical names mentioned in this paragraph are both of them names of men whose work has a dignity of its own as philosophical work. They were neither of them apologists of Christianity; indeed, Lord Russell's avowed atheism has only recently been tempered by a gentler, agnostic note. But they were considerable philosophers with whose philosophical work any serious student of the subject must engage at their own level; Russell's "method of logical constructions", Kant's "synthetic *a priori*"—these are the names of serious opposing options in respect of some of the most perplexing and continuing problems of the subject. Neither Kant nor Russell will be of much service to the man who wants to prostitute his faith and his intellectual integrity alike to the caprice of something called a "Christian philosophy of life"; but for the man of faith who is also a philosopher their work will continue to raise most serious and most searching questions, questions that clearly touch the things of faith, yet without finally overthrowing their interior castle.

The world of philosophy is one world; the world of faith is another; and yet in the mind of the individual these worlds continually interpenetrate, and it would be illusion to deny the reality of their conflict. Here of course there is nothing unique in the case of philosophy, which is, after all, only one human activity among others, although one with a very great and a most serious dignity. There is nothing to commend one piece of philosophizing against another in the fact that the former lends itself more easily to the role of *ancilla theologiae*; the philosopher who is a Christian knows that sometimes he will have to sacrifice his own image of what the faith is to the claims of the discipline he professes. He will owe much in such moments to the mystery of the communion of saints in which he lives,[1] much also to the extent to which he can come to see his own experience in relation to the substance of the Christocentric ascesis. It is a terrible and a testing experience; yet there is nothing *altogether* unique in it; others have known it on the plane of actual human conduct and choice. One thinks of the inspiring example of those Spanish Catholics of whom M. Albert Camus wrote at the end of his *L'Homme Révolté*.[2]

The choice these men made was a terrible and a bitter one; but their place *sub specie aeterni* in the history of the mystical body of Christ is sure, and their protest against the willingness of ecclesiastical authority to enforce its claim upon men, by reliance on lawless armed force, on murder and on tyranny (as the Spanish Church has certainly done since 1936), is a thing maybe of deeper eschatological significance than the often quoted examples of the resistance of high-placed Church dignitaries to Communism in eastern Europe, and in China.

In Christ's name, a man may have to choose that which seems not of Christ; and in the cause of the knowledge of God, a man may have to turn his back on more than the silly respectabilities of so-called religious philosophy.

[1] Cf. H. U. von Balthasar, *Elisabeth von Dijon*.   [2] Paris, 1951; pp. 375 f.

No one, however, who has come even to the frontiers of the conflict between faith and philosophy can lightly esteem its *Angst*. Today, of course, it usually takes the shape of a sense of deep powerlessness to attach meaning or intelligible use to theological and religious expressions, or to set out the sort of ground on which they can be treated as valid.

Now this impotence does not have its source in a wilful refusal to recognize the sort of tasks religious language actually performs. We are not dealing with an intellectually undisciplined anthropomorphism, or with a philistine unwillingness to acknowledge the claims of poetry as well as of prose; we are not face to face with Bentham *redivivus*, repeating parrot-like the cry: "poetry is misrepresentation". Of course no one supposes the *pro nobis* of the phrase "crucifixus *pro nobis*" to have the same sense as the words "for us" in the sentence, "Uncle John kindly settled the hotel bill for us", or even the same as "for his friend" in the sentence (referring to a shipwreck), "if ever a man gave a life for his friend, Hector did by surrendering his place in the boat". Yet it is insisted by those who believe the creed that there is *some* resemblance between the uses, that *pro nobis* in "crucifixus *pro nobis*" is not a mere ejaculation, or (more seriously) that the language of the creed has something in common with the language in which we describe and communicate matters of fact as well as with that of, e.g. Keats' poetry, or even of the *Aeneid* or *Iliad*.

Certainly it may be pointed out as the discussion develops that the fundamental language of religion is prayer, perhaps a statement in the formal syntactical mode of speech of the familiar thesis, Religion is adoration. Others may point out how important in religion is the language of address, of "I" and "Thou", of the sermon addressed to individuals and calling them to decision;[1] others may point to such phenomena as the "prophetic actions" of the prophets,[2] and indeed of Jesus himself in cursing the fig tree,[3] bidding us further extend our view to the sacraments. Thus in a Catholic devotional near-classic,

[1] Cf. Prof. H. H. Farmer, *The Servant of the Word* (1942).

[2] These actions were minutely studied by the late Principal H. Wheeler-Robinson.

[3] Cf. Prof. C. H. Dodd in his essay in the volume *Mysterium Christi*.

Father W. Roche, S.J., speaks of the "*hic est calix sanguinis mei*" as a "deed rather than a word";[1] and even those who do not share Roche's understanding of the sacrifice of the mass may well allow that he brings out something of the special linguistic character of the "words of consecration". We may, we must, work further, more exhaustively and more minutely, and lay bare for instance the precise character of the language of the Gospels; for the Gospels are certainly unique in the matter of their literary form, equally certainly have "their own sort of logic". But is it a "logic of illusion", a logical *Unding*? Is the enterprise of representation which they attempt something inherently incapable of attainment? Is there a logical lie here, a kind of cheating through failure to acknowledge the authority of the necessary forms of human thought, and description? For however complex, diverse and rich the world of Christian language, that language in the end draws its point from the belief that some things are the case; but if the content of this belief is something to which no sense can be given, and in respect of which we can specify in words no conceivable test (the word is not used in a restricted laboratory sense) for deciding whether it is true or false, the axe is laid to the root of the tree. This, of course, is supremely true when the theological belief in question stresses concrete factuality in the way of one which insists on the primacy of the Christology. If we speak of the "fact of Christ", what sort of fact is this?

These difficulties, it must be insisted, do not disappear when, for instance, with Dr Friedrich Waismann, we reject a rigid Kantian paradigm of the limitations of the human intellect.[2] The question of fact cannot be by-passed; the "factuality" of God in Christ sets us an inescapable problem, and it is simply not fair for the Christian *bien-pensant* to accuse those who experience its bitter pressure of, e.g. being in bondage to a mistaken view of theoretical physics as the paragon and canon of human knowledge. Christian believers who are serious philosophers, and not the purveyors of dubious apologetic wares for the edification of Church congresses and ecumenical gather-

---

[1] In his *Mysteries of the Mass in Reasoned Prayer.*
[2] Cf. his paper on "Verifiability", *Ar. Soc. Proc.*, Suppl. Vol., 1945; reprinted in *Logic and Language* (1st series), edited by Prof. A. G. N. Flew, 1950.

ings, have to face them in their own terms, and know on their pulses the virtual estrangement from this substance of their being which that facing brings.

Something too of the same sort of virtual estrangement from the substance of himself may be known by a man who is compelled, by his psychological condition, to submit to the ordeal of deep Freudian analysis. For such a one, as for the philosopher, and even for the one who rebels against the sickening cruelties of the clerical spirit, in the name of human mercy and pity, the temptations are grave indeed. He may take the ordeal (for it is an ordeal), too lightly; or he may take himself as he undergoes it too seriously. He may treat as of little importance the challenge to his faith, and fail that way; or he may allow himself to forget that, by baptism, he is unchangeably set upon a way, upon that way which is Christ himself, movement from God to man, movement back from man to God; upon that way which is also the communion of saints.

Here are analogies, perhaps, for the predicaments of the philosopher who is also a Christian. But the essay cannot end here; for if it did so, the author might suggest the illusion of a happy, or a satisfactory ending; and that would be to deny the rule acknowledged in its course that thought must follow being. We will end where we began, with the problem of contingency; but first we must pay attention to some aspects of it of which so far we have not said enough.

No theology whose axiom is the sovereignty of Christology can escape the problems of *history*. For such a theology it is not, for instance, a light thing that e.g. Codex Vaticanus omits from its text of St Luke's Gospel the so-called "first word" from the Cross. For such a theology, the establishment of principles for the proper interpretation of the Fourth Gospel is a matter of very great significance; it cannot, for one moment, treat the obscurity of the features of the earthly Jesus as a matter of little importance. A theology in which the Christology is sovereign is one which cannot escape the question of historical reality by such familiar escape-routes as that offered by an idealist philosophy of religion, or by the ideas of early twentieth-century "Catholic modernism". Its underlying temper of realism, its sense of the primacy of the deed done by Christ in flesh and blood, must deny it the use of such expedients.

It is of course, again, the issue of *fact*; overlapping with, but of course distinguishable from, that raised a few paragraphs back in connection with the philosopher. Did these things happen? It is crucially illustrated, of course, by reference to the old-fashioned "problem of miracle". Certainly the evangelists themselves distinguish carefully between the various events and actions we now bracket together as miracles; they have no general concept of miracle in our sense. Men saw what they recorded; and the unity which they bestowed on the diverse occurrences we tend to group together as miraculous was one of their setting in the ministry of Jesus, and his movement from life to death. But that movement has undoubtedly assumed its status as the structural framework in which these events have been set by the synoptists, because "the Father raised Jesus from the dead". Of course this "raising" was something that none could see, none could perceive; it is not an event in time like the burial of Jesus or the visits of mourners to his tomb. But (to speak very crudely) the emptying of the tomb is in some sense such an event, or group of events, as those; that is to say, if the tomb was empty, there must have been a moment in time when the body of Jesus was in the tomb, and a moment afterwards when it was not. And if we say this (and it is the present writer's view that we must), we are in some sense putting ourselves in bondage to the settlement of questions which are questions of historical fact.

The question: "What is an historical fact?" is, of course, in a real sense a philosophical question; but it is one that cannot possibly be tackled by philosophers without attention to the actual practice of historians, any more than, for instance, a logician can determine the criteria of a good physical hypothesis without attention to the practice of theoretical physicists. But the philosopher has important work to do in disentangling confusions and illusions, which may have their source in the imposition of a restricted and inflexible paradigm of what it is to be a fact, upon the domain of the historians concerned. Yet although there are different sorts of fact, they are different sorts of—*fact*, of *actuals*. Of course actuals do not form a class, or a species, or a genus, like the entrants to a college in a given year, or cats or mammals. But all the same we are fudging if we allow ourselves to suppose that we do not recognize a distinction between the actual and the non-actual, between the eruption of Vesuvius and the murder of Caesar on the one side, and the birth of Venus from the foam, and the exploits of St George with his dragon, on the other; and it is a matter of crucial importance for Christian belief that the resurrection of Jesus belongs with the former, and not with the latter.[1] This does not imply that the word "Resurrection" is the name of what men could have seen, felt, touched, even smelled; but it does imply that between the ultimate mystery of the raising of Christ by the Father from the dead, and a certain perceptible event or set of events (the emptying of the tomb) there is a necessary relationship.

It should be clear from the foregoing that there is a very important work of ascetical discrimination to be done in respect of the status of the sort of experience of radical doubt which we have been describing as likely to be, today, the lot of the Christian who is a philosopher. Inevitably one asks how that experience is related to the sort of thing described by those far advanced on the way of the knowledge of God, who have spoken of, e.g. *dépouillement*, dereliction, the destruction of the images, and the rest. Clearly the two are not the same; it may be that the former only approaches the latter asymptotically so as never to reach it, but so as still to have some sort of relation to it. Or, more profoundly and more exactly, we may describe the former as some sort of analogue of the latter, itself, of course, only called dereliction because of its remote likeness to, in utter dependence on, the fontally creative stripping and dereliction of Christ.

What is true of the case of philosophy is true also of the possibly sharper and more taxing tension between historical knowledge and faith which remains even when a proper

[1] See G. E. Moore's excellent discussions of the meaning of the word "real" in *Some Main Problems of Philosophy* (1954), pp. 216 ff.; cf. also Lord Russell's *Philosophical Essays*.

self-consciousness concerning e.g. the actual logic of historical descriptions and explanations has been achieved. The fourth evangelist said much relevant to this problem in his profound theological discussion of the relation of seeing and believing; for him the former could no more pass into the latter than, e.g. for Kant, the discursive intellect could pass into the intuitive. Yet faith was nothing apart from relationship to the visible, tangible flesh of Jesus, which is (in Hoskyns' phrase), "the place where it is demanded of men that they should believe". It would be a serious mistake, of course, to treat the problem of the relation of faith and historical knowledge, as it has been raised for men after the advent of New Testament criticism, as if it were on all fours with the theological problem of which the evangelist is speaking. Again, there is perhaps a kind of asymptotic relation, and analogical correspondence between the two; the spiritual combat of faith with unbelief of which the evangelist speaks perhaps belongs to the same universe of discourse as the writings of saints and mystics on the inwardness of *dépouillement* and the rest.

Moreover, the historical critic is perfectly justified in asking whether, as a matter of fact, the author of the Fourth Gospel was justified in seeing this theological problem as raised by the ministry of Jesus. No doubt it is an important fact that this problem, and not another, was raised and faced by St John, just as it is important that the special framework of a journey from Galilee to Jerusalem for passover was adopted by Luke, and used by him in the way it was. But this importance is the importance for a man attempting a piece of historical reconstruction, simply of an item of historical evidence. If it is also more, if for the man who believes it tells him much of the very arcana of the way of believing, this is not by itself something that absolves him from the tension of engaging with the historical problem at its own level, even if it shows him the context in a Christ-centred spiritual life, to which that engaging, as all other things, belongs. But to treat something as the index of an all-inclusive setting, and to treat it as historical evidence for something else, is to treat it in two ways which, even though they must crucially overlap, are and must be logically distinguishable.

The involvement of faith with history is close-knit indeed, and historical uncertainty can sap the very foundations of faith, especially when the theological primacy of the Christology is demanded and accepted. Yet faith is most certainly not another name for historical certainty, nor does the achievement of a greater measure of such certainty make faith itself less a problem and a mystery. Faith is something which goes before historical reconstruction, and is something which even conditions its most radical exercise, relating it to its own intense and searching discipline.

Here, certainly, we are again conscious of the communion of saints, of the membership enjoyed by Christians one of another, in faith, in hope and above all in charity. The ultimate ground of this communion is, of course, the *ultimately* mysterious *perichoresis*, the *circumincessio* of the three Persons within the abysses of the Trinity.

There is certainly some sort of correspondence between the experience of the saint, and the dry intellectual struggle of the man who is battling in his study with the historical problems of Christian origins; there is, *mutatis omnibus mutandis*, an analogy between his efforts, as a historian, to achieve a *relative* security concerning the temporal beginnings of Christianity, and the patience with which men of faith have awaited the "revelation of the mystery". It is clear that, according to the Catholic tradition, there is in that latter patience something reflecting, *per speculum in aenigmate*, because participating in, the fontal and creative patience of the Son who acknowledged, and accepted, that the secret of the last hour was the Father's only, learning here as always obedience by the things that he suffered.

The perplexities of the historian, like those of the philosopher, are certainly not out of relation to the central mystery; and yet they do not lead directly towards it. For that mystery involves and encompasses them. The kenosis of the Incarnation, the self-emptying of the Son, his conformity to the limitations of human particularity, all alike reveal concretely, decisively and effectually the manner of the presence of God, in his changeless love and all-powerful humility, to his creatures. As has been said above, we cannot see that love apart from the kenosis; and

it may be remarked that if we keep the two inseparably together, part at least of the contradiction between those who
insist on divine impassibility as necessarily involved in God's
transcendence, and those who, like the late Geoffrey Studdert-
Kennedy,[1] were moved by their knowledge of the reality of
human suffering to deny it, may be resolved. Kenosis is an ontological mystery; that first, but, as men like Gore, Scott-
Holland and Weston realized, it is one that has a profound
bearing on the way we represent, for instance, the manner of
Christ's consciousness as incarnate. It enables us to take the
familiar philosophical cliché, "the limitations of human knowledge", and ask what happens to it when its sense is revised
against the background of, and in terms of, the obedience of
the Incarnate, the circumstances and manner of his mission.

Moreover, kenosis is, *mutatis omnibus mutandis*, a crucial
category of ascetic theology; this comes out most clearly in St
Paul's second epistle to the Corinthians. Here again, of course,
if we invoke its aid we must remember that its background is
ontological; what Paul speaks of is not something that he
records as "the contents of his consciousness", but a sense of his
mission and its significance that he has won through daring to
see it in the light of the Cross. He knows that the ground of his
mission, to which it belongs, is all. So there is a deep movement in his language between what is almost autobiographical
description, what is theological interpretation, and what is, in
effect, the expression of a deepened understanding of the
mystery of the Cross through the refraction of that mystery, in
the arcana of his own spiritual life and suffering. And yet, because all is under the sign of kenosis, the final note is of a
radical self-abandonment.

So indeed it is with all the saints, who provide, for those who
know the kind of perplexities of which this essay has spoken, at
once reminders of that encompassing perplexity into which
Christ himself entered and sure promise of succour in them.
There is only analogy between the perplexities; but those who
face without flinching the contradictions of which this essay has
spoken, whether in Franco's gaols, or in their studies, are some-

---

[1] Cf. his *The Hardest Part.*

times aware that the prayerful compassion, for instance, of the true contemplative is to them the effectual sign of that "which it has not entered the mind of man to conceive".[1]

Only there is no escape from contingency. If Barth protests against, e.g. the offering of the "argument from contingency" as a possible preamble to faith, it may be partly because he sees clearly how the coming of Christ "as the place where it is demanded of men that they believe", has radicalized and transformed the notion of the contingent. The sheer contingency of Christ provides a new sort of use for the logical ontological notion, a new standard for its employment; for in the Incarnation there is contingency so sheer and unequivocal that inevitably at all levels we shrink from it, preferring "necessary absolutes", whether abstract values, or institutions, or even spiritual experiences. As the saints have, however, known, the Church herself is involved in that contingency, and the sin of her rulers is always in the forgetting of it. Involvement in its consequences runs right through the whole life of the believer, almost in a kind of downward spiral, in all his relationships; but this burden is laid upon him because he is also partaker of its strange glory. For the believer knows that the supremely revealing and the supremely authoritative moment in human history (the hour which the Son received from the Father) was that in which he cried upon the Cross: "My God, my God, why hast thou forsaken me?" Thus it was made plain that in the Son of God's acceptance of the ultimate triviality and failure of human existence, whose deeps at that moment he *finally* plumbed, the whole language of perplexity, uncertainty, bewilderment, hopelessness and pain, even of God-forsakenness, was laid hold of and given a new sense by the very God himself and converted into the way of his reconciling the world unto himself.

---

[1] Cf. Pierre Henri Simon's remarkable novel, *Les Raisins Verts.*

OUR CONTEMPORARY CHRIST

T O SPEAK of the truth of the Christian faith is to use language as familiar as it is embarrassing. Presumably those who profess and call themselves Christians believe their religion to be in some sense true; but in what sense? Perhaps indeed if they are challenged, they hedge or seem to hedge, and plead that the nature of its truth is proportionate to that for which truth is claimed, namely the Christian faith. It is not true in the sense in which, for instance, it is true that the weather has improved in Cambridge during the forenoon; or that the Conservative Party has suffered considerable reverses in the municipal elections; or that the powers of decision of the Prime Minister as against those of the Cabinet have increased in recent decades; or that a molecule of water is composed of two atoms of hydrogen to one of oxygen; or (if indeed it be true) that any even number is the sum of two primes. The truth of the Christian faith is the truth of a faith, or a way of life which shows itself true by authenticating itself for those who live it. We have moved, it is claimed, away from questions relating to the truth of propositions; we are in that world where "I" responds to "Thou", and the imperative mood of address is answered by the personal response "*Magister, adsum*".

But is it as simple as that? There is more to faith than assent to propositions; but to allow that there is more is not to disallow that assent to propositions has its place in faith. So Paul indeed included in his first letter to the Corinthians a record "of the facts which", he said, "had been imparted to me: that Christ died—that he was buried: that he was raised to life", etc. The translators of the New English Bible do not scruple to use the word *fact* here, as if to indicate their conviction that what was imparted to Paul was a series of propositions which corresponded with what was actually the case. If there was no such correspondence, then the sense of the language is plain that Paul's complicated and subtle theological argument concerning the resurrection of the dead, which the sentences I have quoted introduce, is robbed of its starting-point. Christians are men who believe that, as a matter of fact, certain events happened. What theologians call faith includes much more than belief that this or that was the case; but unless the belief is present, faith is without one of its necessary constituents.

All this may seem trite and elementary; but the history of Christian thought displays many examples of the eagerness with which earnest and intelligent men, who have wished to further the cause of the Christian Gospel, have sought to escape from the precariousness seen to be involved in this dependence of its claim to truth on the truth of certain contingent, empirical propositions: that is, certain propositions of which it is perfectly good sense to say that they are not true, and whose truth is established by empirical observation, or vulnerable to refutation by such observation. We cannot deny a sort of attraction to the view which would make Christianity in some sense independent of certain events actually having taken place; or indeed would enable us to treat these events as mere illustrations of some more general principle of spiritual life which in their bare bones they dramatically illustrate. (One thinks here of the handling of the Christian tradition by those who have studied deeply in the school of Hegel, or who have made their own an existentialist ethic of freedom, derived supposedly from the work of Martin Heidegger.)

Moreover, we have to reckon with elements in the tradition itself which seem to encourage us to free our religious imaginations from too tight a bondage to Jesus in the days of his flesh. There is the Johannine theology of the Paraclete, and above all, perhaps, that obscure saying of St Paul which has so baffled exegetes; when he writes (in II Corinthians) of "knowing Christ no longer *kata sarka* (after the flesh)". Were not the Hegelians justified in construing the *Noli me tangere* of the risen Christ to Mary Magdalene in the record of the fourth Gospel as a concrete mythical expression of the demand that Christians discard the bondage of a false attachment to the details of a particular history, and adhere within themselves to a way of life which they must realize in circumstances altogether strange to those who first listened to Jesus? Was the saying not best taken as a mythical expression of the principle of *Aufhebung*? Paul himself stressed the eternal, and the future; he only occasionally dwelt on the past, as if such preoccupation would deflect his mind from the abiding verities, and the promises of fulfilment that lay ahead.

The works of Rudolf Bultmann and his school, distinguished alike in the fields of New Testament study and of religious philosophy, have sharply revived those issues, and we must not ignore the relative novelty of the form in which they are presented: this although the student of the history of religious thought will find more than mere echoes of the issues canvassed, for instance, in the searching correspondence between Loisy, von Hügel, and Blondel, following the publication of Loisy's famous *L'Evangile et l'Eglise*, and recently made available.[1] Blondel's letters showed a subtle theological penetration and a robust common sense in their judgment of Loisy's argument; in fact Blondel showed himself at once a good deal more hard-headed and a good deal more perceptive than von Hügel concerning the implications of that argument. It was Loisy's hope to establish Catholicism unchallengeably as a supreme tradition of spirituality on the foundation of boldly radical ideas concerning Christ's purpose and the way he saw his own mission. Blondel asked, for instance, just how credible it was to esteem Jesus a deluded fanatic and to suppose him validly identified with the Logos by whom the world was made. His argument at once subtle and common-sensical is wholly relevant to the Bultmannian claim that it matters nothing how Jesus saw himself provided that in the words he preached and the words preached by those who continue to preach him, the Word of God addresses men. If in Bultmann there is less emphasis

* This may be found in the volume, *Au coeur de la crise moderniste*, ed. by R. P. R. Marlé (Aubier).

on development than in Loisy, there is a theological occasionalism which is wholly vulnerable to Blondel's arguments.

To such a Catholic modernist as Loisy, Jesus was significant as causally instrumental in the establishment of an elaborate system of sacramental and mystical religion, a *Heilsanstalt* that was unquestionably a school of saints. His divinity resided in, was in fact constituted by, the fact that devotion to him made these things possible. He was established as founder of the Church by the faith he elicited and the practice in which that faith clothed itself. So for a radical Protestant today of Bult-mannian sympathy, however much he may, as Bultmann himself supremely does, qualify his purpose, Jesus is constituted Christ in *praedicando*. *Christus est Jesus praedicatus*. Sometimes men argue as if preaching were the informing of the amorphous matter of Jesus-tradition with the form required to constitute it Christ; Christ, who is then sometimes spoken of as in this proclamation, which alone constitutes Jesus as Christ, the 'eschatological event" wherein by response men are "issued into freedom".

The underlying theory of knowledge is obscure, and hard to summarize, because of the radical inconsistencies of its exponents, including here Bultmann himself whose Gifford Lectures on *History and Eschatology* alone show him a prophet too intoxicated with his vision to attend to precision in its formulation. But that there is an underlying theory of knowledge is unquestionable. It incorporates a particular attitude to the New Testament documents which, in Bultmann's own case, combines a radical scepticism of their historical worth as sources concerning the ministry of Jesus with many passages of profound exegetical insight, particularly in the large commentary on John in the *Meyer Kommentar*, which is not yet available in English. But the theory of knowledge to which I refer makes of this inaccessibility of the historical Jesus something to be welcomed, as if it ensured that the only Jesus we shall concern ourselves with is the Jesus who in preaching is rendered our contemporary Christ. I say "our contemporary Christ"; for preaching which makes or converts Jesus into Christ, converts him into *our* Christ. Even as Croce said that all history is contemporary history, so Bultmann would imply that the only Christ for us is the contemporary Christ, fashioned by the transformation of Jesus into Christ-for-us by his being preached to us.

The constitutive, creative role of preaching, of kerygma, is vitally important. One is tempted to say that this kind of philosophical theology is a theology which makes the kerygmatic experience its fundamental subject-matter, and then seeks, almost in Kantian style, to uncover its transcendental conditions. The description "Jesus of Nazareth" must answer to an element to be found in a complete inventory of the elements that make up the world of space and time; moreover in the actuality of the kerygmatic situation, that element as object of reference *must* have its place. No Jesus; no kerygmatic situation. But only in that situation where by words of men the Word of God addresses men and women, Jesus is constituted Christ, and apart from it he is simply one who played an insignificant, and relatively unknown, role in history, dying horribly at the end.

One could conceive a kind of debate between Bultmannians and Catholic modernists, the former stressing the cruciality of the world of preaching, the latter that of the world of liturgy, of sacrament, of contemplative prayer. Both are incurably religious in the sense in which Bonhoeffer in his prison-cell warned his correspondent of the perils of religion. The pulpit and the altar; if we ask how these institutions are possible, seeking their transcendental conditions, we may well be tempted to the answers given by Bultmann and the Catholic modernists. Moreover, because the preacher requires a message, while the celebrant of a liturgy may content himself with mastery and improvement of its prescribed form, we may well seek a modern content for that message in the introspective metaphysical self-scrutiny of *Existenz-philosophie.*

The impulses behind the movements of thought I have sketched are various. There is a discontent with the particularity of historical Christianity, a desire for that which is universal in contradistinction from that which is particular. But there is also recognizably present a desire to escape from bondage to that which could have been otherwise. The image of the eternal changelessness of God, whether we conceive it in terms of immediate and synoptic comprehension at once of himself, and of his creation, or in terms of unshaken, unchallengeable, all-determining will, is one which besets every theist, and sets him on edge in the presence of the contingent. Cook-Wilson indeed pointed out in his lectures on Plato's *Republic* that once Plato had established the reality of the forms, his problem was to find any *raison d'être* for the particulars which copied them, or partook of their being; and this edginess in the presence of the actual world characterizes a great deal of transcendent metaphysics. Christianity faces men with the paradox that certain events which could have been otherwise are of ultimate, transcendent import; and this without losing their character as contingent events. The propositions, *Crucifixus est sub Pontio Pilato*; *passus et sepultus est,* are contingent propositions; their subject-matter moreover is altogether innocent of miraculous undertones. Yet this judicial murder, its pain and its end, form the substance of the confession of faith.

Moreover, we must go further. We cannot allow any seriousness to Christianity's claim to truth unless we can also claim factual truth in a simple, ordinary sense, for propositions concerning the way the subject of that suffering approached his end. How right Julius Schniewind was in his commentary on Mark to take seriously the inconsistencies that threaten the credibility of the Gethsemane narrative: if the three witnesses slept, whence the evidence that Jesus thus wrestled in prayer and asked that the cup might pass from him? This issue must be faced. To ignore it is to ignore the rootedness of the very heart of the Christian faith in what is logically contingent, in what was in principle observable, in this case audible by tired men!

We can understand the impulse that leads men to seek escape from perplexity concerning these details to the interior certainties of a profound religious experience, subtly articulated, courageously aware of the circumstances of human existence. Why bother concerning the precarious foundation? Yet if this foundation is ignored, or is treated as of little import, we shall surely find that we have lost precisely that which distinguishes Christianity from every other faith, namely its claiming, among its fundamental truth-conditions, the truth of propositions that might have been otherwise—and this as an aspect of its central affirmation that in human flesh and blood the ultimate secrets of God were disclosed, and by pitifully human action the ultimate contradictions of human existence resolved.

But the inadequacy of the theological programme I have been criticizing is not simply confined to its handling of the New Testament material—or, rather, to the way in which it thinks possible that the problems raised by that material can be dealt with. The mistake of supposing that one can translate propositions concerning actual historical transactions into propositions relating to the spiritual lives and religious activities of individuals and of groups is a radical one; perhaps a crowning illustration of the entrenched habits of the idealist of supposing that the inner life of the subject is alone truly significant, and that when we deal with its supposed, evident realities, we are on firm ground from which the onslaught of critical reflection, whether historical or philosophical, cannot dislodge us. Once we can convert statements about the actuality of Jesus as the Christ into statements concerning our response to him, we may be tempted to suppose that we have set our theological convictions upon the rock-like foundation of unchallengeable spiritual experience. But it is not only our ordinary Christian common sense that is outraged by this procedure. We have in fact committed ourselves to an anthropocentrism in theology that could be criticized as a most dangerous species of mythological illusion. For is it not dangerous illusion so to conceive the supposed ultimate Reality that we deliberately, and of set policy, preclude ourselves from thinking it in other than human terms? Are we not committing ourselves to an anthropomorphism far more radical, far more uncompromising, than that from which the old-fashioned "substance theology" sought to liberate our fathers? And this, let us not forget, on the threshold of the new "Copernican revolutions" of the space-age.

To say this is not to offer anything in the way of positive solution; only to warn against a theological *cul-de-sac* into which a self-conscious modernity might seem to beckon those who consider themselves adventurous. In fact this *cul-de-sac* bids fair to be no more than an enclosed playground from which the fundamental intellectual challenges to the faith in our age may pass unheard. The issues between faith and unbelief go too deep, and cut too sharply, for revival of metaphysical idealist gambits effectively to resolve them.

ORDER AND EVIL IN THE GOSPEL

"He was in the world and the world took
its origin through him and the world did
not know him. He came to what was his
own and his own people did not receive him."

SO THE writer of the fourth gospel prepares for the climax
of his prologue, the declaration that the Word became
flesh. He finds the beginning of his story in the transcendent world; he is compelled, by the nature of what he wants to
set forth, to site its origin not in Judaea or Galilee, not indeed
in time and space, but in the trackless, timeless realm of absolute
being; yet before he reminds his readers that the Word through
whom all things take their origin became flesh he insists that
when that Word so came among his own he was rejected.

The prologue of the fourth gospel is by all reckoning a
classical statement of the doctrine of the cosmic Christ, of the
role of Christ in the creation of the world. But at the same time
it forms the introduction to a book which with good reason has
been called the "gospel of rejection". "He came unto his own
and his people did not receive him." It is as if the author would
warn his readers at the outset that if he finds in the Word now
become flesh the very ground of creation, they must not forget
that the Word was rejected. So he binds together at the start
of his tale the transcendent and the familiar, the glorious and
the bitter. Whatever may be true of the subsequent history of
Christian thought, the antithesis between an optimistic Logos
theology, which finds the ground and goal of all things in Christ,
and a more sombre "theology of the cross" does not exist for
this writer. For him, as his prologue makes plain, the two are
warp and woof of the tale he would tell.

We are concerned with what the gospel is; and this causes us to consider what it was to those who first heard it, men and women who lived in a world utterly different from the one in which we find ourselves. Sometimes it must have seemed as if their world was so different from ours that what was good news for them is for us, if we are honest, something sheerly irrelevant, something that we must dismiss out of hand as worse than boring, and altogether remote from human existence as we know it. "If such be the gospel then the gospel is simply not 'with it'." To say this is not to question the value of recent writing, or the honesty of the writers. Indeed it is simply to bring out what no doubt it was its intention to convey, that Christianity is a strange and nearly incredible thing, tied up in such a way with the thought of bygone ages that the effort to extricate and present its core must seem a nearly impossible task. The Logos theology of the fourth gospel itself must seem to many but another example of the sort of metaphysics that a modern must find incredible, remote from his experience, intelligible, if at all, only as a period piece that one can appreciate but hardly take seriously.

Yet behind the language of the prologue something more can be discerned, something whose appeal is universal, even if that appeal is grounded in the author's appraisal of the One concerning whom he writes. In these verses the reader finds himself raised to a level that is beyond optimism and pessimism, as one usually understands those two contrasted attitudes. The author is sure that the ground of the world itself is good; he is sure of this because he identifies that ground with what men have heard and seen in Jesus; yet Jesus was rejected, and his glory was most fully revealed when he was lifted up from the earth upon a Roman gallows. John tells the story of Christ's passion with the fullest possible use of tragic irony; his story ends in a cry of triumph, τετέλεσται; but it is a triumph purchased at the price of appalling catastrophe. Judas has departed into the night and before Pilate's judgment seat the chosen people have confessed that they have no king but Caesar. The light has shone in the darkness, which has failed to overcome it;

but the darkness remains, and of the end of the traitor there is no record.

So far I have confined myself entirely to the gospel of John. I shall now turn to other traditions of the ministry and work of Jesus. Anyone who like myself is professionally concerned with the grounds and foundations of religious belief must sometimes ask himself what it is that, in spite of all, keeps him in some sense within the Christian tradition. It is a difficult question to which to give an honest answer. It is easy to plunge into elaborate and subtle apologetic, which somehow leaves unreached the grounds of one's adherence, however precarious and uncertain that adherence may be. But as I explore the elusive frontiers between reason and emotion, where lurk the ultimate grounds of adherence, I come back repeatedly to the narrative of Gethsemane.

If I am honest, I think that I must say that I should cease to believe altogether unless I believed that Jesus had indeed prayed that the hour might pass from him, had indeed been left alone to face the reality of absolute failure. It is fashionable nowadays to speak of Christ as victor, as if the agony and disillusion, the sheer monstrous reality of physical and spiritual suffering which he bore were a mere charade. The idiom of a superficial cosmic optimism, often expressing itself ritually in patterns of liturgical symbolism, is currently fashionable, as if a world that knows, as ours does, extremities of terror as well as hope, could be consoled by a remote metaphysical chatter. But the gospels, including that of John which does not chronicle the episode of Gethsemane, recall our imaginations to a figure prostrate on the earth, afraid and desolate, bidding men and women see in him the ground of all creation.

It is sheer nonsense to speak of the Christian religion as offering a solution of the problem of evil. There is no solution offered in the gospels of the riddle of Iscariot through whose agency the Son of man goes his appointed way. It were good for him that he had not been born. The problem is stated; it is left unresolved, and we are presented with the likeness of the one who bore its ultimate burden, and bore it to the end, refusing the trick of bloodless victory to which the scoffers, who invited him to descend from his cross, were surely inviting him.

What the gospels present to us is the tale of an endurance. "Christ for us became obedient unto death, even the death of the cross." The writer of the fourth gospel invites his readers to find in the tale of this endurance the ultimate secret of the universe itself. For the ground of that universe is on his view to be identified with the agent of that endurance. So his teaching cannot easily be qualified as optimistic or pessimistic. He is no pessimist; for he is confident that we can find order and design, the order and design of God himself, in the processes of the universe and in the course of human history. But if men would understand that design, they must not, in random speculative mood, look away from the concrete reality of Jesus of Nazareth, from the bitter history of his coming and rejection. Where the speculative intellect finds answer to its furthest ranging questions is still the same place where the bruised spirit may find consolation from the touch of a man of sorrows.

To suggest that Christianity deals with the problem of evil by encouraging the believer to view it from a cosmic perspective is totally to misunderstand both the difficulty and the consolation of its treatment. Rather Christianity takes the history of Jesus and urges the believer to find, in the endurance of the ultimate contradictions of human existence that belongs to its very substance, the assurance that in the worst that can befall his creatures, the creative Word keeps company with those whom he has called his own. "Is it nothing unto you all ye that pass by? Behold and consider whether there be any sorrow like unto my sorrow." It is not as if the passer-by were invited immediately to assent to the proposition that there was indeed no such sorrow; he is asked to "consider". It is a profound mistake to present the Christian gospel as if it were something that immediately showed itself, that authenticated itself without reflection. It is of the manner of the coming of Jesus that he comes so close to the ordinary ways of men that they hardly notice him, that they treat him as one of themselves. "There stands one among you whom you know not": so the Baptist in that same first chapter of John to which I have so often referred.

But how, except by coming so close to men, could he succour them? A Christ who at the last descended from the cross must leave the penitent robber without the promise of his company in paradise; and such a Christ we may dare say must also deprive himself of the precious comfort in his own extremity that he received from the gangster beside him; for it was that gangster who in Luke's record continued with him to the very end of his temptation.

I am not here offering an apologetic, only bringing out certain elements in the complex reality of Christianity that seems to me of central importance. I would say that nobody these days, who is concerned at all with issues of faith and unbelief, can afford to treat them as opportunities for being clever. If men still believe—in spite of the strong, even overwhelming, case of the sceptic—it must be because they find *malgré tout* in Christianity the revelation of the eternal God, a revelation that touches them in the actual circumstances of their lives, whether in the common fear of a week of international crisis, or in the more personal extremities of sin, failure, bereavement, of unresolvable conflict of obligations when they find themselves pulled in two directions by claims of pity and by claims of truth. Is the so-called gospel in any sense good news to one who has bestowed love and care upon another whom he is forced in obedience to the claims of truth to acknowledge as worthless and corrupt? If it has no word of consolation in such extremity, how can we call it good news to the individual? What value is there in a cosmic optimism which leaves unplumbed the depths of human grief?

So I come back to the place where nearly I began, to the figure prostrate on the ground praying that the hour might pass. It is the claim of Christianity that men find God there, that in some sense all who came before that one were thieves and robbers, that he indeed it is in whom all things consist, through whom they take their origin, and by whom they will find their consummation. Men may well find in the end that this claim is beyond their acceptance, that it demands assent to what they cannot, if they are honest, say yes to. But those who believe its truth as long as indeed they do believe it must at least make sure that what is rejected is the substantial reality and not a counterfeit bereft alike of pity and of glory.

It may seem strange that I have gone so far without even mention of the Resurrection; but my reticence in this respect is of design. In one sense belief that Jesus was raised from the dead, that the Father pronounced a final Amen to his work, is a *prius* of my whole argument. To discuss the issue of the historical evidence for the Resurrection of Jesus and the complex theological problems that it raises would take me beyond the limitations I have deliberately imposed upon myself. Yet it is the *prius* of my whole argument; for it is in the Resurrection[1] that we find the ultimate source of that peculiar tension between optimism and pessimism which I have judged characteristic of Christianity. One thing, however, in conclusion, I would dare to say, and that is this. It is a commonplace of traditional theology that in speech concerning God and the things of God "the negative way" must precede "the way of eminence". If men would give sense to what they say, they must be agnostic before they dare invoke the resources of anthropomorphic imagery; they are always properly more confident concerning what they must deny than concerning what they may affirm. So with what men intend when they speak of the Resurrection of Jesus; they know what it is not in a way in which they cannot know what it is, inasmuch as its ultimate secret rests with the Father who raised him.

In knowing what it is not, they know that it is not a descent from the cross postponed for thirty-six hours. It is not the sudden dramatic happy ending which the producer of a Hollywood spectacular might have conceived. In the stories as we have them, it is only to his own that the risen Christ shows himself with the marks of his passion still upon him; his commerce with them is elusive and restricted, as if to guard them against the mistake of supposing that they were witnesses

---

[1] On the subject of the Resurrection the reader is referred to the discussions in the volume, *The Resurrection*, by G. W. H. Lampe and D. M. MacKinnon, Mowbray, 1966.

of a reversal, and not of a vindication, of those things which had happened. It is a commonplace of theology to speak of the Resurrection as the Father's Amen to the work of Christ; yet it is a commonplace to whose inwardness writers on the subject often attend too little. For if it does anything, it drives one back to find the secret of the order of the world in what Christ said and did, and the healing of its continuing bitterness in the place of his endurance.

"Come down from the cross and we will believe." Many Christians have joined in this cry; many continue indeed to make it their own, even when they pay lip service to the gospel of the Resurrection. But it is only in the light of the Resurrection that those Christians can learn rather to say with understanding the profound words of Pascal, that Christ will indeed be in agony unto the end of the world.

ATONEMENT AND TRAGEDY [1]

(cf. S. Mathews Atonement & Social Process) ∴ task of being self-critical.

I T IS now regarded as a commonplace in critical discussion
of Anselm's theology of the atonement that he was in
unconscious bondage to the ethical ideas suggested by the
social order of his age. But those who are quick to recognize the
extent of his limitations in this respect are sometimes less
willing to extend similar principles to the criticism of their own
ideas. Yet fundamental theology must always reflect both the
unacknowledged personal prejudices and the inherited moral
assumptions of the theologian. In theology worthy of the name
we are always involved with faith seeking understanding of
itself; this understanding is rendered perpetually precarious by
the relativity that must infect even the most disciplined effort of
the one who seeks it. There is no field in which these considerations press more urgently upon the thinker than the
doctrine of Christ's atoning work.

It may be indeed partly for this reason that we encounter

[1] Related aspects of the topics treated in this paper, which was presented at a
colloquium on the philosophy of religion at the State University in Rome in
January 1967, are developed in two other recently published papers, *viz.*, in the
essay on "Subjective and Objective Conceptions of Atonement" in the volume
Prospects for Theology (essays presented to Professor H. H. Farmer, Nisbet, 1967) at
pp. 167–182, and in an article, "Theology and Tragedy," which appeared in
Religious Studies, Vol. 2, No. 2 (April 1967), pp. 163–169. These two papers overlap
in some respects, but comprise together a tentative exploration of the significance
of tragic drama, both classical and modern (using the latter term to include
Shakespeare and Racine), for metaphysics and for Christian theology. All alike
are indebted to the neglected pioneer work of Professor D. Daiches Raphael, *The
Paradox of Tragedy* (Allen and Unwin 1960), to which reference is made explicitly
in the article in *Religious Studies*; a work that has suffered the neglect from British
moral philosophers which is so often the lot of writings which attempt something
at first sight (though not on deeper consideration of the very best contemporary
work) unrelated to dominant habits of thought. While I differ a great deal from
Professor Raphael's book, I am deeply indebted to him for writing it. This whole
topic will receive extended treatment in my forthcoming Gifford Lectures, *The
Problem of Metaphysics*.

today among writers who practise the arts of demythologization, a tendency to welcome the so-called "classic" conception
of the work of Christ, revived by Bishop Gustaf Aulén, on the
ground that it is in form and content so unashamedly mythological that it lends itself to translation into any terms likely to
commend themselves to the translator. To speak of the Cross
as "a victory over the powers of darkness" is to use a mythological variable to which determinate value can be assigned almost
to taste. The range of options within which these values can be
found is of course extended by the fashionable and now well
grounded uncertainty prevalent among competent students of
the New Testament concerning the intentions with which Jesus
himself approached his passion. We characterize his endurance
in mythological doctrine as "a victory over the powers of
darkness" and thereby endow it with a profoundly therapeutic
significance where, for instance, our own fears concerning a
future largely unknown but sometimes deeply menacing are
concerned.

To write in these terms may seem to some at least to indulge
in uncharitable caricature; but at least it enables us to recognize
the extent to which some of those who have made play with the
notion of demythologization in this field have deliberately
abdicated from the task of evaluating Christ's work in ethical
terms; they have avoided the risks implicit in doing so, risks
which in the theology of the atonement there have been from the
certainly ran, and which any contemporary who seeks to
follow in their steps must also run. One who, like the present
writer, approaches the study of the history of theology from the
point of view of a moral philosopher is aware of the extent to
which in the theology of the atonement there have been from the
period of the New Testament onwards determined efforts to
present the sense of the work of Christ in morally significant
terms. This attempt includes of course innumerable examples of
theologies so morally horrifying in their implication that to
understand them clearly is to be moved to discard them, or even
to say that if they embody theological truth human beings are
morally justified in revolting against the monstrous deity whose
ways allegedly they portray. Yet when this fact of intellectual

history has been admitted, it must be allowed that it is within the context of the theology of the atonement that some of the profoundest Christian explorations of the human situation have been achieved, and that this has only been possible as long as Christ's work was regarded as something morally significant. To say this is not for one moment to deny that it has often been found in itself a source, indeed an ultimate source, of moral significance; undoubtedly men and women have found the horizons of their moral understanding enlarged and trans-formed by its contemplation. Yet the horizons in question remain horizons of the moral understanding. The enlargement was only won at the cost of the tremendous risk of diminishing the ultimate to the status of the relative, of failing to recognize the inevitable poverty of the images and analogies employed. But the underlying assumption was plain that here we were engaged with a reality that touched the substance of our moral life.

To speak in these terms necessarily took for granted that we were not condemned to a complete agnosticism concerning the manner and circumstances of Christ's human life. In one sense it took for granted an approach congruous with certain elements deeply present in contemporary depreciation of the mytho-logical. There was an element of attention which, it was argued, corresponded with the style of the Gospel narrative, from the overtly miraculous to the humanly profound, from mighty acts of power that moved witnesses to wonder and to a half-faith, dangerous at once to themselves and to the one they confessed, to a supreme act that could be presented with a more or less complete abstinence from apocalyptic and miraculous embroi-dery, using only a subtle and searching irony to convey the presence of the transcendent. But the kind of moralization of which I am speaking took for granted that it corresponded with the reality of the affair. The movement from the miraculous to the moral was adopted (to borrow Wittgenstein's useful phrase) as a "system of projection" because more than any other it enabled men and women to capture the inwardness of revela-tion; this because the work done and the ordeal met in human flesh and blood was something whose outskirts we could

99

genuinely trace. What we said and wrote concerning it was logically contingent and epistemologically matter of perception and of memory. But this was inevitable consequence of incarnation, indeed its reflection at the level of human awareness.

A study of the history of theology will, as I have said, remind us continually of the depth of perversion to which this effort to grasp the inwardness of Christ's work in ethical terms has led, and we can understand the extent to which those who would claim that a proper appraisal of the historical material shows it to be impossible have welcomed this alleged recognition as a liberation. Yet moral reflection belongs to the depth of human self-consciousness and it may be that the historical failure of the traditional doctrines of the atonement, both objective and subjective, both Anselmian and Abelardian, is in part due to a failure to find the form of moral reflection least wholly inappropriate to the analysis of the Christian material. There is a sense in which Christian theology may be much more than it realizes the victim of the victory won in the person of Plato by the philosophers over the poets, and in particular the tragedians. It is true that Aristotle sought to modify the significance of this victory; but he failed to reverse it and in the rest of this paper I wish to ask the question whether in fact the theme of the work of Christ may not receive effective theological treatment when it is represented as tragedy. This I say remembering the supreme significance of the resurrection, but also continually recalling the extent to which in popular apologetic understanding of the resurrection has been deformed through its representation as in effect a descent from the Cross, given greater dramatic effect by a thirty-six hour postponement.

It is of course often remarked that a great deal which is characteristic of the world views to be extracted from tragic drama, both ancient and modern, is incompatible with the Christian understanding of existence. Thus it is alleged that we are continually made aware in Sophocles, in Shakespeare, in Racine, of the intractable surd element in the scheme of things, a destiny which shapes the history of an Electra, a Hamlet, a Phèdre, which is their ineluctable inheritance. Even where Racine's explorations of derangement and bewilderment are concerned it is impossible to avoid seeing in his work, as in that of the other two writers I have mentioned, a paradoxical affirmation at once of human freedom and of an irresistible element in the scheme of things that brings even the most steadfast moral fidelity to nought. No determinist could write an effective tragedy, could achieve the sort of deep exploration of responsibility, justice, guilt, that we find for instance in Electra or in Hamlet. Both Sophocles and Shakespeare take for granted, even if they do not explicitly admit the fact, the reality of a "freedom of open possibilities". Electra could have gone the way of her more accommodating sister, and thereby avoided the kind of disintegration that was the price of her refusal to compromise with the truth of the situation in which she found herself. It was her steadfastness which betrayed her, her refusal to pretend that things were other than they were which twisted her into the shape of a human being obsessively dedicated to a revenge that in its execution could be judged no more than a simulacrum of justice. Again, where Hamlet is concerned it is a comparable instance that the truth of his father's death shall be revealed in action which unleashes for instance the emotions which destroy Ophelia.

In such works there is a presence to the reality of moral evil, to the ways in which its power is experienced as a destructive force which makes the writings of most philosophers and theologians seem somehow trivial. This because the writings which I have mentioned are more nearly in accordance with the facts of the human situation. Even if we are tempted to write them off as works of imagination, the imagination displayed in them is one powerful in the disclosure of what is; it is not the servant of idealist fantasy in the way in which we must surely judge that the comfortable musings of theologians and metaphysicians often are.

What then of the Gospel narratives? It is almost a convention of Christian practice to read them as if they were orientated towards a happy ending, as if the resurrection-faith which gave them birth was powerful to obliterate memory of the sombre events which they describe. It is certainly an important commonplace to remember that as we have them they are expressions of the faith whose origins in some sense they present. But if their composition belongs to the history of Christian consciousness, we are surely justified when in critical evaluation of their contents we see their authors trying to come to terms with a revelation of the ways of God with men too strange to admit of decisive comprehension or representation.

Where to a philosopher particularly interested in problems of epistemology much modern theological discussion seems weakest is its failure to explore in depth the many problems connected with memory. Although the apologetic elements within the Gospels as we have them and the material out of which they are composed demand continual stressing, there is also the extent to which alike in the books themselves and in their sources there is a reaching back towards the past, a coming to terms with it. It is not of course enough to say that the secret of the whole affair is thought to reside in the past; to say anything of the sort would indeed be a sheer mistake. But it is there in the past that the presence of the Son of man to the intractable element in human existence is to be found; it is there in the past that he was betrayed, and by that betrayal with all that it entailed for its agent went his appointed way. In flesh and blood he revealed the depths of human nature; but in the time and place in which he was manifested as the judge of all the world he was also identified beyond shade of equivocation with the condemned. It is indeed from recognition of the paradox of his situation in this respect that both subjective and objective doctrines of atonement have sprung.

Yet it may be that we have failed to notice that when we speak of these doctrines as doctrines we are using the word in a different sense from that in which we employ it when we speak of the doctrines of the Trinity, or even the Incarnation. For what we speak of is essentially a deed done in history; (and we should never forget the extent to which the archaeological discoveries of the post-war period have re-activated general awareness of the historical context of Christian beginnings). A doctrine of the atonement is the projection of a raw piece of human history in a way calculated to admit the man who attends to it to some perception of its inwardness and universal significance, to some glimpse indeed of the way in which it expresses and conveys the will of God for his creation. But such a doctrine inevitably fails if it encourages the believer to avert his attention from the element of sheer waste, the reality of Christ's failure. To speak of Christ's readiness to embrace failure and defeat is familiar in the almost casual language of traditional piety. In consequence it is easy to forget that the words should be used and should be understood as being used to state simple fact. Again we have only to recall historical actualities and reflect for a moment on the element of abdication of responsibility for his people's welfare involved in the way that Jesus took. It is admittedly speculation to ask whether by other methods he could have helped to avert the catastrophe that was to overtake the Jewish people less than forty years from the crucifixion. It is at least arguable that he had enough influence to achieve at least a little; but he seems to have preferred a road which, if it led to the unmasking of human motives, also involved many of his contemporaries in a terrible guilt and provided inevitably an excuse for his followers in later years to fasten responsibility for the crucifixion upon the Jewish people and their descendants. If for the Christian it is in the events of the first Good Friday that the sense of the final judgment of the world is to be glimpsed as well as the foundations of its hope, he must also remember that part of the price paid for the accomplishment of these things in human history was the unmentionable horror of an anti-semitism whose beginnings can perhaps be traced in the New Testament itself, and whose last manifestation in our own time was Christian acquiescence in the "final solution". To say this may seem wilful exaggeration; but we have to come to terms not only with the work of Christ, but with the ways in which from the beginnings the Christian Church has come to terms with it. Always there has been besetting temptation to convert deed into idea, to fail properly to do justice to what is involved in finding the very foundation of human excellence in a raw piece of history. So the cutting edge of the doctrine is blunted by refusal to recall the concrete detail of the events with which it deals. So the mystery of God's presence in human existence

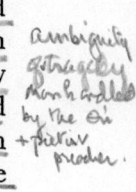

unspoken tragedy of Xs death, involves then his birth — death to the innocent.

ambiguity of tragedy Montgomery by the Ou + pietian product.

is diminished through induced forgetfulness of the depth to which he descended.

And that depth is at least as deep as those abysses of human circumstances we find explored in great literature. It is a lesson to be learnt from tragedy that there is no solution of the problem of evil; it is a lesson which Christian faith abundantly confirms, even while it transforms the teaching by the indication of its central mystery. In the Cross the conflicting claims of truth and mercy are reconciled by deed and not by word. The manner of their reconciliation is something which lies beyond the frontier of our comprehension; we can only describe and re-describe. But always we must guard against the failure of supposing that by a formula we can exorcise reality of which in its beginnings Christian memory showed itself at once to be aware and at the same time to fear so much that every sort of device was invoked to blunt its bitterness. Yet in this respect the principle *lex orandi lex credendi* has prevailed across the centuries, and/even if Christian men and women have been disappointed of a doctrine of atonement adequate to capture the sense of the Cross, they have continually found in its recollection the assurance of divine presence and mercy. It is indeed as witnessing to this historical fact, that the oscillation between subjective and objective conceptions, between Abelardian and Anselmian schemes, has borne witness. Here is the revelation of God; but here also is that human deed in which the abysses of existence are sounded and the ultimate contradictions of life plumbed and explored.

SCOTT HOLLAND AND CONTEMPORARY NEEDS

IN A proper study of the influence of Thomas Hill Green on English life, a space would have to be found for the deep inspiration which undoubtedly he provided for Henry Scott Holland. In Stephen Paget's life of Holland[1] the examples of their correspondence given to the reader show that the Balliol philosopher was much more to the young ordinand and priest than teacher and tutor: he was in a strange, perhaps unique, sense spiritual director as well.

If a reader of Holland's sermons to-day begins with the opening sermons in *Logic and Life* (1882), he may well judge Green's influence dominant: but he will be wrong. By Green Holland had been exposed to the full impact of a particular stream of the humanistic culture of his age. The integrity of the man, the subtlety of his idealist "metaphysic of experience", the passion of his social concern—all these deeply affected the young student: his days at Balliol marked him for life. But if Green had taught him to look always for spiritual continuity, the New Testament spoke to him of life out of death, of gulfs crossed not by the development of an immanent spiritual principle but by the act of God.

Holland gave his theological work to the world largely in the form of sermons: he apologized for publishing them, but he argued that he had decided that he must be a preacher, and that therefore what he might more easily have done in his study he was compelled to do from the pulpit. His "torrential eloquence" is often mentioned: so too his consuming passion for social righteousness. But it is less often realized that he was a considerable theologian. He was very emphatically not one of those who appeal to an abstractly conceived theory of incarna-

[1] John Murray, 1921.

tion to justify some previously formed attitude to social evils. His sermons continually bear witness to the restless search and sweep of his theological thinking. Of course, it does not have the formal order rightly demanded of the academic theologian: but it does not neglect the duty of completeness. I mean Holland was never a man to hammer one aspect of the Christian verity to the omission of others: he had a profound intuitive sense of the unity of the faith committed to him. It was not that he ranged wide in choice of subject (he certainly did that); but that in lapidary sentences he would suddenly bring together a whole range of topics showing the tightness of the unity in which they were held.

For instance, this in a sermon on "The Mind of the Church" in *Creed and Character* (1887)[1]:

> Let us consider this (the compassion of the Father) in its depth, and width, and height. It is the compassion of the entire Godhead that builds the Church—the compassion of God, the great Father, made known to us through the tenderness and tears of a human heart, in flesh and blood, in Jesus Christ, his Son, our Brother. That compassion, as it is in Christ Jesus, offers itself in a shape that enthrals and subdues with a touch of human kinship; but nevertheless, it is, still, in him but a revelation of that supreme compassion which moves the Father to send his Son into the world. The compassionate mercy of the Father sends his Son; and it is made manifest and sealed to us in that hidden, yet felt Spirit, whose very Name is given him for his pity, the Advocate, the Spirit of Consolation, the Comforter.
>
> The Ministry of the Church, then, arises out of the deep compassion of the Triune Godhead.

Holland is talking about the foundation of the Church. Therefore he must talk about the Father who sent the Son. Yet he must not neglect the particularity of Christ's incarnate life: nor the abiding ministry of the Paraclete, who takes the things of Christ and shows them to us. The whole paragraph reveals a deep theological self-discipline.

Again, in the sermons on sacrifice in *Logic and Life* you find the same impatient, yet disciplined, anxiety to leave nothing

[1] *Op. cit.*, pp. 113 f.

out. Of course, again they are sermons, not a treatise on redemption; but Holland sees that here pre-eminently the preacher must show a width of sympathy that acknowledges no other command to emphasis or integration than what is enjoined by the rich complexity of the New Testament. For instance, he is utterly emphatic that here we have at the very centre an act of God, unique, unrepeatable, costly: there is nowhere in Holland the slightest deviation from the central evangelical assertion. Yet this act of the Cross somehow at once illuminates the abysses of the divine love and the age-long problem of innocent suffering. Holland will never say that the Crucifixion is *merely* God's way of dealing with human guilt: it is that, but unfathomably more. So in the sermons on sacrifice he ranges passionately, restlessly, invoking now one scheme of images, now another: but always eschewing the deadly, sterile *merely*, conscious that here he is dealing with the ultimate mystery of the divine will, made accessible ("pity" is a word never long off his lips, for his thoughts will never stay long away from the ministry of the Galilean plains), yet inaccessible still; as concrete as the nails that fastened Jesus to his Cross (those nails and not others did the job), yet as universal as only the will of God can be.

Again in *Creed and Character* he turns to the theme of the Atonement. Here at once his language recalls that of John McLeod Campbell and anticipates that of R. C. Moberly.[1] But it has its own peculiar force.

God's forgiveness issues out of Heaven in the shape of Man, bearing human flesh. Jesus Christ is the Forgiveness of the Father. The Father had already forgiven the world, when he sent his Son to be born of the Virgin Mary, to be crucified under Pontius Pilate. He arrives, bringing with him the pardon of the Father; and this pardon is effectual. For there is now in man one spot, at least, clean from defilement, on which the eyes of God's purity can afford to rest. There is now, amid the loveless hordes of sinners, one Heart, at any rate, upon which the Father can risk the outpouring of his love; one Body, amid the hopeless and the

[1] The first edition of *Atonement and Personality* was not published till 1901. I must thank the Archbishop of Canterbury for pointing this out to me.

faithless and the diseased, which can admit the rushing power of the transfiguring Spirit. The love, hope, purity of God—long homeless and unhoused—have found at last a footing within our flesh, a resting-place, a habitation, a temple. They had looked, and there had been in man—not one that doeth good, no, not one!—not one that could respond to that appeal—not one that could surrender himself to their intimacy—no, not one; and, therefore, not one whom God could forgive. But now there is the Son of Man in and through whom God's forgiveness can begin to work. Christ, the Forgiveness, becomes the one forgiven Man: the one Son, who has sanctified himself to do the Father's will.[1]

The language is extremely bold: but it comes in the third and last of a group of three sermons on the Law of Forgiveness, and shows how surely Holland grasped in practice the principle that Christian thought must accept the discipline of Christology. If we plot the rules governing the use of a fundamental noun like forgiveness, and a still more fundamental verb like forgive, we must see that their very claim to be fundamental stands only when their use about and in relation to Christ is made plain. Something of what Holland is after here has been more recently canvassed by Dr C. H. Dodd in his arresting use of the idea of manhood's *transparency* to God in Christ.[2] In Dodd as well as in Holland the treatment of Christ's manhood is seen to involve not merely the issue of its relation to that divine nature to which it is united: at the same time, the theologian must fasten on the relation in which both that human nature and that divine alike (for it is the Son who is incarnate) stand to the Father. Holland's boldness of language is an expression of his relentless recognition of this crux. Now, it may seem strange at first that sensibility to a major theological crux makes a man bold. Yet the boldness that issues from a slapdash over-simplification of the complexity of the Gospel is not of course real theological courage; it is the brash bravado of the spiritual Philistine and only serves to strengthen the prejudices of a falsely scholastic orthodoxy. Holland's boldness is that of the man who sees that it is at the points of greatest difficulty that

---

[1] *Op. cit.*, pp. 224 f.; cf. Karl Barth's view of Jesus as *der Erwählte*.
[2] Cf. his *Benefits of his Passion*, Lutterworth Press, 1947.

the most precious insights lie, and that bold, almost extravagant language is warranted at once to advertise and safeguard such treasure. To speak of Christ as the Forgiven Man is startling, especially if at the same time he is called the Forgiveness of the Father. But if it is startling, it is also crystalline clear, although the clarity is that of the deepest waters, not of the muddy shallows.

Earlier in this group of sermons Holland had spoken most poignantly of the mystery of Christ within us:

And what, if around and about this poor, this impoverished will, there were wrapped the irresistible might of a will that had not been broken, a will, new, fresh, undaunted, tough as steel, endurable as stone, firm as adamant?—What if the warmth of a love were about it to which the emotions of impure appetites are impossible?—What if we were given up to this love, so that it abode within us and possessed us and held us fast, untroubled by our disaster, unhurt by our sins?—What if, after all our sinning, we still could turn back again and again to find this loving will there still, pure and strong, as ever within us, still pressing with unwearied patience, on towards the beauty of holiness, with its unwavering eyes ever fixed on the face of God.[1]

The language is severely ethical. Holland displays an extreme sensitivity to the reality of human guilt and the irreversibility of human choice. As a good Anglican he sees in the doctrine of "justification by faith"[2] an assertion of "our absolute exclusion from the creative act by which God acquits us; in that act we have no more part or lot than in the act of our first begetting". Yet our healing is in Christ Incarnate: and Holland sees that if we most certainly must remember the Cross on Christmas Day, we must not forget the "honour God did to man in the Incarnation" (a form of words he often uses) on Good Friday; nor on either day forget the Resurrection and Pentecost. There is a wholeness in the faith that is wholly reconciliable with the sharp discontinuities one discovers within it. That wholeness commands us to mark well the otherness of Christ and his strange-ness: but it is the otherness of one who is Man, who makes the

---

[1] *Op. cit.*, p. 217.   [2] *Op. cit.*, pp. 221 f.

healing of our human state possible in, not apart from, manhood. Thus as man, now risen and ascended, he is within the very body of our lives, their sweet, sound heart and centre. "Love would not be moral if it were not vicarious."[1] And that for Holland is true pre-eminently of that love which is the source of all love, the love of God whose definitive expression is the mystery of Christ.

Holland's treatment of redemption is the very core of his preaching and work, and it has a remarkable completeness of view. His emphasis on forgiveness of sin shows that he accepted as partly valid juridical categories: but if, like so many Anglicans, he seems nearer to McLeod Campbell than to Dale or to Denney, it is because he discerns in the Cross an outpouring of divine love in humanity that just cannot be contained by any quasi-juridical scheme. He is always moving behind such a network of conceptions as if somehow he would show them less than quite ultimate. But his theology remains for that obstinately a *theologia crucis*: one may even say that it is most obstinately so just when this mood is on him. For there he is intoxicated by the sense of Christ as the "revelation of the mystery", as himself concretely the key to all the riddles of existence. It is his passionate Christocentrism that somehow is on edge in the presence of all that seems in any way to diminish the depths of Christ's penetration of the stuff of our humanity.

This comes out clearly at points where one might expect the influence of Green to be strongest—in a group of sermons in *On Behalf of Belief* (1889) where he deals with human history. They reach their climax in a sermon on the Circumcision which is, in my judgment, one of his very greatest. In the whole group he is concerned with the obstinacy of human things, the backlash of stupidity and evil that will not be subdued to purposes of God. He shows a certain kinship with, as well as a real difference from, F. J. A. Hort in his exposition of the way theological progress has been achieved. When he sketches the wide canvasses of historical progress, Holland the preacher shows a sharper, clearer sense of the realities than recently fashionable theologians like Niebuhr sometimes command. For he does

[1] *Op. cit.* p. 218.

take with an utter, an almost desperate seriousness that "God is like Christ". In earlier years he had preached on "Christ, the justification of a suffering world": but now quite simply, with a curious freedom from any air of triumphantly demonstrating a truth, he points to the suffering Christ, the revelation of the Father, as the only key we have to the inner ways of God, and the only sure guide to the posture befitting us in the world he has fashioned.

The sermon on the Circumcision is the climax of this group. Its ethical gravity recalls the minute, devastating argument of Butler's *Dissertation*, or his sermon on self-deceit. But it is more than an eloquent uncovering of the sin of the man who makes his own purposes the measure of being, who dreams of a *tabula rasa*, and dares himself to clean the slate. We are enabled to see the falsity of such an attitude as pointing beyond itself to the Incarnation.

As we glance down that long list of our Lord's forefathers in St Matthew or in St Luke—which looks so stiff and legal, and monotonous—how pathetic, how profound the significance becomes, as we remember what that list embodies! There, in those dry names, lies the record of the burden which the centuries had slowly built together for the Lord to carry. Through that line of names the story of man's life reached him. It arrived to him charged with all that those men had made it—their struggles, their hopes, their joys, their woes, their sins, their pains. Out of the nameless years which had come and gone, a certain sequence had preserved itself through those remembered men, links in the long chain from Abraham and David. A tradition had handed itself down, a story had been prolonged, a memory had survived and grown, and accumulated details, and gathered in continuous experiences. Passions, aspirations, miseries, losses—all had stored their results within this unbroken and enduring movement. Such strange exaltations, such untoward reverses, such patient persistence, such stubborn obscurity, had all gone to the fashioning of that family of David! Into it had passed much that was worthiest and much that was worst of human character and incident. Ruth, and David, and Zerubbabel, pastoral loyalty, royal glories, heroic deliverances—yes, but also, as St Matthew seems to suggest with frequent emphasis, Tamar, with her terrible scandal;

Rahab harlot of Jericho; and Bathsheba, the wife of David's sin. And all this inheritance, just as it stood, at the particular moment when Caesar first prepared to lay the bitterest mark of servitude upon the race which once had tasted the free royalty of David— all this, without turning one jot or tittle of it aside, without shrinking, without refusal, our Lord assumed for his own on the day when he was carried to the Temple as the Child of Mary.[1]

Holland is not talking about the Old Testament types for their own sake: he is speaking of Jesus as fulfilling God's work as himself the very Will of God. He is pointing to his self-identification with the particularities of Israel's history as the ultimate sanction of an obligation to an analogous acceptance of the conditions in which we in our day and generation must act. We must avoid false archaism as well as utopian scheming: no fight is the "last fight" (save only *Christi gloriosi proelium certaminis*), nor does any age, Carolingian or Caroline, Innocentian or Elizabethan, qualify to tempt us to waste our days in dreaming nostalgically its faded glories. We are where we are, even as Christ was where he was.

Certainly Holland's Christology could be called kenotic: but his use of the idea of kenosis serves to show how rich and complex as well as hard of definition it is. The reader of his sermons will not find in them any detailed technical discussion of the relation between the Logos in the bosom of the godhead and the Logos incarnate. The kind of theological issues so delicately and subtly canvassed by Bishop Frank Weston in his truly great book, *The One Christ*, pass by his attention.

But the reader will find three different aspects of the kenotic idea brought sharply to his attention:

[1] *On Behalf of Belief*, pp. 193 ff. Holland's understanding of history is echoed in a remarkable way by Hans Urs von Balthasar in his recent essay, *Theologie der Geschichte* (Christ Heute: 1. Folge, 8. Heft—Einsiedeln, 1950). Like Holland, von Balthasar finds the key to the doctrine of providence in Christology, and that Christology of a strongly kenotic emphasis. He starts from a profound discussion of Christ's attitude towards that hour which lay in his Father's hand, of the utter reality for him of time, and moves on through a massive argument to the conclusion that the innermost sense of history lies for the Christian less in the conflict of the "two cities" than in the struggle of the Bridegroom with the Bride. If he goes beyond Holland, he agrees with him in a radical Christocentricism (learnt perhaps partly from his effort to come to terms with Karl Barth) and in emphasis on the patience of God. I am most grateful to Prof. T. F. Torrance for calling my attention to this work.

(1) In his understanding of civilization and culture, as we have seen, Holland moved a long way from that of his master, T. H. Green. For him the patience and meekness of God were almost identical with his providence. As we have seen, too, for him the sanction of this view was Christological: and it is a Christology which has a markedly kenotic flavour.

It is no accident that, when he preaches profoundly on culture and civilization in the group of sermons already marked, he shows how far he has moved away from Green: for in them he is bedding down a positive attitude towards the things of this world in a most serious Christology. It was precisely seriousness about Christology that Green's immanentism would not allow him.

We are so accustomed to the accepted superstition concerning the *Lux Mundi* school,[1] that its members were in bondage to Oxford neo-Hegelianism, that we forget that perhaps one of the most important things about them was the zeal they displayed in breaking out of that prison. From Green men like Holland learnt to expose themselves to the whole manifold impact of contemporary culture: admittedly they learnt from him to pierce the contradictions of the associationist theory of knowledge; but what he gave them before all else was a sense of the world as under the providence of God and of the worth of taking seriously its problems and causes. The technical philosophical criticism of Hume and the utilitarians Green offered owed a good deal to the critical philosophy of Kant and the speculation of Hegel: but in impressing on his pupils the stamp of his own character he furnished them less with an introduction to continental speculation and analysis than with an attitude towards the world they lived in. This became part of their whole intellectual and emotional make-up; but so too was their penitence and that which lay behind it. How to fuse together a sense of historical conflicts as capable of mastery, with a knowledge that it is Christ who has "opened the Kingdom of Heaven to all believers", that in him alone the Father has seen the travail of his soul and been satisfied? To

---

[1] Even the Archbishop of Canterbury is not immune from this. Cf. his *F.D. Maurice and the Conflicts of Modern Theology* (C.U.P., 1950).

these problems Holland turns in these very great sermons, and to them he sketches an answer that comes perhaps more from meditation on the Passion than from familiarity with German and French thought.

Here then we see kenosis as in effect the principle that bids us measure the Logos-Christ by the *Christus-patiens*. Holland is optimistic: but his optimism is the optimism of the man who has made the Cross the measure of his world. If he believes that persuasion is superior to force in being (τῷ ὄντι) as well as a method of dealing with the obstinate, intractable burdens of our human lot, he does so because in Christ's life the ways of God have been revealed to him. Paradoxical though it may seem, he is far less Hegelian than many modern writers on these topics, whose apologia for trust in providence is much more like confidence in an Hegelian "cunning of the idea" (*ruse de l'histoire*) than "in one who has overcome the world".[1]

(2) Holland's Christology is also one that stresses the antithesis of Crucifixion and Resurrection. The sermons on the Resurrection in *On Behalf of Belief* are famous: but in preaching on the foundation of the Church, again and again he stresses the reality of the divine incognito. For him the hiddenness of Christ's glory is the thing which makes necessary the training of the twelve, their intimate initiation into his secrets. This belongs not simply to the necessary economy of his self-revelation: it lies deep-bedded in the nature of his work. Here again it is the primacy of the *Christus patiens* that is being stressed: but now in a different way. For suffering and glory are shown as correlates: and the context of the Passion is revealed as the way to resurrection and ascension, to the eternal ministry of intercession and the gift to his own of the Paraclete.

Although Holland's arguments always show his mastery of a truly theological dialectic, it could be justly said against him that he did not clearly perceive the extent to which "eschatology shows us the true historical and cosmic proportions of the

---

[1] Cf. in justification of this judgment the impressive Hegelian studies of M. Jean Hyppolite, not least his long review of Prof. Georg Lukács' work on the young Hegel in *Études Germaniques* for April-June 1951 and January-April 1952.

Resurrection".[1] Although his sermons on eschatology are vivid and arresting, they are not closely enough linked in thought with his treatment of the Resurrection. The fact remains, however, that his understanding of the latter is most deeply theological, and shows us the incisive penetration of which he is capable, catching in a phrase, "When he rose, his life rose with him", the very heart of the matter. We see Christ incarnate *through* his Resurrection: and this because in his glory his work is consummated and made perpetual. But that work was one which could be done only in concrete particularity and in settings of deepest humiliation.

(3) But finally Holland's Christology is kenotic because he allows its full pressure to be felt by his doctrine of God. He speaks continually, as I have said, of God's pity, his patience, his very meekness: for him the temper of Christian asceticism is determined by the Christian remembrance that God has "honoured" mankind in the Incarnation.

His language here is, if you like, infected by mythology—that is to say it is a product of an obstinate, hardly dissoluble marriage of the metaphysical and the concretely descriptive. He would have accepted the indictment: for a man, who had felt the impact of Green and yet held to his faith, must have measured the preciousness to his articulation of Christian verity of such language. Green was, as I have implied, actually greater as a social theorist than as a metaphysician (indeed, it is interesting that when Holland himself canvasses a philosophical theme, like the limitations of science, his argument is much nearer to James Ward's than to that of his master in the "Greats" school).[2] But the perspective from which his social theory was developed was one from which, for all its professed value as a critique of *laissez-faire*, the abysses of human conflict

---

[1] R. Mehl in *Ecumenical Review*, April 1952, p. 292. Cf. also H. A. Williams, *Jesus and the Resurrection* (Longmans, 1951).

[2] In a sermon on hope in *Christ and Ecclesiastes* (1888). Ward's famous first series of Gifford Lectures on *Naturalism and Agnosticism* were given at Aberdeen in 1896. When Holland's philosophical temper is under discussion, it is well to remember the influence exerted on him by Butler, to whose *Analogy of Religion* he devoted his impressive Romanes lecture of 1908. Some of his wisest *philosophical* words on faith are to be found in the sermon on μαρτυρια in the Fourth Gospel in *Pleas and Claims*.

could be delicately obscured. And therefore Holland knew the theory would not stand. But because he had learnt from Green the preciousness and the wide possibilities of things human, he did not abandon humanism, but sought a profounder and, we may say, a more deeply gentle humanism. Its foundation was laid in the love of God.

Note, I do not say in the fact that God created us, but in something at once more simple and more profound, his love. Hardly a day passes that we are not reminded of the menace of materialism, of the need of a "return to God", who is the true foundation of our western culture *et tout ça*. But Holland, who cared greatly for our civilization, and is regarded indeed, or was till recently, by the theological *avant-garde* as a "this worldly" type, did not preach so. He took with a simple, penetrating seriousness God's self-revelation as love, as love active, concrete, working. He saw that the coming of Christ broke up indeed the foundation of our little world, our cosmos made to measure presided over by an idol fashioned after the image of our passing idealism. He turned his hearers towards that which was at once most ultimate and most intimate, at once universal and yet concretely particular. We must measure our world by what we know of its source through his self-revelation. He is in a most searching, because most human, way a theologian of revelation: from Green he learnt (as Hort insisted in his Hulsean Lectures that a theologian must always learn somewhere) of the richness and the diversity of things human, but from his master he departs when he sees the ground and the security of those things resting not in themselves but in the being of the Triune God.

Holland preached constantly on texts from the Gospels; for in the life and death of Christ he found that love of God made concrete and accessible. It is not an accident that he would repeatedly expound the feeding miracles; he never let go of the sharp historicity of Jesus of Nazareth. Yet what was made accessible in his compassion remained in its source inaccessible because inexhaustible. It was the love of the Father manifested to men in the mission of his beloved Son, and of the Paraclete who for ever takes the things of that Son and shows them to the Church.

Holland does not learn to speak of the transcendence of God in general terms: for he presents that transcendence as something by which we are apprehended in the Crucified. The movement of his preaching is continually concerned to protect his hearers against the fallacy of conceiving the relation between God and man abstractly. It is often said of the *Lux Mundi* school (indeed its members sometimes described their work so) that they separated the so-called "physical" attributes of God (omnipotence, omnipresence, omniscience, etc.) from the "moral" (benevolence, mercy, justice): and their critics blame their Kantian inspiration for this metaphysical philistinism. Certainly Kant's austere moralism was important to them, if only as a corrective to Hegelian elision of ethical distinctions. But their Christology rests on a surer foundation than philosophical confusion. In reality they are challenging just that sort of classification of divine attributes and doing so on Christological grounds. What they are protesting against (and Holland's sermons bring this out) is the Church's unconscious *Entmythologisierung* (demythologization) of its message, of its understanding of being and of God. For what matters in the end is that we should see the power, the wisdom, the presence of God in terms of his love and compassion: something that we could never have so seen apart from the Incarnation.

What gives the work of Holland a vital contemporaneity is the extent to which he thrusts this matter upon our attention. If we speak of him as expressing (in Archbishop Temple's phrase) a "Christocentric metaphysic", we have to remember that for him behind Jesus is the Father who sent the Son. His spirituality swings between a Christocentric and a theocentric pole. Perhaps when he is speaking of the *imitatio Christi*, he sometimes forgets the mystery of Christ's relation to his Father, which he himself elsewhere brings out so well in speaking of the Resurrection: we could wish that his sense of eschatology were more flexible and more pervasive.[1] But in the end he sees that our final concern must be with God: the God whom Jesus reveals, but in the same moment discloses as hidden, the one from

[1] Cf. from a Reformed point of view the fusion of eschatology and Christology in Théo Preiss, *La Vie en Christ* (Delachaux et Niestlé, 1951).

whose hand he receives the burden of his mission and his hour, whose nature indeed is shown to men in that receptivity[1] of his.

It is here that we find the ultimate sanction of Holland's optimism. I am not saying that he always sees it himself like that: only that when he reasons his case through, as he very often does, he thus wings his way back to the ground of the world in the love of God. And this makes him a teacher for our age as well as for his own.

For we need to be reminded of the ultimate sweetness of things, in a time of wrath to be recalled to mercy, and in a time of violence to be told again of persuasion. We will not be fobbed off by a trivial optimism: we can easily be betrayed into a nihilistic despair. But our greatest teachers are those who remind us that the law of God's being is pity and meekness, although a pity and meekness revealed in the Cross. In those who witness to this God there may be a strange companionship. Thus a thinker like Canon C. E. Raven, with his deep sympathetic understanding of the vast achievement of modern science of nature as well as his personal love of the natural world, may be nearer than he knows to Karl Barth, whose *Dogmatics in Outline*[2] throbs with a kind of ground-bass of joy and hope strangely reminiscent of Holland's own. (British readers are always ready to ignore Barth's radical Christo-centricism, but it remains the axis of his work.) A profound union may bind such men in their insistence that the Christian message of hope for the world shall not be exploited in the interest of abstractions like "western values", but shall be manifested in its wholeness and sweetness as the succour of God's own pity for his own.

It is for the Christian preacher to stand himself in the shadow of the Cross, to catch there the music of God's promise, and joy, of his abiding purpose of love there fulfilled. Too often

---

[1] Cf. Dr C. H. Dodd's discussion of Philippians II in his Bampton Lectures—*Gospel and Law* (C.U.P., 1951). Cf. also von Balthasar's treatment of Jesus' attitude to time in his *Theologie der Geschichte*.

[2] S.C.M. Press, 1949. The great *Dogmatik* is itself fundamentally an optimistic work, a point excellently brought out by von Balthasar in his study of Barth (Hegner, 1951).

to-day we fob off men and women crying out for a word of hope with an academically precise pessimism, which seems to glory less in the Cross than in the disintegration of human societies and in the coming of despair. We have reached the truly appalling position of pointing to the threat of the atom bomb as an evidence of the disorder of our being and at the same time, like men in a trance, accepting and preparing to follow to the end the way to which such expedients belong, calling it our "western way of life". The Stalinists[1] are quite right to say we welcome our theologies of despair simply because they confirm us in this nightmare refusal of revolt: they are our necessary dope.

But not so did Holland see the ways of God. He saw them otherwise: perhaps more as R. P. Louis Bouyer in his *Le Mystère Pascal*,[2] when he wrote:

It seems that in the love of God, in the love which is God, there is something which only sin can let us understand. The paradox is bold: but the Church has made it her own in singing on Holy Saturday, *O Felix culpa!* Sin kindles divine wrath. But approached, as it were, across his wrath, God's love is shown us anew: and it is us if we enjoy by his favour a sudden piercing insight into the eternal secrets of his very heart. This is the incomprehensible mystery of the kenosis, of the God who becomes poor to make us rich, who compels himself to feel bodily the blows we inflict on him in order to pardon the infliction. On the Cross the godhead seems to lay itself waste. God the ultimate judge of all the world interposes himself as a screen against his own anger. Better—the Almighty gives himself up to sinners, and they work their will on him. But had the creature never seen this *Deus patiens*, would he ever have understood the limitless self-giving which is the very inner stuff of God's being? So maybe this torrent of fire had to be poured out upon the world that in the floods we should catch some far off echo of the eternal springs.[3]

[1] Cf. the *Modern Quarterly* and the *Daily Worker* (*passim*). (This essay was written in 1952.)

[2] Op. cit., pp. 338 f. (Eng. trans. *The Paschal Mystery*, Allen and Unwin, 1952). Bouyer owes something at least here to Serge Bulgakov: *Du Verbe Incarné* (Aubier, 1944). It is interesting to compare his treatment of Kenosis with the treatment of Krupsis by R. P. René Thibaut, S. J., in his valuable *Le Sens de l'homme Dieu* (Museum Lessianum, 1949).

[3] Eng. trans. *The Paschal Mystery*, p. 233. The translation here given is my own.

The very language of the last sentences recalls Scott Holland's eloquence. But more important: the message of hope these words convey is near his own, and it is a message of which our world is in direst need.

SOME NOTES ON KIERKEGAARD

OF THE making of books on Kierkegaard, there seems to be no end; but it will be a very great pity if their number causes Dr Croxall's *Commentary*[1] to be overlooked by those concerned to understand and to evaluate this strange, ambiguous, even contradictory Danish genius. He has written his book under the conviction that "the primary need for English readers" is that of "explaining, sorting out, and commenting upon the actual words that Kierkegaard wrote"; and it is a measure of his achievement that he has fulfilled the promise of his title by a work that is hard to read without close attention to the texts on which he is commenting, but that provides to a student of those texts continual illumination and suggestion. He has accompanied the publication of his *Commentary* by a volume of Kierkegaard's meditations,[2] many of them drawn from the largely untranslated *Papirer*, and by doing so has undoubtedly enlarged his readers' debt to him.

Few men have suffered more than Kierkegaard from their idolators on the one side and from their detractors on the other; and sometimes one suspects with an irony which would have appealed to S.K. himself that they only agree in having failed to read him. This of course is not to suggest that where he is concerned, scholarship is the road to understanding; Dr Croxall's book is certainly the work of one fully at home in Danish language and literature, but he is too deeply in tune with his subject ever to claim that by his scholarship alone he has been able to open the doors upon that subject's secret. One who exalts the category of the individual as Kierkegaard does, almost deliberately sets every obstacle in the way of systematic

[1] T. H. Croxall, *Kierkegaard Commentary*. Nisbet. 25s.
[2] T. H. Croxall, *Meditations from Kierkegaard*. Nisbet. 12s. 6d.

exposition and criticism of his views; if one says even that the key to the understanding of the works of his aesthetic, pseudonymous period is to be found in his broken, obscure and elusive personal history, especially in the crisis of his relations with Regine Olsen, one is in danger of showing that one has not read those works themselves, with proper attention to their many-levelled, sinuous, yet always ironical dialectic. Certainly Dr Croxall well brings out that his subject is a master-ironist, and if we are to say of Kierkegaard that he learnt in his own life the inwardness of that distinction between the genius and the apostle, of which he wrote so profoundly towards the end of his life, we must be prepared, if we are trying to understand him, to take his writings, and not our own concept of what they must contain, as the articulation of that lesson. Even in the prophetic anger which he displayed in his attack upon the Danish Church after Mynster's death, we can still discern the lineaments of the ironic, half sceptical student of the different modes of human seriousness, seeking by reflection now on Don Juan, now on Faust, now on Job, now on Abraham, to evaluate those modes, and to separate the relative from the absolute, the serious from the half-serious and the trivial. If in the later works, which Dr Croxall quite rightly finds easier for the general reader than the earlier, Kierkegaard's playfulness is less noticeable, and the rich, almost luxuriant virtuosity of his psychological insight less obvious, both are still there beneath the surface; and it is no accident that some of the most remarkable of the overtly religious *Meditations*, which Dr Croxall has translated, are those in which he is able (for instance, in his treatment of certain of Christ's parables), to display his sensitivity to the ironic.

Kierkegaard must be received as Kierkegaard; for then even if he does repel, as sometimes he must repel, he will at least not be pigeon-holed as the "father of existentialism", or given the place in the progress or decadence of theological thought that the pigeon-holer thinks he has best deserved. Dr Croxall brings out how surprising his writings often are, how well deserved, for all the differences that separate them, the comparison drawn between Kierkegaard and Socrates; by both alike, men are disturbed, in respect at once of their cherished assumptions and also of their hardly purchased intellectual sophistication. It might be that for some at least Kierkegaard's main service will be to drive them back to study with increased perception and renewed excitement the Socratic dialogues; for if he is sometimes almost obsessed with the necessity of criticizing Hegel's doctrine of the "concrete universal", he is also aware of a far wider philosophical environment than that in which the German Romantics and their successors moved, and shows himself able to avail himself, and to make available for others, its forgotten resources with the freedom of genius. Certainly as M. Jean Wahl has excellently brought out, he is perhaps the most searching of all Hegel's critics; and we badly need a book which will trace the working out of this criticism, point by point, in relation to Hegel's *Jugendschriften*; but it would be disastrous if the execution of such a task seemed to assign to Kierkegaard his place in the "history of philosophy". It is of the nature of his interrogations that they can have no such place, and that those who have best learned from him will often be those who quote him least, but who suddenly reveal in their discussion for instance of Kant's ethics (a subject on which, in spite of the character of Judge William in *Stages*, Kierkegaard has left very little) that they are aware of the profound criticism of Kant's formalism implicit in what S.K. has written, both in his earlier and in his later works. But it will be Kant's doctrine that is being discussed, not Kierkegaard's; for in a sense the latter has no doctrine, only the capacity by the range of his psychological insight as well as by the depth of his understanding of what is involved in faith, to set a question mark against the outlines, at once firm and flexible, of Kant's conception of the form of the universal moral law. Odd though it may seem, this kind of questioning may sometimes strangely resemble the protests made in the name of his understanding of our actual human nature by Joseph Butler against the more naïve[1] formalism of Wollaston, who attempted to derive all human duties from a single overriding obligation to the truth, and seemed to forget what Butler always remembered, namely the

[1] More naïve, that is, than Kant's.

extent to which contempt for that obligation itself is rooted often for men in "the plausible casuistry of the passions"; it must always, Butler insisted, go ill for an ethic that forgets the concrete stuff of which human beings are made. And if the idiom of his protest was, as Matthew Arnold pointed out, deeply overcast by the characteristic styles of the eighteenth century, he has this in common with S.K., that he recalls men from the abstract and the general to the concrete and the particular, that he insists that no moral teaching can possibly bear upon our condition which neglects the multiplicity of our concerns, the irreducible complexity of our nature, the fact that for us men the way to a final simplicity must lie very often only through the painful dealing, stage by stage, with all that that complexity involves for us. There is a curious spiral movement here whose impression remains even when the "infinite qualitative distinction" between God and man, between faith and reason is acknowledged.

If the reference to Butler is surprising, the surprise is deliberately intended. It is of the nature of the study of Kierkegaard that he should illuminate by turning us back to find new perceptions in familiar and superficially different writers. Both the style and the stuff of his psychological insights are vastly different from Butler's; but when, with the very horizons of the notion of psychological insight itself enlarged by our study of Kierkegaard, we return to Butler's *Sermons*, we see the minute and subtle descriptions of the latter in a new way and are certainly able to learn from it that which otherwise might have escaped us. It is particularly important that we should let Kierkegaard teach us fresh lessons about such a moralist as Butler; for if the two agree, in spite of all their differences of style in stressing the concrete, Butler is immensely superior in his stronger, less prejudiced sense of the claim of utilitarian considerations upon our conscience. Rationally informed and disciplined concern for the welfare of mankind at large is not the whole of virtue; but it is a very important part of it, as Butler clearly recognized. Kierkegaard claimed for his work that it was a "corrective"; and one who makes such a claim must always be the first to allow the necessity of corresponding correction, where his own insights are taken hold of, and converted into a kind of incorrigible and necessary truth. It is easy to fasten on those elements in his outlook which are sombre, even pessimistic, and forget the irony that suffuses so much that he has written; it is easy to make of the legacy of this most painfully individual of writers, a kind of warrant for every sort of anti-humanist excess. Certainly there is excuse for this; but if we try to invoke his authority to justify our indifference to social reform, or our sense of the death-penalty as somehow "intrinsically fitting to a proper seriousness concerning our human estate",[1] we are surely making of his insight something it was never intended to be, showing how little we have taken the measure of his painful apostolate. We do that last best when we ourselves take part in the dialogue, and offer our own corrections.

The same sort of unexpectedness is displayed in Kierkegaard's explicitly theological writings. Those who think of him as the grisly exponent of a crude substitutionary view of atonement are fitly reminded by Dr Croxall that the orthodox of his day found in his soteriology an exaggerated tendency to exemplarism, to emphasis on Christ as pattern rather than redeemer. If we turn to his Christological writings, and to those *Meditations*, translated by Dr Croxall, which deal with the life and the sufferings of Christ, we are often reminded of the passionately humanist onslaughts made by the late G. A. Studdert-Kennedy on the formal doctrine of the impassibility of God. If Kierkegaard makes no explicit use of the notion of *kenosis*, he shows by his practice how indispensable that notion is for any intelligible doctrine at once of the Incarnation and of the Trinity itself. Dr Croxall rightly stresses how curiously unfinished and incomplete his writings on the figure of Christ and his person often seem; his deeply perceptive reflections on the divine Incognito, his treatment of faith as "contemporaneous discipleship" seems suddenly to end and to be followed by brief, almost harsh quotations of the language of conventional dogmatic theology; it is as if Kierkegaard's characteristic indirectness and reticence must somehow display themselves even

[1] The language is the sort we have often heard on official ecclesiastical lips.

when he has deliberately ceased from speaking in parables, and display themselves now by a conscious choice of the stereotyped idiom of the catechism. But those who find, for instance in the *Meditations* an approach to the *mysterium Christi* which attracts them to the point of wishing to follow it further, may be referred to the remarkable volume of meditations on the Sacred Heart by the Roman Catholic theologian Hans Urs von Balthasar, entitled *Das Herz der Welt*, wherein they will find a treatment of the ultimate mysteries of the faith as searching and disturbing as for instance that fashionable among self-conscious Anglican Thomists, like Dr E. L. Mascall, is ultimately trivial and sterile. Von Balthasar achieves a completeness of outline, a wholeness of theological view lacking in Kierkegaard; but his debt to the latter is as clear as his debt to Barth, and all alike show that if men like Studdert-Kennedy in their polemic against the formal doctrine of impassibility were sometimes unbalanced and often indisciplined, they were at least insisting that no theology of divine transcendence has any right to call itself Christian that does not see the very transcendence of God in terms of the crown of thorns.

It is no use reading Kierkegaard unless one is prepared to work; but if one is prepared to work, then even when one is repelled, one will learn. For apart from the wealth of psychological insight his writings contain, there are few who raise so sharply the problems of the relation of faith to reason, of religion to ethics. He raises the problems, now in one way, now in another, and he provokes us to face the problems too, not (if we have learnt from him at all) in his own terms but in ours. No one has understood or begun to understand Kierkegaard who can talk profoundly of the "teleological suspension of the ethical", and discuss it learnedly; but the man who remembers the history of Kierkegaard's relations with Regine Olsen and the former's often repeated, winding reflections upon his bitter, even cruel decision as he reads the account of Will and Anna Brangwen's visit to the cathedral in D. H. Lawrence's great novel *The Rainbow*, may be driven to most searching consideration of the actual relation between the absolute of religion, and the absolutes of human conduct. So insight may be won, more effectively even than by the systematic opposition of Kierke-gaard to Kant, of the religious writer who insists that men are related to the universal through the absolute and the moral philosopher who insists that relation to the absolute comes only through a preceding and an abiding relation to the universal. We may certainly regret that his obsession with Hegel, his readiness to identify the universal as such with Hegel's concrete universal, prevented Kierkegaard from seeing more clearly the claims for moral goodness made by Kant, and from passing comment on those claims; but we understand him best perhaps when we make the opposition between the two our own in concrete terms, even letting the contrast convey itself to us by way of the opposition between a passage in Kierkegaard, and one in, let us say, George Eliot or Lawrence.

And so it is too when we turn to the contrast between faith and reason. No doubt Kierkegaard always adhered to the principle contained in the saying of Hugh of St Victor,

"In things which are above reason, faith is not really supported by reason, because reason cannot grasp what faith believes; but there is a something here by which reason becomes determined, or is determined, to hold faith in honour while it cannot fully understand it" (Croxall, *Commentary*, p. 29);

or rather we should say that the language of this principle conveys the way in which Kierkegaard was always, now in one way, now in another, allowing his understanding of the relation of faith to reason to be shaped and reshaped. But it is hard to escape criticizing him on the ground that just as his universal was too much the concrete universal of Hegel, and that alone, so for him reason was the all-embracing, all-recon-ciling synthesis of the Hegelian dialectic. Some at least of those who find that Kierkegaard has nothing to say to them turn away from him because his philosophical culture is too narrowly that of the German Romantics, his conception of human rationality too continuously overshadowed and dis-torted by his preoccupation with their arguments. It has already been remarked that as a matter of fact Kierkegaard was able to cast much of his most subtle and characteristic teaching concerning faith against the very different background of e.g. Plato's *Meno*. But we may still regret that here again Hegel concealed from Kierkegaard the depth of Kant's achievement with its remarkable anticipation of our contemporary understanding of the nature of the *a priori* and its function in knowledge. Certainly we can never to-day receive as a last word an account of the relation of faith to reason which draws its understanding of the latter from Hegel's logic, and is consequently able to dodge so many issues by simply pointing to the uncriticized extravagance of Hegel's metaphysical pretensions. But the problem is still with us, and it is for us to restate it in our own terms, drawing on Kierkegaard's profound insights concerning the nature of faith, as for instance his notion of "contemporaneous discipleship" to enable us to do so. So he teaches us best again when he does not deliver to us a doctrine, but rather suggests to us a method; his word is never a last word. And just as Karl Barth, who owed much to him in the domain of theology, moved on to receive in part at least the methodological principles of his dogmatics from St Anselm, so those who would learn from him concerning the relation of reason to faith must not seek to take over from him, as it were ready-made, a concept of the former; rather they must fashion their own paradigms of rationality, and then fearlessly acknowledging their authority, be met by the problem of faith. Kierkegaard's world was certainly a different world from theirs; but it remained true that some of those who have been most certainly among the masters and makers of their world, have numbered him with Augustine, Pascal, and Dostoevsky as a man from whom they have learned much. In such possibilities is surely Kierkegaard's secret.

Part II

ETHICS, POLITICS AND
PHILOSOPHY OF HISTORY

THINGS AND PERSONS

I T IS a commonplace today to say that metaphysics is impossible. Indeed, the demonstration of the impossibility of metaphysics has assumed the status less of an exercise for philosophers than a stock in trade essay for students. Yet one may question whether some of those who with such assurance rule the claims of the metaphysical philosopher out of court have altogether taken the measure of what he is about.

Now the subject of this paper is a metaphysical theory— that is to say what we shall be concerned with is something which Collingwood might have called a set of presuppositions, but whose character can perhaps be described without the use of that question-begging term. Of course, metaphysical theories differ enormously in character, but at least it seems that they resemble one another in this, that they prescribe absolutely the kind of discussions their champions think worth undertaking, and at the same time dictate the moves they make in the course of their argumentation. Thus, even if one agrees with those who say that philosophy can be more or less reduced to logic or the study of the inter-relation of the various current systems of common sense and scientific description, one has to allow the presence in the background for this conception of unsuspected presuppositions concerning what is worth saying as well as what is sayable. It is hard to see how one can offer a purely logical criterion of what is sayable, even though one may concede the character of logical to those operations whereby one determines the formation and transformation rules of some individual system of representation. The problem of what can be said, the analysis of "can" in that phrase remains one of the cruces of contemporary philosophy. And we are perhaps not much further on than Kant was, at least in the elaboration of a method for solving it.

None the less it remains true that those philosophers who have gone furthest in the direction I have indicated would repudiate altogether the suggestion that their concern to restrict philosophical inquiry in this way was governed by anything other than a recognition of its proper scope. The suggestion that all utterance, which does not thus fall within the scope of the "language of science" or those languages whose logical relation to the "language of science" can be plotted, should be dismissed as trivial or meaningless is commended as a surgical operation demanded by the nature of things. It is, perhaps, unfortunate that one cannot resist the sense that this conception of the nature of things, however subtle its characterization, does retain something of the character of a metaphysical theory. And that in effect however much the playing of the game may essay standpointlessness, that standpointlessness is by no means completely achieved.

Now in this paper I want to revert to a very crude and primitive essay in what may be called the elimination of the metaphysical, so crude that the metaphysical characters of the presupposition of the operation itself are hardly concealed. I am referring to an aspect of the work of the so-called utilitarians. I take this example deliberately because the subject matter of this symposium is presumably primarily ethical, and it seems to me that the utilitarian attitude towards ethical problems illustrates excellently, in the field of ethics, the extent to which the attack on metaphysics is itself governed by a kind of metaphysical bias. Utilitarianism remains enormously interesting, not simply for what it is as an ethical theory, but because it represents an explicit attitude towards the problem of conduct, that reveals how that problem must appear to anyone who tries resolutely to eliminate from the discussion any appeal whatsoever to that which transcends observation.

In a textbook on ethics you will find utilitarianism usually listed as the theory which insists that the rightness or wrongness of actions be judged by a reference to their consequences. But if you read widely the history of the subject you find that the contours of the doctrine cease easily to be contained by this description. For utilitarianism as professed by the most important of those who argue and develop the theory was much more than a series of propositions. It could much more accurately be described as the programme of a campaign, whether on the plane of philosophical analysis or at the level of social reform. Of course the whole argument pivoted on the ancient question of the relation of the "ought" to the "is". True the logical apparatus at the disposal of the utilitarians was as defective as their psychological theories of the spring of conduct. But their purpose was fundamentally clear; and likewise their assumption. They insisted that ethics must be regarded as nearly as possible as a system of fact, albeit a system of fact of a very special sort. When Godwin in his *Political Justice* described morality as a system of public advantage, he wrote as a utilitarian. Although the psychology the utilitarians employed was crudely introspective in technique, there underlay their attitude to human needs and wants the conviction that these were in no way typically different from any other fact in the world.

Of course to understand them, to understand the game they were playing one must understand also what suggested to them that this was the way to play the game, and moreover one must understand the game their opponents were playing. In other words, of course, one must study them historically, in the circumstances of their origin. And it is, I would insist, a gross mistake to suppose that such a method is incompatible with concern for the truth or falsity of their doctrine. Rather it alone helps one to see what actually that doctrine was, and in seeing to judge something of what philosophy always comes near being to the empiricist. Thus if one points to the extent to which the utilitarians found their inspiration in Newtonian physics, one is ignoring neither the importance of e.g. Bentham's concern with legal reform nor the permanent significance of the utilitarian outlook. One is neither confining the inspiration of the utilitarian to the methods of the exact sciences, nor suggesting that the utilitarian attitude belongs in a peculiar measure to a particular moment in the development of scientific method and understanding. Fundamentally, the utilitarian champions the ideal of an ethics not mysterious, of principles of human behaviour most related to, because derived from, the scrutiny of the facts of that behaviour and from the latent possibilities of adjustment and harmonization to which it is judged to be open. Neither in that behaviour nor in the principles by which it is to be judged is there anything mysterious. Observation will reveal its nature, and observation too will suggest the kind of modification to which its initial springs are susceptible.

Here one should emphasize two points as of fundamental importance:—

1. In the language of the late Professor John Laird, utilitarianism is an act-ethic—that is, an ethic concerned to study primarily the properties of acts. As nearly as possible the utilitarian, for all the fact that his psychological method is crudely introspective, thinks of an act as a transaction, as a change in a medium whose form is conceived as being as closely as possible analogous to a physical system: granted that such transactions are malleable, can be modified in their direction and consequence by legislative interference, it is still insisted that fundamentally the moralist finds his field in acts, a very special class of event, with the difference between them and physical events reduced to a minimum.

2. In utilitarianism you have a doctrine that from one point of view appears rigid: whereas from another it possesses a curious flexibility. It is rigid in its insistence that acts be judged by nothing apart from their result. Moral judgment need take no account of the deliverances of any intuition or moral sense: no traditional sanctities can defend themselves against criticism by appeal to a sixth sense. It is rigid too in its insistence on happiness as something relatively simple, possessed of no interior complexity of structure. Yet it is flexible in its conviction that human nature is sufficiently malleable to permit our finding our satisfaction in vastly different kinds of objective.

You may ask why we should waste time on such familiar considerations. Simply for this reason. In utilitarianism one encounters a clear example, clear to the point of a caricature of the approach to ethics which refuses altogether to take personal existence seriously. You see this in the insistence that the notion of happiness is fundamentally simple, that in effect happiness can be so defined as to constitute the twin of the whole analysis. It is insisted that in human satisfaction there is nothing mysterious. As James Mill boasted, "given time, one should be able to make the human mind as clear as the road from Charing Cross to St Paul's". Now it is perfectly true that the contemporary empiricist has seen the logical contradiction in the notions of absolute simplicity and of absolute clarity. As Ramsey said "One can make nothing clear but one can hope to make many things clearer". But for all that it remains true that in that process of clarification the contemporary successors of the utilitarians will insist that the idea of satisfaction can be invoked to clarify, rather than referred to as something requiring clarification.

In this criticism of the utilitarian doctrine in the form which we encounter it in Shaftesbury, Butler attacked it on the ground that you could not derive from the utilitarian doctrine a satisfactory conception of the virtuous life. Yet in effect a utilitarian might reply that this was simply to miss the mark inasmuch as it implied that it was the virtuous life which mattered and not the system of public advantage. To say, as Butler does, that benevolence is not the whole of virtue is to insist that the life of the morally good man is not necessarily achieved simply by disinterested concern for the good of others. The relations in which a man stands to his fellows are not exhausted in terms of benefactor confronting beneficiary and so on. There are other kinds of situations which morally engage a man; for instance, there is the promise made or the demand of justice. Butler protests against the utilitarian refusal to discriminate satisfactions, against his readiness to treat goods as homogenous. But he does this because he has in effect departed from the whole method characteristic of the utilitarian, and indeed of act-ethics in general. He argues that the proper subject of the moralist is the individual or person in his nature and in his relations with his fellows, and he refuses consequently to allow that we can, so to speak, absorb ethical reflection in discussion of the means of promoting good or find the primary field for the application of our ethical ideas in (to quote Godwin's phrase again) a system of public advantage.

All this I mention because it seems that the work of such thinkers as Kierkegaard, Buber, Marcel and the rest, is best approached if it is seen in relation to an opposition with which every student of ethics is familiar—that is to say, the opposition between the assessment of ethical principle as significant primarily in relation to the promotion of a system of public advantage, and that which insists that the primary sense of such ideas be found in the personal existence of the individual, in his relations to his fellows. I have said nothing of Kant who perhaps more obviously than Butler in his doctrine of the good will repudiates at once the idea of goods as in any sense homogeneous and the possibility of treating moral relations and principles out of relation to choice and its determination. But clearly his position is one that insists on acts as significant to the moralist *qua* "pieces of living" and not as transactions.

To set the writers I have just mentioned in the tradition outline may seem strange: especially in view of the fact that Kierkegaard from whom both Buber and Marcel in varying ways derived is best known as a critic as Hegel, and Hegel surely must be thought of as standing not so much in the following of the utilitarian as that of their opponents. It was, however, primarily against the impersonal element in Hegel, his doctrine of the sovereignty of the universal idea, that Kierkegaard sought to defend the significance and ultimacy of personal existence; and for us the significance of what he was about is perhaps equally clearly seen if one reflects on what ethics must rot away into if the assumption of the homogeneity of satisfaction is accepted, and ethical principles construed primarily as the means of constructing a system of public advantage.

I suppose that the student of traditional ethics coming first to such writers as I have mentioned is impressed by the sense that in them the frontiers between philosophical analysis and literary description seem to have been passed. Would you describe Kierkegaard as philosopher, theologian, psychologist, writer of dramatic dialogue? His aversion to generalization goes much further than hostility to "the system". The enunciation of general theses of any kind seems to dissolve away into a prolonged series of descriptions. His comparison of lives and attitudes of mind, even though in places it recalls Plato, is concrete: Socrates, Abraham, Job, Don Juan, and—he will never withdraw from the particular into the characterization of some form of life as good as such. One is far withdrawn from Kant, for instance, in Kant's insistence that the form of the good life can be characterized apart from the matter; there is nothing remotely resembling the sort of formal logic of moral conduct you get in the *Grundlegung*. At times one cannot resist the impression that principle is altogether abandoned in the interest of an inwardness realized perhaps as much by the rogue as by the saint. One cannot talk easily in brief about Kierkegaard: one can only commend him, as perhaps he would have wished to be commended, as a corrective. For in the last resort, as he insists, his work can only be understood in relation to himself: it is the record of his own pilgrimage that he has left. One cannot detach principles or criticize their absence: fundamentally, his most important communications are always in his own phrase indirect. Yet perhaps it is only to be expected that it is just this fact that his ideas are so hard to catch hold of that makes the professional philosopher so impatient with him. None the less he must be reckoned with; for no one has seen more clearly than he that the category of individuality is that on which any generalized speculation must suffer shipwreck. What it is to be an individual is not something whose contents can be expounded: it can only, he argues, be shown and that indirectly.

So too in other ways with the other thinkers I have mentioned, both alike are on edge in the presence of the general or the abstract, and argue, if I understand them aright, that the sense of such fundamental ideas of personal existence as meeting, encounter, hope, loyalty, is lost if we seek to offer of them a general definition irrespective of the circumstances of the individual. The only definition one can possibly offer is by way of example. For it is of the very nature of such relations that they engage men as individuals, exposing them not as instances of such and such abstract characters but as this or that man. Whereas certainly such an ethic as Butler's or Kant's is fundamentally right against the utilitarian in insisting that ethical ideas find definition in the field of personal existence, they are wrong if they suppose that such can be conceived in terms of a general formula. The use of any such formula can only have the effect of drawing an artificial boundary to contain that which in its nature cannot be contained. The responsiveness of men to men, the "disponibility" of a man in the presence of his fellows, the diversity of human love—these are not things that can be mapped. You cannot set out even in the most rarified formula what is that which through the intimacies of personal exchange a man is called to become. Although certainly in human life it is the discipline of the ego that is at issue, you cannot simply define that discipline in terms of the submission of inclination to principle: to do that is to run the risk of conceiving the fundamental business of becoming human impersonally, in terms less of a man's relations with his fellows than of submission to the impersonal discipline of reason. If one identifies goodness with the taking of an objective view of one's behaviour, one is in danger of conceiving goodness out of relation to the actual situation in which it is realized: one runs the risk of that unconscious solipsism, of that withdrawal of oneself in idea from one's actual relations with one's fellows which for men like Buber and Marcel constitutes the fundamental state in ethics.

Whereas in Kierkegaard the idea of the individual takes shape in the exposition of an extraordinary complex and ultimately religious dialectic (in a dialectic that is almost Hegelian in its sinuosity and is throughout unified by the "leap" of faith), men like Buber and Marcel, although the temper of their thought is religious, are much more concerned with ethical realities. That is to say, one can trace in what they are discussing a more evident kinship with the discussions of traditional moral philosophy. The situations they consider include familiar ones like the giving and receiving of promises;

only they urge us to ponder the inwardness of such situations and to see them in relation to the men and women who, they urge, come into being through them. One might say that whereas for the Kantian moral worth is constituted through the individual's submission to the discipline of practical reason, for writers of this school such worth is realized by the extent to which the individual so to speak opens and deepens himset through his relations to his fellows. But there is a kinship with the older intuitionism in the insistence on the hard inescapable facts of personal existence. Or so certainly it seems in some writers of this school who speak as if they sought to substitute for elementary consciousness of the Cartesian sort at the outset of reflective construction, a man's sense of himself as standing over against his fellows, who make demands on him. And this for all the extraordinary subtlety, the attention to individual detail and the rest; their thinking is less self-absorbed than Kierkegaard's, less sheerly religious in its movement, and, as I say at the outset, appeal is made to that which has something of the character of an *a priori* intuition.

Thus it is insisted both that the facts of personal moral exchange are unanalysable, and that they are evident to anyone who reflects on what he knows. Linguistic usage attests them, and here of course the well-known distinction between the language of "I" and "Thou", the language of address, and the language of "It", that of description is invoked. Certainly it is more and more recognized that where ethics is concerned, the language of conversation, of advocacy, of entreaty even is more important than that of description: it would be admitted that if we are to approach ethical study linguistically, it is to the function of such language that we must attend and its logic or principles that we must try to plot. But clearly writers of the kind I have mentioned go much further than that, and insist not simply that in ethics we concern ourselves with what such language expresses, but that we rate as of prior ontological significance the kind of reality to which it calls attention; and it is argued that we only have to think in order to see that this is so. Maybe the appeal is not simply to intuition: but it is implied that the kind of reflection necessary to establish the authority of this kind of experience is comparatively short, even though of course, the content of the experience is practically inexhaustible. *One might perhaps say that with Buber we have seen a transformation of the older intuitive ethics into a thesis concerning the prior ontological significance of particular forms of speech*; and again one returns, of course, to the question of the authority of such an intuition. With Kierkegaard it is different: his descriptions either do or do not establish themselves; and their elaboration and subtlety give them every chance to do or not to do so.

But to recapitulate: writers like those I have mentioned are significant because in various ways they raise the problem of the individual. In a way they recall one strand in Kant, even though he would have regarded their thinking as lawless, and they are on edge in the presence of the rigidity with which he insists that we can plot the form of the good life. Yet they are one with him in insisting that the ethical problem is not one which can be reduced to a study of the mechanics of adjusting satisfactions. That is, they take the ethical problem seriously and insist that it is a problem. Or perhaps I make a mistake in using that general singular: it is problems that they take seriously, the problematic elements in human existence. Only of course in doing this, there is nothing self-authenticated. If with Mill we say that it is better to be Socrates dissatisfied than a fool satisfied, we have still to recognize that this thesis does not simply authenticate itself. If one rates personal existence seriously, if one judges the work we have been concerned with as significant, one has still to justify that judgment. One still has, for instance, to vindicate the significance one claims for Kierkegaard's religious dialectic, and that problem, which is part of the problem of the possibility of metaphysics, is of course ultimately the problem of distinguishing things and persons. It seems to me that traditional ethics of what used to be called a non-naturalist pattern has always taken this distinction more or less for granted; it has of course usually found the differentia of the person in the presence of reason, both practical and theoretical, and in consequence, perhaps, it has failed adequately to schematize what personal existence is. It is to this problem that some contemporary writers, such as Buber and Marcel, have turned their attention; while others, engaging with a more profound problem, have called attention to the extraordinary difficulty with which one retains hold of a sense of the person as significant against the manifold arguments in favour of treating it as somehow reducible to something other than itself. The problems which confront the moralist today in this connection are twofold. There is the problem of what exactly it is to be a person; and there is the further problem of how one authenticates the claim that one is inclined to make for characteristically personal existence. There is, of course, the further question of what precisely becomes of ethics as traditionally pursued outside the utilitarian school if one refuses to give any significance at all to the idea of person as distinct from thing. It is perhaps the status of our sense of the unconditional worth of the personal that lies back behind our controversies concerning ethical intuition.

JUSTICE

IT WAS Coleridge who said that all philosophers were
either natural Platonists or Aristotelians: there is perhaps
no matter in which this contrast is more immediately
illustrated than the discussion of the virtue of justice. One need
go no further than compare Plato's *Republic* with the fifth book
of Aristotle's *Ethics* to recognize this. Whereas Plato's elaborate
investigation of justice in the *Republic* is in fact an examination
of the foundations of morality itself, Aristotle, after an introduction in which he shows himself vividly aware of the reach of
the Platonic discussion, devotes himself to a characteristically
minute anatomization of the different forms of justice as more
narrowly conceived. Thus, it is to Aristotle that we owe
historically our distinction of forms of justice as corrective,
distributive, commutative, etc. At the outset, however, of his
discussion Aristotle says that in the popular mind the description "unjust" is held to apply both to the man who takes more
than his due and to the man who breaks the law. It follows, he
continues, that the man who does not break the law and the
man who does not take more than he is entitled to will be
"just". "Just", therefore, means (*a*) lawful, and (*b*) what is
"equal", that is fair. One can see in the stress upon fairness and
equality the source of the later Latin definition, which has
become almost conventional, of justice as *suum cuique tribuere*.

Whereas for Plato the discussion of the virtue of justice
extends to attempted refutation, however successful or un-
successful, of the contractarian view of the origins and function
of morality, with Aristotle we enter upon a more restricted
view of the scope of the virtue. In Plato it is treated as one of
the four cardinal virtues; but in fact he assigns to it an architectonic role; for it prescribes to each of the other excellences

of the soul its proper place. Thus the just man for Plato is the man who rightly esteems temperance, courage, and wisdom; he is not betrayed by the attraction of Spartan ideals into giving courage a role which is more than its due, or a dignity that is beyond its proper esteem. Courage is the servant of wisdom. Again, there is an important place in human life for the prudent management of one's own affairs, for the careful and diligent apportioning of means to ends, and for the well-directed use of one's talents; but the excellence of a man does not consist in the skill with which he manages his affairs with an eye to the supposedly obvious advantage both of himself and of his society. What matters is that the direction in which that advantage should be sought shall be rightly conceived and that mere functional efficiency shall not be regarded as an end in itself. All this is a crude and inaccurate summary of a long complex argument: but at least it brings out the extent to which for Plato *iustitia suum cuique tribuit.* But the elements over which, to speak metaphorically, the virtue of justice presides, are elements within the human individual; it is for Plato a kind of second-order virtue; it is the virtue of the man whose virtues are themselves properly ordered in relation one to another.

Such an approach to the virtue of justice must never be neglected; for historically, it has surely been influential in giving to men the sense that where justice is concerned they are near the heart of the moral matter. Indeed the very vagueness, the very generality of the language which people habitually use concerning this virtue, suggests that they think of it as having uniquely a kind of pervasive "everywhere, nowhere" character. If it is illustrated most obviously in fair dealing, in the giving to each his due, this is entirely compatible with the recognition that the situations, in which we are called to give to each his due, range far beyond the competence of the courts to decide. If we move dialectically (in the Platonic sense of dialectic) from situations in which disputes demand immediate recourse to an impersonal arbiter to other situations more intimate and searching, we find that what the latter call for is something of which the former is an analogue.

To try to make this point more clearly, it is a commonplace

of political and juristic theory that no man should be judge in his own cause. Part of what we mean when we speak of "rule of law" in society is that disputes bringing an individual into conflict with the executive itself shall be submitted to an impersonal arbiter concerned to determine whether the executive with its peculiar responsibility has in this or that case exceeded its proper bounds. Thus students of the nascent democracy of Western Germany (rightly mistrustful of the elements in German society who had been partly rehabilitated by re-armament policies) were cheered by the apparent determination of a properly irreverent public opinion to make sure that the executive had not violated this principle in the "Spiegel" case. No man shall be judge in his own cause; for human beings invariably see their own case more favourably than the case against them. Or if (as occasionally happens) they are scrupulous, they may tend, by way of compensating against this prevalent danger, to see their opponents' case in too generous terms. Aware of the temptation to bias in favour of their own advantage, they may compensate by a kind of exaggerated unfairness to themselves and indeed to that for which in dispute they are bound to stand. It is not always good to give way and, without the service of impersonal arbitrament, good men may by their goodness be betrayed into concession, morally damaging to themselves and to their opponents.

Now it might be suggested that this procedure is an analogue of what, echoing Plato's language, we may call "justice in the soul". Kant insisted, as indeed Butler did before him that men were laws to themselves; and by this he meant, not that they were able to invest their prejudices and personal preferences with the character of supposedly universal authority, but on the contrary that they were constrained by their rational nature to submit the springs of their conduct to a judgment analogous to that which an impersonal arbiter passed in cases of dispute between men. In their own most intimate causes they were compelled *in foro interno* to be judges; for none other could execute the intimate personal judgment to which they were impelled by their nature. I say, impelled by their nature; for Kant saw human beings as almost bond-servants of the claims of objectivity. They had to strive after an impersonal objectivity in respect of their own affairs. If they tried to dodge this imperative, they were running away from themselves. Kant formalizes the virtue of justice even as he revives in modern terms something curiously akin to its Platonic interiorization. His sense of what justice is owes more immediately to the tradition which defines the virtue as consisting in *suum cuique tribuere*; but he recognizes that the scope of this demand to give to every man his due extends to the whole of human life. Here indeed Kant is in agreement with Butler who brings the virtue of justice into close relation with that of truth. Benevolence, he says in his *Dissertation on the Nature of Virtue*, is the whole of virtue *"only within the limits of justice and veracity"*. He is no utilitarian in that he refuses to allow in the *Dissertation*, as indeed by constant implication in the detailed analyses of the *Sermons*, considerations of general welfare to provide men with sufficient guidance concerning the moral conflicts in which they find themselves. Their nature is too complex to allow resolution of their moral dilemmas by recourse to so simple a formula. A principle of rational benevolence has great authority; but its authority is limited by the independently authoritative claims of justice and veracity. Certainly, for Butler, justice consists in the giving to every man his due, and the refusal to give to each his due he sees clearly illustrated by an indifference to the special relation in which for instance we may stand to our friends, to those to whom we are bound by ties of special attachments, to parents, to husband, to wife, to personal friends, etc. Here, as always, Butler is the moralist who emphasizes the irreducible particularity of the various strands that make up the complex unity of a human life. The utilitarian esteems these special bonds too lightly; he does not attach anything like proper weight to them; he is a man of the general formula who sacrifices proper attention to the particular in the interests of over-simplified general principle. But Butler who has criticized Wollaston for his attempt to reduce all human virtue to the duty of truthfulness even as he criticized Shaftesbury for his attempt to make rational benevolence the whole of virtue, none the less finds particularly close connection between justice and veracity. It is indeed these twin virtues that prevent our regarding the utilitarian model of the good life as complete, and it is to the deep insight present in thus closely connecting them that I would now turn.

We are bound to try to see things as they are. The extent to which in dispute between men the courts enable us to see the issues in dispute between us impersonally, is of course limited by the reach, by the competence, by the validity in moral terms of the law the judge must interpret. This one can say, although one must never forget the important role fulfilled by the judiciary in filling up gaps by creative interpretation in the reach and the scope of the laws administered.[1] Still, the sense in which judges make law is derivative from that in which laws are said to be made by legislators. There is, therefore, a clear limit to the extent to which positive law is an effective instrument of justice and of truth. Where the pursuit of justice in human life is concerned, there is no limit that must be recognized. This point indeed Kant tried to bring out by his extreme formalism, whereby he sought to give to justice understood in terms of obedience to rule great dignity, without the devastating mistake of identifying the moral life with obedience to the prescriptions of a detailed code. Again one has to remember always in Kant that if conscience is presented as a kind of judge, this is an analogy. It is indeed Kant's view that the judicial process derives its validity from the extent to which its procedure catches the universal morality whose form, he argues, is perfectly familiar to the individual however hard the task may be of achieving obedience to it.

There is in Kant and Butler an insistence that law, seeing things as they are and responding to them as they are, and fairness in dealing with oneself and one's fellows, are very closely bound up together, and that these things belong to the very centre of the enterprise of human life. Thus, in both these moralists the virtue of justice, while nowhere losing the relation to fairness in the legal sense, to equality, etc., which it receives in Aristotle, is interiorized again; but the interiorization is of a

[1] Compare here the excellent treatment of this matter in Mr Justice Cardozo's *The Nature of the Judicial Process*.

different sort from that which one finds in Plato and this because for both these moralists a sense of the sovereign authority of moral virtue, of virtue as the ultimate authority under which men stand, prevails over the conception with which in the *Republic* at least Plato seems to flirt, of virtue as the supremely attractive form of human life, as the heart's true home of humanity. With Kant the question concerns the nature of the final authority in human life, of that by which a man shall be judged. It is his view that men's judgment is committed to themselves, and that unless it were there could be no such thing as morality; for to Kant "ought" implies "can". But what are we to say in the light of this analysis of the relation of justice to the humdrum human situations in which we are called to practise the virtue more specially? What indeed also are we to say concerning the crucial issue of the relation of justice to mercy?

Very tentatively it might be suggested that we must learn to see justice and expediency as sometimes virtual correlatives. In modern life if we want to explain what we mean by the claims of justice, we have very often to begin by setting out what seem to be the dictates of a rational expediency. In social ethics we are all utilitarians now. For this very reason we do well to recall how often human history has in fact confirmed Butler's insistence that rational benevolence is the whole of virtue only within the bounds of justice and veracity. Mrs Cecil Woodham-Smith's study of the Irish potato famine, and the principles which informed the attitude towards it of outstanding members of the British ruling class (the spiritual progenitors of those one would expect to see on the Christian Frontier Council), is signal evidence of the folly as well as the cruelty, of which those who claim to be guided by the rule of utility, are frequently guilty.[1] That book abounds in lessons for those who are concerned with the future of the railway system in the British Isles and who plead that considerations of what can be rationally established as profitable shall override all claim to special consideration, for instance, from men and women who would keep their roots in the remoter areas of Scotland. To say

[1] *The Great Hunger* by Cecil Woodham-Smith, Hamish Hamilton, 1962.

this is not to deny the claims of expediency; it is only to insist that if we would understand justice in the concrete to-day, we have to see that it presents its special claim most effectively as an *intrusive* voice breaking in upon our ready assumption that rational expediency is all we need attend to. So regarded, justice is recognized as at once conservative and radical, conservative in that it bids us attend to the actual circumstances in which men and women of flesh and blood have come to lead their lives, radical in that it counsels a readiness to protest in the name of what has a mysterious absolute quality against those whose admittedly superior expertise encourages them to adopt the pose of wise "know-alls", gifted with infallible assurance concerning what must be done.

Earlier in this article reference was made to the "Spiegel" case. It was Jeremy Bentham, perhaps the greatest and certainly the most rigorous of the utilitarians, who spoke of publicity as the atmosphere in which justice flourishes, thereby admitting in his own way the close relation of justice and truth. If, in affairs as well ecclesiastical as temporal, justice and not expediency alone is to be acknowledged, Bentham's point must surely be given weight in the purlieus of Lambeth, the Cabinet offices, and the Athenaeum as well as in the apartments of Cardinal Ottaviani and the Holy Office. What made the circumstances surrounding the appointment of the first dean for the new cathedral at Guildford scandalous was precisely the absence of the sort of publicity which Bentham rightly discerned as the very atmosphere of just dealing. Justice may have been done; but it remains unfortunately true that it has not been seen to have been done, except by the minority "in the know", and those who find themselves able to accept their actions without question.

We come finally to what to the theologian must be central to the kind of inquiry which we are pursuing. Just as there is no escape from the reality of the conflict between the claims of justice and expediency, so there is no escape from the reality of the conflict between the claims of justice and mercy. This conflict does not exist in God, and almost one is tempted to say that what one means when one thinks of the difference between

God's goodness and human goodness is that in him this conflict does not exist. But it may be that what we mean when we say that in the Incarnation God took human nature upon himself was that he made this conflict his own and deepened it to the level of his own perfect humanity. Certainly we must not be nearly so cavalier as we often are in dismissing conceptions of the atonement, which, however crudely, present the Cross as the "trysting place where Heaven's love and Heaven's justice meet". For here is the stuff of irreconcilable conflict. We see things as they are; it is our obligation to try to see them so and not to run away from them by pretending that they are other than they are. We regard sentimentality as a temptation especially when this sentimentality leads us into taking, or attempted taking of the burden of other people's guilt upon ourselves. This is a viciously sentimental attitude of mind, a kind of imaginative making of ourselves scapegoats so that we can dodge the far harder thing which is to face the fact that other people, even those whom we love, are sometimes evil. Of course there *may* be no genuine moral distinctions; it is not for nothing that discussions of justice all down the ages have tended to raise the question of the foundations of morality; it may be that this essay would be better occupied with that problem than with justice in the narrower sense, or in the rather futile and half-baked attempt to bring narrower and more inclusive senses together. Yet there is a distinction between good and evil, and justice consists for the individual sometimes in recognizing the distinction, allowing that when it comes to judging others we do not know all the facts, and yet that what we know compels us to condemn. We may well say that if we had been in the position of the men who administered the German Concentration Camps, or of those who acquiesced in their existence, we should only have been spared from their guilt by the accident of our own relative inefficiency, or ignorance. (We should sometimes indeed thank God for the fact that we are not as efficient as some of the inquisitors and butchers of history and are spared their sin by a kind of muddle-headedness with which Providence has endowed us.) But we must condemn, even while we question whether we ourselves would have survived the testing; we cannot in humility treat evil as other than it is. It is not being honest with ourselves to say that we cannot condemn because we should have done worse or no better. We might even by this kind of thing be subtly excusing ourselves by suggesting that all alike move in a night where all cats are grey; but there is white, there is grey, there is black in the world. An Eichmann is wicked beyond the measure of many of his fellows; their weakness which they must not deny is less than the actual guilt which is certainly his.

To think in these terms is at once to lay oneself open to the charge of moralism; and perhaps the temptation for the just man (that is the man who takes justice seriously) is always to topple over into a kind of moralism. But human life is complex, and moralism is an element in it; so too is the resolute determination to see things as they are. It is from justice that we must cry for mercy, even as we recall that Christ prayed to be delivered from the burden laid upon him of unmasking men for what they are. Kant was right to say that we are constrained to justice. We are constrained to the sort of impersonality which he tried to characterize; but he was also wrong in refusing to attach validity to the extent to which men shrink from this.[1] There is a validity, a partial validity in our turning aside from seeing things as they are; for although the claims of justice sometimes override those of compassion, yet compassion has its place in human life, and unless we hold the two together we mutilate ourselves.

The Christian would say that there is no place at which they can be so held together except at the foot of the Cross of him who is the truth of what men are, even as he is of one substance with the Father, who also by the action of his Passion works the reconciliation of the irreconcilable.

Thus in this review we have seen how the study of justice touching clearly as it does such things as the limitation of the claim of expediency and encouraging our will to protest against the kind of obliquity we noticed in the Guildford scandal, at the same time plunges us into issues touching the very foundations of morality, not quite as Plato saw them, but

---

[1] Butler was wiser in his balancing of the claims of pity and resentment.

as, maybe in the light of Christianity, we have come to see them. Our morality is paradoxically something to which we are constrained and something from which we would be delivered. The man who plays Christ (and this for some Christians is the ultimate temptation) seeks to execute, or to achieve in himself a deliverance which he can only receive. Christianity does not obliterate the complexity of human life, although it is often presented as doing so. Rather it presents a new context in which that complexity may be seen; the problems are as before, but set in the context of Christ's endurance they are transformed. We must not try to swallow up justice in compassion or overwhelm compassion in justice. We must discipline compassion by reference to justice, even as we temper justice by acknowledgment of the claims of compassion, and if the way of this seems beyond us, as it most certainly will, we must recall that our ways are not in ourselves, but that Christ is for us Way even as he is Truth and Life itself.

ON THE NOTION OF A PHILOSOPHY
OF HISTORY[1]

IN CHOOSING a subject for my lecture, I naturally wanted to select one which had some bearing on the work of the great man we are to commemorate this afternoon; and accordingly I venture to submit some reflections on the notion of a philosophy of history. I say on the notion; what I want to offer is some indication of the sort of intellectual jobs the idea of a philosophy of history has been invoked to perform. Metaphysical theories, and philosophies of history certainly qualify for that title, may be nonsense; but they may be, to use Professor Wisdom's phrase, the sort of nonsense which, by the ways it expresses deep-seated puzzlements or concerns, demands to be taken very seriously. Philosophies of history may be neither true nor false in the sense that truth and falsity may be claimed for the statements or hypotheses of the historian; but they have proved both illuminating and instructive, able to fertilize and to stimulate as well as to perplex and to frustrate.

We are all of us familiar with the type of historical prophecy indicted by Dr Karl Popper in the second volume of his well-known book, *The Open Society and its Enemies*. The forms of dogmatism Popper attacks have undoubtedly been extremely influential; but they do not, I submit, give us a standard of what the term "philosophy of history" should be used to indicate. Later in this lecture I propose to make some observations on Hegel's doctrine; but for the time being I want simply to insist that the term "philosophy of history"

[1] This essay was delivered as the 23rd L. T. Hobhouse Memorial Lecture at King's College, London.

has a certain openness of texture or porosity, to use the valuable phraseology of Dr F. Waismann. Its use has no fixed horizons; we may and must use it for a whole family of overlapping types of intellectual activity. In this it resembles the word geometry which extends, in the spread of its use, from the supposedly intuitively based simplicities of Euclid to a whole group of purely formal hypothetico-deductive schemes. We still call what children learn at school geometry, and there is no reason why we should not, even though the non-mathematical specialist, whose training is interrupted on the frontiers of the calculus, has to make some difficult adjustments when and if he asks the question, "What is geometry?"

Similarly there is no simple answer to the question "What is philosophy of history?"; but only, I repeat, some sort of description of the kind of jobs the notion is supposed to perform, and the way these jobs overlap.

The first time I heard the phrase used was at school in 1931 when in a divinity lesson the headmaster used the phrase in referring to the subject-matter of chapters 9, 10, and 11 of the Epistle to the Romans. Those are the chapters in which Paul tries to consider the fate of Israel. His language is tortuous, and his metaphors often torment the reader. But no one can deny the sincerity of the former Pharisee when he speaks of his heart's desire and prayer to God for Israel. The horror of his people's fate weighs upon the apostle. Certainly if at times he argues as if he would find good coming out of evil, his writing is far removed from the urbane dialectic of the Hegelian professor whose students would greet his enunciation of thesis and antithesis with the refrain "but it is all resolved in a higher synthesis".

Is the difference simply one of style? It was certainly the claim of the young Hegel that his dialectic owed much to his meditation on the fundamental Christian rhythm of crucifixion and resurrection. The memory of this rhythm and its theological implication is certainly not absent from Paul's mind elsewhere in the Epistle, even though he does not openly appeal to it when considering the fate of Israel. I must confess that I think the fact that he does not do so is significant of his continual refusal to carve out of the mysteries of his faith principles of metaphysical explanation. In the passage with which we are concerned, Paul would justify the ways of God to himself and to his readers; and he ends on a note of agnosticism, although of a peculiar sort. The ways of God, he says, are past finding out; but this need not distress us, inasmuch as what we know of them gives us an assurance that they are ways of love.

In the end Paul does not seek here to give the understanding a resting place, a perspective from which riddles of heaven and earth are plain, but rather to illuminate the imagination and to secure the will. The language of his letter is religious, and therefore perhaps more nearly poetry than the prose-poetry of the metaphysician. It is almost relentlessly concrete. Israel is not in any sense the name of a spiritual type, as perhaps it is in Hegel, but rather a concrete community of flesh and blood, men and women.

Was my teacher right in calling this philosophy of history? If we allow openness of texture to the concept, I think that for all the uniqueness of Paul's idiom we may and must allow that he was justified. And this for the reason among others that Paul was concerned with the problem of *evil*, the besetting background of much that is commonly called philosophy of history. Paul was not concerned with this problem as a modern might be; his concern was wholly concrete. He did not enumerate features in our natural environment, the cobra or the tarantula, the cholera germ or the influenza virus, which put a question-mark against any facile teleology; he faced the problem of the rejection of that Israel which had first claimed his spiritual and intellectual loyalty. The reader of his letter must beware of following too rigid a conception of the relation of particular to universal. For Paul the problem of evil was *there* in the awful destiny of his people. In a way it was for him focused where it had been for the Jesus to whose following he had been converted. Jesus had mourned the coming fate of Jerusalem, and had seen in himself somehow the one whose coming had made these woes inevitable for his people. Maybe this seems to some readers of the gospels arrogance; but it was arrogance suffused always by compassion, even as its foundation was certainly an agony.

If we are justified in calling this sort of meditation, of thinking aloud, an exercise in the philosophy of history, we can, I think, welcome the clarity with which Paul presents some of the features of the enterprise. For one thing, to repeat myself, the besetting concern with the problem of evil. Maybe the depths of Paul's spiritual questioning must remain the experience of the few. But still we have, all of us, known the issue of waste. Behind Paul, as I have said, stood his Master, to whom the writers of the gospels did not hesitate to attribute the words: "It were good for that man if he had not been born." The woes of the Son of Man follow a predestined pattern; but the responsibility of the man who was guide to those who took Jesus remained. It is sometimes said by fools that Christianity offers a solution of the problem of evil. That is quite simply a lie, no more no less than sheer falsehood. If, as we read Christ's words about Judas, we remember the infinite tenderness of his regard for the individual, we cannot dodge their implication by speaking of any "solution".

Paul wrote as he did, because he had seen the problem of evil in the same way as the writers of the gospels saw it. He used an idiom which gives some justification to the suggestion that he wrote philosophy of history. But he chose this style not because he believed that the decisive form of religious language was that of philosophy of history, but because by writing as if he were concerned with the "meaning of history", he could show the way in which it was in the biographies of men, and the histories of peoples, that the unanswered and unanswerable questions were raised. Evil was not a theme for abstract treatment. To face the problem of evil one had to look at the place where the problem was set in terms of a unique exposition of its inwardness.

If the language to which I have so far referred seems religious rather than metaphysical, I make no apology, inasmuch as it was surely in a religious idiom that the concern of philosophy of history first received expression. Here as so often in the history of ideas, it is the religious style which prepares the way for the systematic essay of the metaphysician. If Paul writes sometimes as a man in pain, the very depth of his perplexity gives a certain purity to his words; for he writes not as if he would provide a solution, but rather as if he would lay the texture of a problem bare.

If I begin with Paul rather than with Condorcet or Hegel, Marx or even Pareto, I have done so because Paul so well brings out one crucial aspect of the concern of the philosophy of history, namely, its concern with the evil men do to each other, and have done. Where there is history, there is necessarily reference to the past, although it be a past somehow incapsulated in the present.

But what precisely do I intend by the word evil? Pain is certainly evil; among the many great debts which the moralist owes to the school of utility, we must mention, perhaps before all others, the merciless criticism to which it has submitted the vain superstition that pain ennobles. If the world is ordered in such a way that human beings should suffer as you and I suffer when we have mastitis, or even an abscess in our ear, then there is that much in the world which is quite undoubtedly evil. If we go further and recall even for a moment what the word cancer signifies, we must surely sympathize with the Marxist insistence that such things call not for explanation but for elimination.

Nor does this mood leave us when we think not simply of pain but of those who willingly cause, or have caused, others to suffer. If I have spoken first of physical pain, it is not because I would belittle the evil will, but because we can surely discern a symptom of the presence of that will in an indifference, however exalted its inspiration, to the infliction of physical pain. We are all of us familiar with those who, in the name of what is sometimes called "the tragic sense of life", speak lightly of pain, as if it were an inevitable ingredient of a properly human existence. We need not accept Dr Popper's interpretation of Hegel in order to welcome his polemic against the sort of quasi-mystical determinism which would treat the difference between what is, and what is of good report, as ultimately illusion.

Paul with whom I began was not indifferent to evil in the shape of physical pain. No more than Christ does he allow the passion of Israel to pass him by. He will not detach himself from its consideration by any of the more familiar brands of spiritual anaesthetic. He is too deeply rooted in the past of his people to treat their catastrophe as something either to be disregarded or somehow justified by reference to some all-inclusive impersonal purpose. He is too much a man of tradition to forget his past, even if his spiritual perception goes too deep to allow him to suppose he sees that past for what it really is.

So we find philosophy of history in what in the end is maybe meditation. If a charge of justifying evil can be brought against the historical determinist, Paul may himself be accused of distracting attention from the practical task of eliminating the ills under which men labour. Theodicy may be a waste of time; and the historian may join his voice to the moralist in lamenting the manner in which "the search for meaning" can debauch the proper discipline of historical research. Where metaphysics intrudes upon science, there care for fact very easily gives place before the claim of *a priori* pattern. To meditate about the past *sub specie aeternitatis*, it may be said, is not to advance understanding, and a man is always in danger, especially on his knees, of supposing his little insights to be a final vision of things as they are.

Yet suppose Paul had turned away from the mystery of Israel; suppose he had simply said that what is done cannot be undone. There would have been surely in such an indifference a mutilation of self, a deliberate assault upon the springs of his pity. For the past of his people was not simply over and done with, as the usefulness of a tool may pass from it with age; the past of a people is not like the life of a scalpel, nor is it something which a man can just use and be done with. We may have little sympathy with Paul's theology; but we must admire his compassion for the very same reason that we must repudiate historical determination. In both the indifferent and the determinist there is a comparable aversion from that continual remembering to which Paul was held by his effort at theodicy. There may after all be a partial justification for a form of language in the sort of moral perception that it makes possible.

May I go a little further here? One of the most remarkable essays on the philosophy of history which I have ever read was called *The Justification of God*.[1] Its author, Peter Taylor Forsyth, was as outraged by his vision of Hegel as ever Popper was by his! In his anti-metaphysics Forsyth was quite impenitently Kantian! But what I would like to call attention to is the title of his book. He wrote as an evangelical Christian, for whom the cross of Christ was the axis of the world. Yet by his choice of title he seems to imply that God must justify his ways to man. His consciousness of the need of that justification had a sharpness lacking even in John Stuart Mill's similar demand. If we call Forsyth's book an essay in the philosophy of history, we bring out again the besetting concern with the problem of evil that is always sooner or later discernible in those who write this sort of work. In a way one's verdict on philosophy of history as an enterprise will stand or fall with the value we attach to this kind of struggle to find a language in which to expound the mystery of evil.

But am I right in thus emphasizing preoccupation with evil as a mark of what we call philosophy of history? I concede that I am only justified if the concept is seen as one with the sort of open texture that I mentioned at the beginning of the lecture. For it is clear that in those whose concern with philosophy of history has been practical rather than theoretical, the attention to the problem of evil will be differently realized. I am thinking here of the use that Burke makes of the notion rather than of the use to which it has been put by those who have written most eloquently of progress. I do this deliberately inasmuch as those who speak most eloquently of human progress have often turned their backs on the past as if it were a realm of darkness and confusion. There is indeed an almost unnoticed element of paradox in the use of the phrase, philosophy of history, in their regard; at least if the use of the word history must carry with it some sort of implied reference to the

[1] Duckworth. (Reprinted, Independent Press, 1948.)

past. But with Burke we are continually reminded of the presence of the past to his imagination and understanding.

For him, philosophy of history was the inspiration of a moral and political self-discipline rather than a body of doctrine. We call Burke an empiricist; and perhaps we do so remembering most the way a certain sceptical shrug of the shoulders will punctuate his most Hegelian periods. If his conception of the state is sometimes nearer in appearance to that of the idealists than to that of any other eighteenth-century writer, there are times when his language sharply reminds us of his kinship with Locke, or even with Mill. In his famous remarks on the crucial effect the most insignificant individual may have on historical change, he deploys the way in which this scepticism is an expression of his philosophy of history, or at least of one side of it. And if we take these remarks in the light of his whole political doctrine, we see that they are more maxims or counsels than general descriptions. Men charged with the work of government must always remember how much of the depths of human life lies outside their competence, and accordingly they must discipline their vision by a certain reverent agnosticism, an agnosticism whose foundation for Burke is frankly religious.

But there is, of course, another side to his philosophy of history, his sense of the nation, I had almost said his metaphysic of the nation. His hostility to the language of abstract right and even to some uses of the notion of contract springs from his sense of the nation as something providing the proper setting of political life. But if his language in bringing out these points is often exalted, his purpose is clear. For him, as Acton saw, national tradition provided an invaluable resource against tyranny and arbitrary power. Like all serious writers on political philosophy, Burke was deeply preoccupied by the problem of power, that is by the practical problem of the proper exercise and proper restraint of power. Of course he saw the problem primarily in terms of the awful temptation that had beset men who had tried to make their dreams of human betterment come true. Men who make such an attempt must always run the risk of intoxication by their own sense of a final wisdom, somehow put at their disposal. It was in the setting of the rich and complex life of historical societies that these visions must be clothed in flesh and blood. The traditions there embodied could be the saving of the theorist and his dreams, if only he would make those traditions his own.

For Burke the nation was something whose feel a man must have if his contribution to its government were to be effective and to avoid the Charybdis of futility and the Scylla of despotism. So he offers his half metaphysical, half poetic realization of the national idea. Halévy well describes his doctrine as half empirical, half mystical, and is perhaps equally right in judging its foundation to be the principle of utility. If in one way Burke stands with the romantics, in another he stands with the men of utility, and would justify his vision in part by the extent to which it diminished cruelty and increased the sense of pity among mankind.

So here again it is with evil that the essay in philosophy of history is concerned. Burke's problems were very different from Paul's; but in the end both men see the nearness of what I can only call an assault on the springs of compassion. For the one it is the ways of God that must somehow be justified; for the other it is the eagerness of men and their readiness to be cruel in pursuit of their ideals that must be tempered, and restrained. Both too conduct their very different arguments in terms of the way the world is ordered, while neither of them altogether forgets the moral universals which provide a kind of implicit background to their words.

It is, however, the work of Hegel and his successors which today provides the average student of the history of ideas with his model of what philosophy of history must be. It has been one purpose of the argument of this lecture to suggest that we must not allow the discussion of the notion to be obscured by an excessive concentration on the work of such men as Hegel and Marx. Indeed it is not the least of Hegel's claims to greatness that his own work is so deeply rooted in the metaphysical and spiritual traditions of his many predecessors and masters. If comment on his work is not to be exhausted in a sharp criticism of the more illiberal aspects of his political theory, it must, I think, take the shape of a serious engagement with the manner in which, from his earliest years, he tried to make his own the whole spiritual experience of mankind and to provide an interpretation of its course which would somehow overcome the oppositions which its phases seemed inevitably to manifest. His philosophy of history, as well as his phenomenology of spirit, interpret his logic and are themselves interpreted by it.

Too often criticisms of Hegel's works are marred by a failure to understand, or even to admit as possible, the sort of experience to which they give expression. Marx did understand, and therefore his criticisms touch the heart of Hegel's scheme. If the argument between these two intellectual giants lies only on the circumference of the average British philosopher's concern, that is not necessarily a proof of its unimportance. Perhaps it needs a drastic restatement; I admit that I am myself convinced that it does. We have certainly to reckon with Kierkegaard's profound criticism of Hegel, the criticism offered by a religious genius who was at once nearer to and farther from the man he was criticizing than Marx. But in the end, behind the opposition between Hegel and Marx lie two conflicting attitudes to the story of man's historical existence, both of which, if we are honest, affect the way in which we see our world. Looked at from one point of view, they can be seen as examples of something like what Collingwood called "presuppositions".

If I were to try to characterize the opposition between Hegel and Marx, I would say that it in the end concerned the extent to which spiritual experience can be regarded as self-justifying. It is a commonplace to say that in an idealism such as Hegel's, the notion of subject is cast for the role which that of substance played in older metaphysical systems. Such an emphasis throws the whole weight of philosophical construction on the actual spiritual progress of mankind, his language, his art, his religion, his science, his philosophy. Here was a movement into which we could enter, enjoying privileged access to its phases because we were ourselves men, and it was in some sense absolute.

It was, of course, precisely the autonomy of this movement of spirit which Marx challenged. In the narrow domain of political theory this challenge took the shape of a subordination of the state to the economic and social realities on which it rested. No longer could a constitutional tradition be represented as the organ of a moral discipline. But the same principle, pursued mercilessly all along the line, assailed the whole representation of the life of spirit as self-subsisting.

Some may think that even so brief a reference to the controversy between Hegel and Marx is an indication of the pathetic, even dangerous, fallacies on which philosophy of history rests. No doubt historians can extract principles of method from their writings; but these principles stand or fall simply by their heuristic value in detailed historical work. But here I would like to make some reference to that remarkable English thinker, the late Professor Collingwood. No one would deny that Collingwood was concerned with the sort of things historians were doing. Much of his work reads not unlike a transcendental analysis (in the Kantian sense) of modern critical history. He did not write anything which we would find it natural to call a philosophy of history. Yet it seems to me that some of the things he wrote about history may be said to derive from a perhaps unconscious awareness of the problem raised by the controversy between Hegel and Marx.

Does this sound far-fetched? I do not think any reader of Collingwood's work would fail to see that history was for him the name of something more than the technical products of research. History is important because it is a way in which men come to terms with their human environment. Human beings are inescapably historical animals; this does not, of course, preclude, in his view, their tending to write the history of the past in the image of their own present. Collingwood is often highly relativist in his opinions; his pervading hostility to realism always prevents his doing justice to the element of "extended memory" which there must be in history. But for all his relativism, he admits the way attachment to a past poses to men some of their most searching human problems. For it is by history that men become aware of the tragic element in human life; they take stock of the way human finitude so often discloses itself in agony. There is what Sophocles suggested by the figure of Oedipus, the man betrayed into evil-doing by his very effort to avoid its perpetration;[1] there is, of course, what Hegel tried to convey by his dialectic of master and slave. But also the serious political philosopher has to remember what Burke sometimes forgot, namely, that tradition may be a source of corruption as well as discipline; and yet the man who would fight against such corruption has to do so within the situation it has created, and may even in the fight against it find himself its victim in the end.

So in history, in this way and, of course, in others too, perhaps more fundamental, men come to terms with themselves and face the problems of their lot. All this is, of course, in Hegel sometimes below the surface, but there. And it was, of course, this temper of mind that Marx assailed. Reconciliation, which Hegel had somehow seen as the goal of mankind's spiritual pilgrimage, came not in bloodless reflection but through action. "Not to understand, but to change." As I think Popper sees, Marx assails Hegel in the name of pity. For both in the end it is history that raises the issue of evil, and for both too in different ways their philosophy of history is their answer to the problem. For Hegel reconciliation is an idea; for Marx it is the sure reward of informed action. So both offer solutions; in a sense, as I have said, their philosophies of history are their solutions.

Paul too, as I have said, was tormented by this same issue of reconciliation. For him, as indeed for Marx, it was found in a deed, a deed with which all the New Testament writings are somehow concerned. Yet the knowledge of this deed did not give him solution as Marx or Hegel understood the word; for his writing remains obstinately a meditation, as if by any other style he might trivialize temptation and agony, and make Gethsemane a kind of charade.

But this is not to gainsay the depth of the debt we owe to Hegel and to Marx. These men open one's eyes; through them

[1] I owe this point, as I owe much else in this lecture, to Professor H. A. Hodges; but he has no responsibility for the use I have made of what he has taught me.

one sees the human situation anew. They lay bare, in different ways, the depth of the problem of reconciliation, revealing it as in part a problem set by the inheritance we have received from the past. They give us, as Collingwood well brought out, a new purchase upon the divided substance of our being. After all there is a sense in which the quarrels of the past are still alive in each one of us. Think for a moment of the way in which we are engaged in the religious conflicts of the sixteenth and seventeenth centuries. These conflicts touched the roots of our culture, and unless we accept as a final word the Marxian analysis of their substance, we find that we are still in some sense divided by them. The historian who by his detailed work makes the course of these conflicts present to us sets us the question of their meaning. Of course, to this question, the partisans have their answer; they dodge the problem of reconciliation by an artificial taking sides. I am speaking here, of course, of a problem that no man living has seen more clearly than the poet T. S. Eliot. Because he has seen the problem at so deep a level, he has given us in the course of his poem "Little Gidding"[1] a treatment of the issue that has something of the peculiar decisiveness that we can only find in poetry.

I am speaking of the third section of the poem, and I would like to offer a short interpretation of its sense. I do this because in this brief exploration of the notion of a philosophy of history I have suggested that the peculiar style of the enterprise lends itself in some ways better to the form of meditation rather than systematic exposition. (Here I may seem to side with Hegel against Marx; may I simply say that in any modern essay in this style of reflection the issues raised by Marx may suddenly intrude to the very centre?) I find in these lines of Mr Eliot a quality of poetic meditation, a curious precision of language bringing out exactly the distinctions we have to draw in a spiritually disciplined approach to the pain of the past. We cannot be partisan and follow an antique and silent drum. There is a kind of make-believe in trying to fight the battles of the past as if they were our own. Yet the answer to this attitude

[1] The last of *Four Quartets* (Faber, 1944), pp. 40–42.

is not found in a sort of superior detachment, altogether disdainful of issues for which good men were prepared to die. And so we have to commit ourselves, but in such a way that we are ready to see how much we owe to those who were on the other side from that to which in some sense we have given our allegiance. Yet to talk in this way is not to commit ourselves to some vision of a synthesis in which reconciliation is achieved. Men died; others were banished and knew the loneliness of exile. These sufferings were real enough; yet if we recall their reality, it is not to summon up our animosity. Rather it is a remembering that must have an ascetic quality. It should at once enforce a sense of the concrete reality of what these men endured and yet give us a perception that they served in their conflict a cause greater than they knew. I would suggest that in this poem we have an example of the attempt to present "the meaning of history". If that phrase has any sense, it may be the sort of thing that can only achieve its definition in poetry.

I say this in spite of the fact that Mr Eliot ends this part of his poem with a quotation from the work of Mother Julian of Norwich, surely one of the greatest of the English mystics.

> And all shall be well and
> All manner of thing shall be well
> By the purification of the motive
> In the ground of our beseeching.

If for Eliot the ultimate solution is religious, it is one which he is prepared to realize for his readers in the poetic medium. It is as if by the choice of this medium of expression, he can offer his readers a vision that is freed from the possibility of irrelevant confusion. May I explain? Others than the strict logical positivists have set our teeth on edge in the presence of speculative metaphysical construction. We are alive, in a peculiar way, to the intellectual and spiritual perils of metaphysics. Indeed, I am fully aware that by speaking of philosophy of history as a sort of metaphysics, at the outset of this lecture, I must have damned the enterprise in the minds of some at least of my listeners. Yet Mr Eliot, by writing philosophy of history as poetry, makes both that, and indeed his own religious vision, clean. By the way I have spoken of him, I know I must have suggested that I see in the passage I have analysed a return to the style of Paul. But this is not all that I intended. For what is offered us in the poem is more subtle and indirect, more deeply suffused with reference to our own spiritual, and indeed political, experience, than the rigorous simplicities and depths of the apostle. When I call "Little Gidding" philosophy of history, I confess that I remember how Professor Wisdom has said that in the philosopher the logician must sometimes become the poet,[1] and remembering have dared to suggest that the poet sometimes gives us more powerful metaphysical sense than ever the professional philosopher can dare to offer. It is perhaps paradoxical now to remember how the strict positivists thought they had written off all metaphysics by calling them poetry.

The style of Eliot's metaphysical presence to the past is not that of Paul's presence to his people. The poet writes after men like Hegel, and indeed Burke, have made us deeply conscious of the intrusion of metaphysical perplexities into our politics. We can only escape this sort of intellectual ordeal by supposing that our political attitudes can be freed from some sort of relation to the formed traditions of our society. It was Burke's contention that any attempt to shape such attitudes outside such relation must doom the politician to a dreadful choice between impotence and cruelty; it was Hegel's verdict that political theories developed in forgetfulness of historical tradition, none the less showed in their content that it had been unconsciously remembered. So when Eliot writes he sees the presence of evil in the history of a culture, and the consequent presence of the problem of evil to anyone whose political attitude does not escape remembrance of that history, as something from which the very language of their attitudes has been in a measure derived.

Thus the achievement of a proper esteeming of the past is essential to our political health, and the poet dares to take the offerings of the professional historians as a field of meditation. There is safety in using poetry as the medium of this medita-

[1] In his paper "Moore's Technique" in *The Philosophy of G. E. Moore* (ed. Paul Schilpp), 1943 (also in *Philosophy and Psycho-Analysis*, Blackwell, 1952).

tion; for poetry is no more theology than it is generalized history. It is "poetry" even when it is written by a man like Mr Eliot. I say this, remembering what he has written in another place: "For it is ultimately the function of art, in imposing a credible order upon ordinary reality, and thereby eliciting some perception of an order *in* reality, to bring us to a condition of serenity, stillness and reconciliation; and then leave us, as Virgil left Dante, to proceed toward a region where that guide can avail us no farther."[1]

I confess that in these words Mr Eliot seems to me to succeed in saying a great deal about the enterprise we call philosophy of history and how its findings are to be received. With their quotation I reach a point when I can venture to summarize this untidy and inconclusive exploration.

Philosophy must often have in it something of the nature of a commentary, an elaborate description of what others than philosophers have done. And this includes what those who have written what is called philosophy of history have offered to the world. To become clearer about what they were doing is in some sense a philosophical task; it also inevitably in places resembles an historical inquiry. It is not easy to generalize the conclusions of our survey. For the enterprises we have surveyed have been the work of individual men; and though in all of them there has been concern whether theoretical or practical with the problem of evil, to some that problem has been of practical rather than theoretical import. The unity that justifies us using the same name for these various enterprises is that of a family, in Wittgenstein's sense; as I said at the outset here we have a perfect example of the open texture sometimes displayed by our concepts. In the end I would simply ask whether these sometimes confused, and often different, styles of intellectual effort have or have not enlightened our understanding and in some way disciplined our emotions and imaginations. Language does not always function in the same way, and we are never free from the temptation of bending what we say to purposes our utterance will not serve. Philosophy of history remains itself; although I

---

[1] In his lecture, "Poetry and Drama", published in the *Atlantic Monthly* for February 1951. This is the concluding sentence.

hope I have shown that sometimes it is nearer to history proper, sometimes to theology, sometimes to speculative philosophy, sometimes it finds its medium in poetry. Its definition must therefore consist in its distinction from these other enterprises, and its vindication in some sort of description of the insight it safeguards, and the human perception it may alone promote.

R. G. COLLINGWOOD AS A PHILOSOPHER

R. G. COLLINGWOOD'S name lives among archaeologists as Haverfield's successor in the systematic study of Roman Britain; but among philosophers he is too easily forgotten as an eccentric, or worse, an idealist. Yet in his prime, he was outstanding among philosophical lecturers in Oxford. I shall never myself forget his lectures on ethics in the autumn of 1933 in the hall of Pembroke College; they conveyed to their hearers an unforgettable impression of the importance of the subject, and they were at the same time notable for the decisiveness with which the lecturer laid bare the texture of conflicting ethical doctrines.

There can be no doubt that the main inspiration in contemporary British philosophy derives from the work on the foundations of mathematics set in hand by Gottlob Frege and Bertrand Russell. Although relatively few philosophers may concern themselves with such problems as the nature of arithmetic, it remains true that British philosophers are today deeply indebted to those who fashioned their methods of analysis in the effort to resolve questions in the logic of mathematics. Yet all the time there was being fashioned an alternative critical discipline to that suggested by the logical revolutions of Frege and Russell; it was one suggested to a considerable extent by the work of Hegel and Marx, and amplified by such men as Wilhelm Dilthey, and it was one to which Collingwood made his own signal contribution—a contribution well assessed by Mr E. W. F. Tomlin's essay.[1] If I say that the inspiration of this discipline was the sense of history, I am not speaking of an achievement which inspired confidence in the

[1] *R. G. Collingwood*, by E. W. F. Tomlin. Longmans (for the British Council, 1953).

methods that made it possible; I am speaking of an awareness which seemed to set a question-mark against all work which tried to by-pass it.

I suppose that if someone turned to Collingwood's writings today, knowing his work only by hearsay, he would expect to find an amalgam of unplausible speculations mainly about history. Yet if he even pursued his way as far as the second half of *Speculum Mentis* (1942), he would find a categorical denial of the possibility of metaphysics. Strange sentiment for a speculative philosopher! Yet Collingwood was in the end no more speculative than Wittgenstein or Professor Ayer; only the inspiration and the direction of his criticism were different. Although he lectured and wrote on the philosophy of nature, it was the problem of historical existence that obsessed him. If he denied the possibility of speculative metaphysics, it was not because he gave an ultimate authority to some "principle of verification"; it was because he remembered that in one age men had taken one sort of view of the world for granted and in another quite a different one. When, in 1940, he published his essay on *Metaphysics* he gave an almost classical expression to the sort of scepticism which must beset any thinker who takes history seriously.

There is a paradox in Collingwood's whole attitude towards history; he saw it both as splendid and as terrible. That men must establish the sort of relation with their past that critical history makes possible was a splendid thing; it showed that men were not as the beasts that perish, but somehow unique because of the way in which their past was incapsulated in their present. But if their historical consciousness delivered men from bondage to nature and gave them a sense of their own peculiar dignity, at the same moment it showed them how much they were the prisoners of their own contemporary circumstance.

Can we transcend historical relativity? Collingwood never thought that it was any answer to point to the fact of mathematics as, since Plato, philosophers have done. Here, no doubt, he showed his own limitation, and betrayed the sense in which he was an idealist. Nothing is more noticeable in the whole series of his writings than his continued hostility to what he called realism. He is as critical of the position or positions to which he gave this name in his *Essay on Philosophical Method* (1933) as in the more passionate pages of his *Autobiography* (1939); and the reader of his *Principles of Art* (1938) will find there a lengthy criticism of the realist theory of knowledge. (It is worth mentioning that this is almost the only English work on aesthetics by a professional philosopher to attract the attention of artists and writers.) When Collingwood talks about realism he is not so much concerned with a doctrine concerning the status of objects of perception as with an attempted flight from the besetting problem of men's historical existence. To him the realists were men who were running away from the critical problem; they sought some point at which men could give an unconditional validity to their commerce with the real. Of course there was an argument ready to hand for him against their work in the sterility of their human understanding: to one who, like Collingwood, saw something of the significance in human life of art and of religion, the peculiarly philistine quality of Oxford realism was an abiding argument against its claim. At least T. H. Green and his followers were men who had seen in philosophical training something more than a mere education in logomachy. But in the end Collingwood attacked the realists as men who had failed to understand Kant's problem; their lack of intellectual subtlety derived from their failure to see what in the eighteenth century had compelled Kant to undertake his three Critiques. Kant had seen the necessity of justifying fundamental assumptions about the order of the physical universe; he had steadfastly refused the escape offered by an appeal to intuitive self-evidence. The notions of space and time, of permanence and change, of causality, possibility, necessity, and existence, he submitted to a laborious transcendental analysis. Collingwood was never any sort of Kantian; but the critical problem was always with him, even though he saw it raised less by the exact sciences than by men's relation to the past of their society and of their world. It was with the fact of history, with the presuppositions of the work of the critical historian that he was in the end concerned.

In his writings on history Collingwood was never much

concerned with "philosophy of history", in the sense of Isaiah and Paul, Augustine, Hegel and Marx. He was concerned with historical writing, with the imaginative reconstruction of the past which it expresses, with the methods historians had used, and with the criticism these methods had undergone. To some extent in his posthumous *Idea of History* (1946) he is content to describe; certainly his own conception of what the critical historian is about emerges by way of a discussion of the history of the idea of history, a discussion sometimes unfair but often of brilliant insight. Yet if Collingwood did not offer anything which could be called a "philosophy of history", it is obvious that in the end history meant, for him, something much more humanly significant than the province of professionally trained historians. It was not that Collingwood ever despised professional history; his work on Roman Britain itself refutes such a charge. Yet in his later writing history had become for him something much nearer to what philosophy was for Hegel in his *Phenomenology of Spirit*, and what it was to some extent for Collingwood himself when he wrote *Speculum Mentis* (1924). In historical awareness he thought that men somehow came to themselves and took stock of their fundamental assumptions; they see themselves for what they are and renew their perception of their relativity and finitude. At the end of the *Idea of Nature* (1944) Collingwood claimed for history authority over natural science; but over history, that is over the sort of self-knowledge by way of history with which by the end of his life Collingwood had seemed to identify both philosophy and history, what rules? Or is history as Collingwood understood it at the end of his life, its own justification and the scepticism it encourages the last word? Is there no sense in which he can use the words "valid" and "invalid" of the deliverance of history? Always as we read the writings of his last period, we remember we are reading the work of a sick man who died before his work was done, but to whose courage in continuing to write we owe so much.

Some who have written about Collingwood look back regretfully to the period of his *Essay on Philosophical Method* (1933). In that work he certainly did, by means of the notion of a "scale of forms", achieve a positive conception of the peculiar domain of philosophy and of the status of the concepts philosophers are most concerned to analyse. The subtle and delicate illustrative explorations of such notions as goodness, the discussions of induction and deduction in relation to philosophical method, the analysis of "new level analysis" alone entitle the book to a place of distinction in the philosophical publications of the Thirties. It is true that in his *Autobiography* (1939) Collingwood failed to do justice to the difference between what he said in it about philosophy and the conception of the *Essay*. Yet perhaps in the untidier, more passionate works of his last years, he was raising problems still more fundamental, and suggesting a conception of philosophy at least as significant as that so finely expounded in his *Essay*. It is a pity that his sense of the Nazi menace distracted him from his work on history into the writing of the *New Leviathan* (1942); that work is certainly valuable as a contribution to political theory, and the courage shown in its completion moves one to reverence. But one must regret that Collingwood never fully developed his picture of the sort of self-analysis to which, in his work on *Metaphysics* (1940), he called his readers. Certainly it demands for its practice a very considerable knowledge of the history of ideas; but as Principal Knox has pointed out, it can also be seen as a contribution to the philosophy of religion, which suggests certain connections between Collingwood and Kierkegaard, and even Barth.

If Collingwood did not always see clearly what he was inviting his readers to undertake, he was not afraid to speak of it sometimes in specifically religious terms. He was always deeply sensitive to the problem of the relation of religious faith to scientific progress and to philosophical criticism. He wrote often of Christianity, which he saw as the *via purgativa* of religion. But here, as so often, he leaves to his readers the task of giving their own interpretation to his frequent comments on the peculiar interdependence of religion and culture. Certainly a man who tried to practise the sort of self-analysis to which Collingwood called him might find it natural to speak of it as a "dark night" of the intellect, a religious experience, although the problems occasioning it were less religious than intellectual. But it would, I think, be an experience promising more for human understanding than the confident acceptance of those who *know* how things are. It was no accident that in the *Autobiography* Collingwood wrote as he did about the Spanish Civil War; the Franco racket was a living symbol of surrender to every sort of hypocrisy and pretence. Those who begin to understand the sort of Socratic self-analysis to which he invited his readers must see something demanding a comparable repudiation in the present anti-Communist crusade. Franco and McCarthy are both enemies of intellectual honesty as well as of human compassion.

The faults of Collingwood's work are obvious and his prejudices are always evident. Yet he had a restless, questioning genius. He was never easily satisfied; like Professor Wisdom, he makes his readers *work*. In the end he raised more problems than he answered; but here certainly he reminds his readers of Socrates, who made his associates face the difficult truth of their own deep ignorance, and of Kant whose doctrine of the categories was, as Professor Paul Tillich suggests, in its essence a doctrine of human finitude. Collingwood's precise concerns were not those of Socrates or of Kant; he belonged more intimately than most professional philosophers to the twentieth century, and the problems in respect of which he urged Socratic self-scrutiny were those he believed lay at the heart of the spiritual experience of his contemporaries. Of those problems he tried to speak, not always in even tones, not always in the same style, but always bravely, always aware that it is in the darkness that the light must shine.

AN APPROACH TO THE MORAL
AND SPIRITUAL PROBLEMS OF THE NUCLEAR AGE[1]

THE GREATEST strength of the report of the Arch-
bishops' Commission on *The Church and the Atom* seems
to me to be its sustained presentation of the idea of the
rule of law as a crucial point in the discussion. Oddly enough
it could be argued that the document is actually more valuable
as an essay in political theory than as a piece of theology. In its
theological sections it is often lame and hesitant; it does, I think,
however, succeed in throwing into bold relief the importance
and influence (in Christian thinking about the problem of
government) of this insistence that power stands under law,
that contrary to appearances power is something whose nature
it is not to escape but to submit and to serve the prescriptions of
practical reason.

Mr Bentley in his talk[2] did not simply commend the just war
doctrine as a kind of middle way between pacifism on the one

---

[1] This essay is the text of a broadcast talk, the third of a series of three, given on
the BBC 3rd Programme in the early autumn of 1948, on the report of a commission set up by the Church Assembly of the Church of England (under the
chairmanship of the late Dr E. G. Selwyn) to discuss the issues raised by the
advent of nuclear weapons. The report—*The Church and the Atom*—is still widely
regarded as a very able piece of work. It included some critical discussion of the
earlier report—*The Era of Nuclear Power*—of a commission of the British Council
of Churches, under the chairmanship of Dr J. H. Oldham, which was published
in 1946. In the preparation of this earlier report I had played a leading part
(although I subsequently became very dissatisfied with it). It was for this reason
that I was asked to broadcast on *The Church and the Atom*, following the Rev. (now
Canon) G. B. Bentley, who had played a leading part in its composition, and the
late Dr H. G. Wood, who spoke as a pacifist. Although I do refer to the attitudes
characteristic of the Church Assembly Commission report over against those of
the British Council of Churches Commission, I decided the whole issue needed to
be treated in a wider perspective and at a deeper level; it is for this reason that
this essay is included here.

[2] *The Listener*, October 14, 1948

side and the doctrine that in war no holds are barred on the other. No: he took this tradition, slow laborious thing that it is, and showed it for what it is—an almost classical essay in the attempted moralization of power. It is easy to smile at the insistence of moral theologians, canonists, international lawyers, that, for instance, the aim of military action is in effect the separation of the soldier from his weapon, the destruction of armament rather than of those who use it. But it is less easy when one sets such a plea in the context in which it has meaning —namely that of the general assumption that the use of force need not be lawless violence but can serve universally valid ends.

So in this report, which Mr Bentley expounded, the moral problems raised by modern methods of warfare are discussed in relation to the decline of a political tradition which, in the minds of its authors, is itself closely linked with the difficult idea of natural law. I myself think it is a pity that they tied themselves in their political discussion to so rigid a conception of natural law: their point could have been made, has in effect been made by Burke for instance, without the uncritical appeal to a self-evident natural law which they offer. But I am sure they are right to insist on a close connection between the spread of doctrines which treat law as the expression ultimately of arbitrary will and our abdication, in time of war, of any sense of possible illegitimacy in means employed. When Mr Vyshinsky said that "Law is the instrument of politics and the reverse theory is untrue", he gave expression to a point of view by no means uncongenial at many points to many of his most vocal western critics. It is perhaps worth noting that many non-Christians share the report's concern at this point. Mr R. H. S. Crossman, in a review of Major-General Fuller's book on *The Second World War*, made criticisms of the policy of unconditional surrender and of the means used to implement it which recall much that the report emphasizes.

It is perhaps a pity, however, that the report says so little of the forces which have encouraged this contemporary acceptance of violence as something belonging to the stuff of life and altogether eluding control. In the minds of the writers it is clearly associated with the decline of any sense of a human norm and with the growth of the illusion that all human problems are ultimately technical. But I confess that this does not seem to me nearly enough; and I am also sure that we have got to ask ourselves how far the mere assertion of the sovereignty of law is itself an answer to the attitude to violence here deplored. Further when the report faces the question what, in a concrete situation, is A to do, it hedges abominably. The concluding sentences of the crucial second chapter assert boldly that if men say that some acts are wrong, and that all the same they suppose they must do them, they are going against conscience; the logic is clear that for such conduct they can no more plead the defence of superior orders at the judgment-seat of God than at an earthly Nuremberg. But there is another strand in the same chapter which tells in a very different direction; it invokes the principle *necessitas non habet legem*; it does not require much insight to see how easily that principle could be used to justify anything at all. When one bears in mind some of the things that trained moral theologians have said and written elsewhere on this topic of the morality of modern warfare, one is left with the uneasy fear that they are often more anxious to quieten conscience than to awaken it to the flash-point of revolt. And it is a great pity therefore that at this crucial moment in the argument this report is so disquietingly ambiguous and evasive.

And here I think we come to the underlying weakness of the whole thing—that it discusses this whole subject as if it were enough first to show how fundamental axioms of just behaviour were transgressed in war as we know it; and then to connect these transgressions with the infection of our whole outlook by the doctrine of the supremacy of blind will, that is, of will differentiated from caprice only by its effectiveness. Admittedly the report concludes with a long chapter on Christianity in an age of power, a chapter that alternates between repetition of the usual *clichés* concerning scientific humanism, and approaches to a level a good deal more profound. But the question is always stated in terms of abstract principle: there is never an attempt to state it in personal terms, in terms of Christian existence today. All through this report the question of what exactly it means to be a Christian in the modern world is subtly by-passed. The issues are converted every time into a clash of opposing world-outlooks: they are never set out as they enter the experience of the individual who has to decide, who has to balance one loyalty against another, who has to make the truth of the Gospel his own in personal terms here and now. Christianity is all the time treated in this report as if it were a complex of ideas from which the relevant cluster could be detached and pitted against those of the USSR or of our uncritical social democracy. We are far too seldom reminded that for us Christianity is a way that is ultimately one with our whole life.

To go further: in this concluding chapter the report rightly stresses the element of titanism in the scientific attitude. More-over it recognizes too that there is much more, very much more, to the scientific attitude than that. Yet how little attempt is made to bear witness to the manifest stirring of conscience among scientists themselves, concerning the use to which their work is put! More than ever, scientists seem to be alive to the extent to which the circumstances in which they have worked have dictated even the direction of fundamental research, cer-tainly that of more practically relevant experiment, and have subtly perverted it. Some, surveying the fruit of their work, have found an interpretation of their experience and a ground of hope in the profound marxist idea of alienation—that process whereby contradictions at the level of production make some-thing demonic of the fruit of man's creative labour, some-thing demonic that stands over against him as an uncontrollable destructive force. Such troublings of the waters of conscience are surely profoundly significant: even when men are led by them to espouse the crudities of marxism they are unconsciously expressing loyalty to the idea of a rational order in things. And what I am sure we have to do, if we are Christians, is to cease from our continual readiness to speak in terms of embattled abstractions, and to think always in terms of men groping in the dark: for it is not the theory itself that concerns us so much as the theory as it is expressed in action and choice, and as it controls in part or whole the movement of a man's actual life. For it is at that level perhaps we see what a theory most surely is.

Perhaps this has something to do with charity, of which oddly enough no mention is made in this report. It is odd too that the Sermon on the Mount is never mentioned: a reaction, I suppose, against the way pacifists have exploited its deliverances.* Yet are its words altogether irrelevant? The biblical theology in the report seems to me on a deplorably low level: the section on the Christian understanding of history is as lacking in profundity and subtlety as any official denominational deliverance on a national day of prayer. It is perhaps no accident that the report shirks altogether asking the question just what is the relevance to Christians here and now of that law of the new Israel delivered on the Mount. I say "here and now" because we cannot ignore the peculiar situation of Christians in this present. To those for whom the truth of the world lies in its relation to God in Christ, the profound unrest of the present cannot be viewed out of that all-embracing setting. Ultimately the significance of what is happening to men as they struggle in the midst of that unrest or are terribly caught by it, is found in Him: it is not sound and fury signifying nothing. Certainly to doubt at a deep enough level the supremacy of law over power is a spiritual experience. But what the Christian has to do is to go further than that: to take as far as he can the measure of the present crisis as it is localized inside all who are living through it and responding to it. In his book, *The Apocalypse of History*, the Russian theologian Dr Eugene Lampert was on to this when he wrote:

We must accept the mockeries of Voltaire, the critique of Kant, the dialectic of Hegel, the atheism of Feuerbach, the strictures of Marx, the reclamations of humanism, Nietzsche's revolt against Christianity, and the nihilistic conclusions of existentialism; we must equally accept and respond to the revolutionary changes and upheavals which disrupt the seemingly solid ground of human existence, however much we may object to their lawless and godless character. *De te fabula narrata!* All these things are a record of the story of every one of us; and we must go through their purifying fire before attempting to question the world's alleged answers and answer the world's real questions.

It is ultimately a kind of intellectual compassion to which Lampert is summoning his readers, an entering into the gropings, the strugglings, the protestations of our own contemporaries which is made possible because all the time they are telling us about our own situation. We are not to escape this mucking-in by appeal to any tradition, however sanctified: it is an imperative laid upon us because we are flesh and blood as our fellows are, for always Christ prayed not that we should be taken out of the world but kept from the evil. There is a good deal in this report that speaks the aloofness of the cathedral close, something, I would insist, poles asunder from the engagement of the true contemplative.

Where the question of war is concerned, this report wisely insists on the merciless character of ideological war, its peculiar impatience of any kind of lawful restraint. It is also alive to the extent to which political realities are in practice subordinate to the assumptions that inform men's choices about what actually is and what is worth having for its own sake. And yet for all that, its argument is conducted for so long a time at the level of the political. Nearly the whole time it seems to take for granted that the problem of participation or non-participation in war is simply a problem in the theory of political obligation. It does not really see how much for men and women today this issue really focuses the whole question of the place of their political allegiance in life. In a way men and women know more clearly than the writers of this report (I except Archdeacon Hartill,* of course) that discussion concerning the authority of the just war tradition is remote and idealistic in so far as it very largely neglects the sort of world in which decisions have to be taken and many of the principles on which they are made. It takes for granted, it is bound to take for granted, an entirely different set-up. This is not to belittle the significance of its insights: but merely to point out that if this tradition is effectively to avail again, we have got to recreate in men's minds the assumptions concerning human life that gave it operative force. You cannot get away from the fact that some at least who plunge into pacifism do so because it seems to them part of a total response demanded by the situation—namely postponing the fulfilment of all other obligations to that of compassion. To them it does seem as if war is today necessarily ideological, however resolute the effort to free it of ideological taint. To them, too, it seems that in approving its methods there lies an abdication of the sense of pity to which they must quite simply say "No", and that because such an abdication decisively mutilates a Christian response to the world, a fact which the writers of this report seem too aloof from savage realities to understand.

Clearly this report could not be expected to endorse the pacifist attitude: but at least it might have conducted its discussion as if it showed some awareness of the conflicts actually going on in people's minds. Or are we to be condemned to think in terms of a text-book scholasticism? It is perfectly fair to accuse those whose position I have tried to outline of political irresponsibility, even of titanism as if they were called to be the saviours of mankind in their own estimation. And yet there is no getting away from the fact that people are talking in these terms, are doing so because ultimately they refuse to turn their backs on faith, on charity—and on hope. Like all mankind ultimately they depend on what was accomplished upon the Cross: but they cannot find any other way towards realizing the content of that dependence except that provided by a readiness to respond, to expose themselves, to open and not to close their understanding and their pity.

In the end this report is a failure. I am not saying that it fails because it does not endorse the pacifist position: I am saying that it fails because it is pitifully lacking in any sense of wholeness, in any imaginative awareness of the depth of the human predicament today. It contains an admirable exposition of a tradition: but there it stops, leaving the questions that arise when one gets off the blinkers of that tradition unasked and unanswered. It remains a strange thing that somehow in this document the vast resources of spiritual wisdom, contained in the Christian tradition have been left untapped as if they had no real relevance to the illumination of our present predicament. Yet it could be that in this time it was the masters of the spiritual life more than the canonists who could have helped us.

But you may say: does anything that I have said take you further? I would like to hope that it did, because I have tried to raise in your minds three questions. If one is a Christian or aspires to be one at all, then one has to take nothing human as alien from oneself. One has got to see that all the time, in ways very strange and surprising men and women in their groping and perplexity are threading the way which is Christ. Mr Bentley clearly has little sympathetic understanding of post-medieval thought: and that is a pity. For it seems to me that in an age like ours, an age of conflict and explosion, if we are Christians at all, we must discern in the conflict and the explosion the outskirts of the ways of God. What we do need and what this report fails to give us, is a new kind of Christian understanding of history that shows its authentic Christianity by refusing to think in impersonal terms. Again this report fails to say very much concerning the redemptive, reconciling function of the church and of the church's life. This is what I mean when I say that I wish its authors had gone to the spiritual writers and not to the lawyers. You can find no guidance here concerning what intercession should mean in a world as radically harassed and frightened as ours—intercession that seems too often to be the prayer of a church severed by a gulf of aloofness from a world it must serve and try to heal. The understanding of history is perhaps in part an understanding of the relation of the Church's prayer to history.

And finally we have got to ask ourselves as Christians whether there is or is not a point at which we must say "No". I agree that the pacifist is all the while menaced by the danger of encouraging in others a political irresponsibility of which he may well himself be personally guiltless. But there is another side. Certainly one can argue quite powerfully that some methods of warfare are so inherently lawless that the cause of law itself bids us abjure them: but has one got to go deeper than that? Is it or is it not the case that Christian assent to the kind of thing atomic war is must infect and poison the spring of that compassion for men and women in their deepest needs that Christian men and women are called to share? The Church exists in part to manifest to the world, albeit in a splintered reflection, that ultimate love whose expression in time is found in the crucifixion of the Son of God—to call men and women to their rest in its unfathomable deeps. Is the fulfilment of such a function compatible with assent to the thing we call atomic war? The word I would like you to ponder here is *assent*. I am sure that each one of us has to ask in his own heart what such assent would be for him. Where I am clear, however, is here: that if moral theologians and canonists write today as if their task were in effect primarily that of justifying obedience to the powers that be, of stifling rather than arousing conscience in this field, of giving nice pat answers to the troubled, their responsibility is a very terrible one. I myself would say that their task is a very different one—that of interpreting spiritually and strengthening the revolt against such things as atomic war that is surely there in the world. It is a revolt which takes many forms but is ultimately one in conviction that human beings were not made to do these things to each other. Is not the presence of this temper of revolt, widely dispersed as it is, in origin and in emphasis, one of the few really hopeful signs in the west today? And are not its standard-bearers Christian fellow-travellers, perhaps before some others deserving the concern of those who bear the Christian name? For we must never forget in our enthusiasm for something we call Christian civilization that it was from the rootless and the outcast that the Christ called his own, and that upon a gallows-tree, between two criminals, He was content to die.

* NOTES

P. 179, lines 5 and 6. In 1968 I should wish to express this differently: "a reaction against the way the writers of this Report have wrongly thought pacifists to have used its deliverances."

P. 180, line 26. The late Ven. Percy Hartill, Archdeacon of Stoke, was the pacifist representative on the Commission.

REFLECTIONS ON THE HYDROGEN BOMB

W HEN WE talk about the hydrogen bomb, we are
talking about something we have chosen to develop
and to use. We are talking about choices we have
actually made; we are not talking about events in which we
have become involved, which, like the Lisbon earthquake of the
eighteenth century, have put a question-mark against our
teleology, our sense of the ordering of natural processes towards
discernible human good. We may say that we have chosen to
develop such a weapon in order that we may *not* have to use it;
and we may mean the paradox most seriously. But we are still
talking about something which we have done; we are referring
to human actions, and not to an impersonal fate.

But who are "we"? Not you and I; true, and the measure of
even direct parliamentary control of such an enterprise is
obviously limited. The "we" is the peculiar "we" of representative government in its modern form; it indicates the responsible
men who know the facts, who are charged with the burden of
executive decision, who are indeed responsible yet not easily
called to answer in the ordinary routines of parliamentary
democracy. Yet it remains hard to see how their decisions can
be altogether disowned; for, they can claim, how can any,
placed as they were placed, have acted otherwise? If there is
here alienation of decisive responsibility, is not such alienation
involved in the very nature of modern government?
  So we are speaking of decisions actually taken, on our behalf
rather than by ourselves, but still decisions. We are not reminded of a process of which we are spectators; but of a whole series
of decisions, which as decisions need not have been taken,
however severe their justification. I think that, at the outset, it is

as important to remember these things as it is to be on guard against such specious slogans as "Ban the Bomb", etc. If it remains obscure to whom precisely such invitations are addressed, we must not, by that obscurity, be betrayed into forgetting that the bomb has been developed by men who have chosen to develop it because the alternative of failing to do so seemed inadmissible. If we are prisoners, the cage is one of our own fashioning.

But, if it is a matter of our own choice, what is there here that particularly frightens us? What is it that makes us wish somehow to disavow responsibility, to treat ourselves as the prisoners of our own technical achievement and not its masters? I suppose, first of all, we are afraid of the scale on which we can now interfere not only with our neighbours but with our natural environment: perhaps almost more of the scale of the latter interference than of the former. This is perhaps paradoxical; but where the number of human beings destroyed by a particular weapon is concerned, we are prepared nowadays to add a nought or two without all that much thought.

Yet we do hesitate a little when we realize that we may be disturbing, by our action, extraordinarily complex ecological patterns, setting up chain reactions whose end is, in a literal sense, an everyday sense, unpredictable. We may say that we do not see how men placed as Truman was placed in 1950, could have taken any other decision than to give the green light to hydrogen-bomb development; we may say, further, that we are not prepared to insist, where the use of what has been developed is concerned, on a rigid control of executive decision by legislative assembly. Yet we are still aghast at what we have done and are about to do; still uncertain, because we have ventured, perhaps illegitimately, into the unknown. So we conceal the inwardness of our hesitation from ourselves by the devices of melodrama, and like to think of ourselves as sleep-walkers carrying on our progress over the cliff edge. Or we take refuge, as an English diocesan bishop did in the language of apocalypse, suggesting that we may touch off the springs that usher upon mankind the *Dies Irae*.

We are afraid of the scale of our interference. Is this fear a piece of blind irrationalism? Or is it the expression of a true reverence? We must be on guard here, for no ethical slogan lends itself more easily to exploitation by the crank, or the servant of unreason, than the notion of the "natural". Yet we cannot be certain that we will in the end be able to bounce all that we do. Butler, one of the greatest British moralists, brought out clearly that there was, at the heart of virtue, a certain reverent agnosticism, a certain refusal of brash self-confidence, of supposing that the world was our oyster, or the oyster of our generation. We were in a sense custodians of the future as well as trustees of the wisdom of the past.

All this is uncongenial to the assured utilitarian temper; but it must be insisted that it is also at a considerable remove from a melodramatic invocation of the "tragic sense of life". Such an invocation could serve, indeed has served well, the recruiting officers of the S.S. To say that we are, in some sense, not the masters of our fate but the servants of a natural law is not to imply that we are the slaves of destiny; rather it is to imply something very different, as Kant's doctrine of autonomy reminds us; it is simply to insist that we remember of what stuff we are made, what posture suits us "as human beings under the sun". If we put such questions to ourselves in the difficult context of a consideration of the ethics of modern war, we do so to protect ourselves against surrender to the impersonal, appealing to the form of a natural law against the blind idolatry of the present moment.

All this is obvious enough. But it is perhaps important to state clearly what it is in our moral traditions which is engaged by this problem of scale, and to recognize that it is just this vaguely admitted sense of a natural law. Professor A. P. d'Entrèves clearly brought out both how precarious a thing this sense is, and how subtly different from the more canvassed conception of a natural right. But his proper caution perhaps prevented him from recognizing how in the hands of such an interpreter as Butler the notion of natural law becomes almost indistinguishable from that of a certain reverence for life, a kind of rational expression of the sense of something to be conserved, at once as elusive and as fundamental as that. When suddenly, dramatically, we are told that to speak in such terms is to fly in the face of reality, of practical necessity, we experience a kind of outrage, the experience being inseparable from a sudden drastic return to the idiom of natural law; a return in its way as unexpected and as searching as that sometimes provoked by, for instance, first-hand experience of the practice of abortion.

But is not this to stray beyond the terms of reference of this talk? Perhaps; yet it remains true that the sense of a natural limit was one of the factors that went to fashion the classical attitude to the problems of war expressed in the "just war" tradition. It is true that this tradition of the "just war" is today dead, at least inoperative. One may indeed smile at the tradition, at its attempted marriage of incommensurables, of order and violence, love and coercion. Yet it stood for something crucially important. It saw, or it embodied the insight, that government was necessary, that the work of government involved the forceful restraint of the wrongdoer, that this principle extended to the more precarious domain of international relations; and yet that just as government must be constitutionally subordinate to law, so, in the defence of right, there was always a *debitus modus*. This tradition was, in every sense, a protest against the idea of total war. It was the declaration that war was an instrument which sometimes must be used; but it expressed a refusal to accept war as a master, as a process which might take charge of its executants and subdue them, even as a totalitarian state its citizens, to its own dynamism.

To speak of the "just war" tradition is to lay oneself open to the charge of being academic. Yet the more I ponder the issues of the morality of modern war, the more sure I am that it is partly because of the vacuum created by the disappearance of this tradition, tenuous as it always was, that we are in the predicament in which we find ourselves. To talk in such a way may run the risk of supposing that certain principles have, as a matter of history, counted for more than they actually have done. We are often made to realize that in government executive action has, and indeed must have, the last word rather than constitutional restraint. Yet in the complex discussion which attended and followed the sittings of the International Military Tribunal at Nuremberg after the last war, it seemed clear that men and women at large still repudiated the idea that military necessity was a kind of moral sovereign, and were even prepared to insist that for certain sorts of action the defence of "superior orders" was no valid plea.

Because we live in an age of extremes, we may run the risk of esteeming too lightly an effort, however, I repeat, practically ineffective it may have been, to avoid facing men with the appalling choice mentioned by a distinguished Scottish divine in the General Assembly of the Church of Scotland—"either Belsen or Hiroshima": either acquiescence in the pitiless methods of the totalitarian state, or the acceptance of the means judged necessary by those with full knowledge of the facts for its restraint or containment. Yet it may be a comment on the state of our civilization that we have allowed ordinary mortals to be faced with that sort of nightmarish choice.

We may say, we do say, in certain moods, that tradition does not matter; that ancient restraints are simply barriers in the way of emancipation; that their authority is dubious, and that utility and human happiness are sufficient to yield us the material of an ethic. Yet it is perhaps a crucial question whether we see any end likely to be set to the sort of experimenting with our natural and human environments implied in the series—atom bomb, hydrogen bomb, cobalt bomb. Is it not perhaps possible that men are, in a profound sense, wrong if they suppose that they can do anything and bounce the consequences, that no holds are barred because none will in the end prove finally, irretrievably destructive? Here at once we are told that we are caught; we *must* behave like fiends because the alternative is worse. The alternative is acquiescence in the sort of method perfected by the totalitarian state for destroying the individual person, whether the assault be made by way of pain, or persuasion, or both. All right; but then let us eschew the word "must" in referring to a conscious and deliberate choice.

For choice is one thing; it is another to describe our decisions as if they were responses elicited from us by some sovereign impersonal process which we see necessarily prescribing what we must do.

History, whatever we may mean by that word, is not sovereign over us; nor—dare I say it?—is technical advance, as such. The mere fact that we can do something does not mean that we must do it; although it may be that we should as the lesser of two evils. We may dislike intensely some of the styles favoured by the existentialists; but perhaps we do not realize how much these styles are provoked by the glib and loose way in which we too often speak of the historical process as if it were something which bore us on its course like a cataract, and by the fact that we are ourselves, more calmly perhaps but still without much question, prepared to accept the nightmare situation of extreme choice as the norm: "Either Belsen or Hiroshima". Still less can we quarrel with the extravagance of existentialist language if we favour ourselves a dubious idiom of apocalypse, suggesting that maybe the world will end with a bang, not with a whimper, and that it is our hand which will let off the fireworks.

We have calmly and quietly to ask ourselves how we have reached our present impasse. This is not irresponsibility, not a counsel of imprudence. It may be true that our political obligations today include a readiness to support the game of diplomatic poker whereby alone the cold war is kept cold, and not to do anything, by public indiscretion, which would suggest our unwillingness to endorse that development of atomic power without which a player in that game must leave the table. Yet there is a deeper question touching the context in which the poker-game itself is played. We need not see ourselves—pathetic fallacy—as saviours of civilization to ask it: How have we got here? Have we made in the past choices that were fundamentally wrong? To say that we cannot undo the past is simply to assert an analytic truth. But one is not denying the consequences of one's definitions if one asks whether, at certain points, certain men made choices which were wrong. For instance, is it true that acceptance of the principle of total war, even when our opponents were men like the Nazis, was acceptance of something which should not have been accepted? To raise these questions is not to encourage a mood of blind censure; it is rather for the sake of present decision that they are raised.

Or again: there may be certain methods of waging war, perhaps the practice of obliteration bombing, about which, at an earlier point, serious questions should have been asked. Certainly, let us never forget, we did not allow the German soldier to plead defence of superior orders; we seemed to exact from him, on service in the field, a critical appraisal of the validity of what he was asked to do which we are slow ourselves to attempt more generally as civilians.

I say, more generally; and you may well ask what, in practice, does this come to? Does it come to more than a plea for serious thought on these problems? A little pathetic because, in the end, what difference can such make? At least, it is a barrier in the way of blind acquiescence, a defence in concrete of the principle of the open society against the bitch-goddess of historical necessity. By trying to look calmly at what we have done, and at what has been done in our name, we assert at least a little the sovereignty of principle over process, of law over blind will. Revolt is the name of an ethical category which needs exploration, and the ascetic theologian might also give it his attention. I have referred to the importance of tradition, of the place of tradition in ethics, and of the difficult question of its claim over against the more obvious claims of human happiness. The revolt I am now speaking of would not necessarily be a revolt against tradition; even in some small respects, at least, the reverse. For it might take in part the shape of insisting that we remember elements in the fabric of human life which we are all of us in danger of forgetting; for instance, the sort of elements which, as Butler saw, compelled that kind of agnosticism which is close kinsman to reverence and lies not far from the heart of true religion, and which touches the penumbral context of our whole existence.

Revolt is an important category; because elsewhere than in eastern Europe is the citadel of the individual person threatened, and not only in Warsaw and in Prague are men compelled to play "Ketman", to say one thing and to intend another in their hearts. Total war (and its shadow is over more of our doings than we like to remember) tends to make such play-actors of us all. It helps to induce a mood, it may be of desperation, more likely of relatively light-hearted cynicism concerning human possibilities. It tends almost unnoticed to diminish the quizzical sense of untapped possibilities of experience, and subdues, with a spurious gravity, the richness of life.

But can revolt be other than irresponsible? And what is this revolt in terms of the individual? Is it, to come to brass tacks, conscientious objection? There the individual must choose for himself; it is the deep reality of the question that I would try to impress on my readers. Modern methods of war are not a kind of sovereign source of moral principles; they are methods, not lords. It is possible that we have made them gods; but false gods never effectively command worship for long. There comes the moment when the idols are slain. In the end we query the insight of those who tell us that the bombing aeroplane has brought us its own morality; and we suspect of blasphemy those who suggest that unbridled technical development may be the occasion of the final Day of the Lord. We have to discuss, to face, these questions as questions of method, of means. If we have converted means into ends, and there are all sorts of ways of effecting the conversion, we must learn to effect a drastic reconversion.

Does this seem to ask too much of the individual citizen? Not, surely, in a modern democracy, a society which tries to give constitutional expression to the asking of awkward questions; nor is it more than was asked of the German soldier who was expected to say "No" in the extremity of the Russian front. To speak of repentance may seem without warrant to invoke a religious category; yet perhaps in our whole attitude towards these problems there is need for just that. Objectivity over these issues is hard; and for us the memory of Munich is still too real and too sharp to let us discuss even now, without a proper sense of shame, what gives its partial validity to pacifism. Yet those who cannot be pacifists, in the sense, for instance, that Dick Sheppard was, must allow the heavy weight of prejudice that prevents a proper attention to the matter of alternative methods of resistance to evil, to those offered by atom bombs. At least war must be seen as a method, its status as such kept clearly before the mind and its problems seen as problems of means. We are not asked to worship; but we will perhaps be judged by the manner of our use of what we seek to employ.

ETHICAL PROBLEMS OF NUCLEAR WARFARE

MUCH IS heard and said in these days of the "great deterrent". We are, it is claimed, committed to a particular conception of the context within which international relations between the two conflicting power concentrations in the world today are carried on. This context is provided by what is called the "deterrent"; it is constituted by a "balance of terror". Those who defend this thesis appeal sometimes to something akin in certain respects to a social contract, whereby the *prima facie* contestants for global mastery agree to stalemate on grounds that the attempt to break out from it would be mutually entirely destructive. The situation is not unlike that envisaged in the second book of Plato's *Republic* where Glaucon portrays as ideal a situation in which the "perfectly unjust man", equipped with power akin to that conferred by Gyges' ring to make oneself invisible, re-fashions the world after his own image. Yet we well know that unless we have such power as that ring bestows, that ideal situation is without our grasp; we live rather in a world where a rough equality in inability to avoid the consequences of even carefully calculated acts of rapacity holds men faithful to a conventional morality. This morality is in the literal sense conventional; it is expression of no natural law, but represents something on which men have tacitly agreed as a kind of *pis-aller*, a second-best in a world where none are endowed with power akin to that bestowed by Gyges' ring. The grounds of men's faithful observance of the dictates of this conventional morality are to be sought in a principle of utility, received as counselling restraint rather than encouraging hope for enlarged possibilities of achievement, conservative rather than radical in its undertones.

It is perhaps worth while, in considering the conception of the "great deterrent", to look back at this model of a society, wherein a common inability to escape the consequences of trusting one's own right arm exacts from its members conformity to conventional restraints. For something of this sort does seem to be envisaged by those who argue that the "balance of terror" makes war impossible by ensuring that if it comes, none will be the victors. If war is an instrument of policy, then in the world of "the great deterrent", war has no place; for an occasion of mutual destruction cannot conceivably be regarded as an instrument of policy. Yet the time has come to ask what exactly we mean by "the deterrent". Let us begin therefore by analyzing the notion of deterrence. We say that a man is deterred from a crime of violence by fear of consequences; and fear is something that belongs to the life of the mind, however we may understand the senses of that phrase, in the simple sense that if a man is so deterred, he is deterred by prospects imagined of what will happen to him. These prospects no doubt include imprisonment; but they also include the likelihood, even the relative certainty, of detection. So in such a case nothing metaphysical is intended if we speak of deterrents as belonging to the life of the mind.

When men speak of the thermo-nuclear deterrent, they sometimes say that it "deters only in so far as it is never invoked or used". Thus they stress the extent to which they believe themselves to talk of a weapon-system which is effective in defence solely in so far as the *idea of its existence operates as a dissuasive from its employment*. Such a system is the necessary condition of an effective deterrent; but it is by the way of the image men form of the consequences of its use that it deters. Indeed it could be argued that if in fact it is used, it is no longer properly called a deterrent or (more accurately) the necessary condition of an effective deterrence. In so far as the thought of its existence fails to deter men from what we must, I suppose, still call "military adventure", it has ceased to provide the conditions of deterrence.

To argue in this way is not simply pedantry. Thus, the apologists for the renewal of nuclear testing claim that their weapons-system deters only so far as it is known effectively to be of genuinely deterrent quality. This does not entail that it shall be established as *superior* to the weapons-system of their rivals. Its destructive power need not even equal the destructive power of the opposed system; it may indeed be measurably inferior in that respect to the opposed system; *but to such inferiority there must be definite limits*. The system must be invulnerable ✓ in its fundamental destructive capacity, to improvements, e.g. development of anti-missile missiles on the part of its rivals. Hence it seems to me perfectly clear that if we accept "the balance of terror", we are committed to tests as alone providing (in the absence of an internationally operated method of inspection) the kind of insurance we need that radical unbalance shall not be introduced into the system.

We might view the fear of unbalance as the fear that someone will discover Gyges' ring and achieve the power of turning himself invisible at will. We are committed to the continued search for anti-rings, and it may indeed seem to some that this state of affairs introduces an element of radical instability into the system.

There is however one pendant to the system of deterrence that should be mentioned, a concession, if I understand it, to ethical tradition. We are constantly told that "we shall never strike first". Rather, we shall strike "only if". Yet according to some writers on the nature of nuclear warfare (if I understand them) in a thermo-nuclear war the first strike will be aimed at the hard bases of the ICBMs of the power which is attacked in order to paralyse that power's nuclear capacity, while the second strike will seek to destroy the social substance of the enemy nation. For these eventualities, for response to the first strike, we are ready; and a critic may ask how this readiness is related to the maintenance of the system of the "great deterrent". Does the maintenance of the system demand readiness of the kind of which I am now speaking as a piece of play-acting, as a condition of the game, or as a genuine resolve? If the readiness is not expressive of a genuine resolve, does not the whole system collapse? We may well ask whether this kind of critical reflection does not reveal an element of sheer myth in the conception of the "great deterrent". To its criticism we must therefore now turn.

Those who defend the conception of the "great deterrent" do so because they believe that this system provides what has already been called a context within which international relations may be carried on. But the business of international relations includes the use of force. The history of the years since the Second World War ended is full of occasions in which force or the threat of force has been used. The business of the world has in fact been carried on, whether in Europe or the Middle East or in Asia, by these means, and those who have meditated the lesson of these conflicts, whose causes in many cases remain till this present, have had to ask themselves what must happen if in fact war should break out, well short of the thermo-nuclear holocaust which we fear but still graver in its potential threat than much which we have known since 1945.

The "great deterrent" still provides the context and it is supposed that none of the great powers involved will be prepared to invoke in service of their interests the deterrent which provides the framework of their intercourse. But it is argued by certain strategists that wars may begin in which the vast preponderance of the so-called conventional forces of the USSR over those mobilized by the west would justify the west in using tactical as distinct from strategic nuclear weapons in the field, to make good numerical deficiency in manpower. Optimists contend that the use in the field of tactical nuclear weapons, sometimes admitted to be of a destructive power as great as that of the bombs which destroyed Hiroshima and Nagasaki, is an act of war which will take place still under the protecting shadow of the "great deterrent". The effect of these weapons is, it is argued, something which can be controlled; damage from fall-out can be reduced to a minimum and destructive impact upon the civilian population in the surrounding country made relatively small. But even those who, because they recognize that conflicts occur in the international field requiring the arbitrament of force, are anxious to secure the use of tactical nuclear weapons to overcome numerical deficiency, recognize the likelihood, even the peril, of escalation.

One thing leads to another; and given the emotional distur-
bance of a war situation, we are perhaps foolish if we suppose
that, once tactical nuclear weapons have been used, we shall
be able to restrain ourselves from the steps leading stage by
stage but rapidly to thermo-nuclear holocaust. There are
many further questions to be asked concerning tactical nuclear
weapons. For instance, what of the genetic hazards involved in ✓
their employment? But it is important to mention this concession which has been made by those who fervently profess their
belief in the "great deterrent" as a context within which
international relations are carried on, to the kind of weapons-
system which may have to be invoked in the carrying on of
those relations themselves. Stalemate in international affairs
becomes eventually intolerable, and if the "great deterrent"
provides the context only for a potential stalemate, then means
will be found for breaking out of it. It is a paradox, but an
intelligible one, that these means may well be found such as to
bring the "great deterrent" itself into play, no longer as that
which provides the setting of international debate, but rather
as a terrible instrument for its prosecution.

I mention tactical nuclear weapons before passing to more
sustained criticism of the myth of the "great deterrent", partly
because in certain Christian circles, for instance the British
Council of Churches and the Christian Frontier Council, the
moral viability of the use of tactical nuclear weapons has been
much canvassed. The problem of escalation has been recognized; but because the very high-minded persons who move in
these exalted circles are at all costs anxious to avoid an open
breach between Christ and Caesar, the perils, even the likelihood, of escalation have been much under-emphasized. Further, it is worth remarking that those who argue that whatever
may be said in favour of tactical nuclear weapons, escalation
must be avoided, are also emphatic that we must not say in
advance where in fact we will draw the line. We should not
indicate clearly in advance what we regard as so morally
impermissible that we would prefer defeat to its use. To advertise this, it is argued, would be to encourage a prospective
enemy to make ready to go beyond what we are prepared to do;

it would be to take from us the very possibility of bluff. It might be said on the other side that this unwillingness to commit ourselves in advance is to lay ourselves wide open to the sort of pressures upon our resolution, of which war time gives us innumerable examples. Unless we make up our mind in advance what we are not prepared to tolerate, unless we commit ourselves publicly to limits which we will not pass, experience in recent history should surely remind us that we are likely to find that no limits in fact exist which we are not prepared to transgress.

Although this section of the discussion may seem relatively peripheral, it is important, in that it shows that even those who subscribe to the myth of the "great deterrent" see that it does not by itself provide a complete rationale of international relations in the modern world. We are not able to write off the problem of the morality of thermo-nuclear weapons by suggesting that they are not weapons at all, that they are rather the foundations of a system in which international relations are effectively transacted. The transaction of international relations frequently involves recourse to armed conflict; and although strategic thermo-nuclear weapons may not be quickly in play, the readiness of Christian casuists to bend their ingenuity to justifying the use of tactical nuclear weapons shows that the road to their invocation in actual conflict lies open. Yet objections to the myth of the "great deterrent" are more fundamental. It represents an attempt to turn aside from the fact that what we are dealing with in discussion of thermonuclear armaments are weapons which men have made and are in the last resort prepared to use. We owe a considerable debt here to Hermann Kahn, whose book *On Thermonuclear War* does at least rub home this lesson. Kahn stresses what he calls the importance of credible first-strike capacity; in other words he begins by insisting that we see the logical independence of what I called the pendant to the principles of our system of deterrence, viz. the claim that "we shall never strike first". He recognizes that these weapons are there for use; they are there for war, which is policy carried on by other means. We must not mythologize them, we must not idealize them as the context in which our international affairs are carried on; they are not that sort of thing at all. What we have to do is to count the cost of using them against that of not using them in certain eventualities. Kahn is the enemy of any sort of escape into the world of ideas. If war is the pursuit of political ends by other means and nuclear weapons weapons of war, we must explore the possibility of nuclear war. We must also ask ourselves such questions as how survival is possible, and whether we can use these weapons without overwhelmingly destructive consequences to ourselves. His thesis is seriously vulnerable, and has been submitted to drastic criticism in the United States, not least by such Christian theologians as Professor John Bennett of Union Theological Seminary, New York. But it has to be seen as a criticism of the deterrent concept, it has to be seen as a return to the understanding of these weapons as weapons, an end to the kind of high-minded idealism of treating them as something different. Of course in his estimate of the capacity of the United States of America effectively to engage in nuclear warfare, Kahn underestimates grossly the traumatic effects of the guilt of having launched or helped to launch this thing upon mankind. He is the slave of his realism, and his gross over-optimism lays him wide open to criticism. But at least he recognizes that we make the greatest possible mistake in discussing these issues if we suppose that the significance of thermo-nuclear armament is exhausted by definitions of its role in a fundamentally unstable balance of power.

There is indeed no escape in the end from the personal moral question of the individual's readiness to acquiesce in the use of these things in the attempted preservation of any values, or way of life whatsoever. Repeatedly in this lecture I have used the first personal pronoun plural "we". "We" have decided this and that; but who have decided and what sort of a decision is this? The ordinary man is far too near a history which is going on around him (and in which he plays his part) to be able to sit back and give intelligible, let alone defensible, answers to questions relating to the authors of those decisions which engage his whole destiny and that of his children. We are so familiar with the jargon of democracy that we fall easily into this first person plural and are encouraged to do so by those whose decisions, sometimes made in conditions of notably imperfect understanding of the issues involved, have brought us where we are. But democracy is the insistence that power shall be made accountable to those in whose name it is exercised, and those who have decided that the nation's resources shall be largely directed, even on the relatively small scale of these islands, to the development of nuclear weapons, must surely justify what they have done. Their argument will be of course that that way and that way alone lies security. (How far such argument in any way justifies the continued possession by Great Britain of an *independent* nuclear force I leave on one side.) But security, the preservation of our way of life, these are the stakes which are invoked as warranting the colossal expenditure of money and resources on thermo-nuclear armaments and in certain circumstances the readiness to use them.

The true democrat will not be satisfied. He is the irreverent man who asks awkward questions and goes on asking; he is not awed to silence by the alleged superior wisdom of those who occupy key positions in the nation's affairs. The word "Why?" is always on his lips; he is an awkward fellow and he glories in it; but the Christian goes beyond; for he should be aware that in these issues of political obligation and the conduct of international affairs great moral issues are at stake. What may men do to one another? What may they do to the actual world into which they are born and of which they are part? Are there no limits to set them beyond which they may not go? Or is anything permitted provided that the sacred name of public obligation is spoken over the most morally dubious procedure? We live in an age in which conscientious objection is a paramount issue; we have seen something of the readiness of servants of a great nation in colonial warfare of extreme bitterness, at least to connive at the use of torture. We are familiar with the endless pleas from Christian *bien-pensants* that we should not criticize those who know better than we do where the nation's need lies; that, whether the issue be Sir Anthony Eden's Suez adventure or the kind of matter with which we are concerned here. We are repeatedly encouraged to put our consciences to sleep; and yet as the story of the indiscriminate bombardment of German towns in the last world war has gradually unfolded, it is not those who kept silent who are vindicated on ground of strategic as well as political good sense, but the lonely pathetic voices, such as that of the revered George Bell, Bishop of Chichester. These men were reviled when they spoke; but it would seem that they have received their vindication after the event. Moreover, we must remember that at Nuremberg, the so-called defence of superior orders was ruled as irrelevant by the International Military Tribunal; and what was done there must surely apply as well to those who judged, and for their future, as to those who were executed or otherwise punished at the termination of the court's proceedings. Do we, or do we not believe that defence of superior orders absolves a man from listening to the voice of his own conscience? If Nuremberg had any validity, its validity lay in its denial of the thesis that absolution could be so given to an individual. If this be so, then the mere command of a superior, allegedly our master in wisdom and insight as well as power, does not acquit us from the duty of considering for ourselves whether on any count the use of thermo-nuclear weapons of war is justified. We must ask ourselves as individuals whether any necessity into which it is alleged our civilization may come, warrants us in unleashing on mankind the horrors of a nuclear holocaust with its consequences to generations unborn only remotely measurable.

I end deliberately on this personal note; for although the issue with which we are concerned belongs to the domain of politics, it also belongs to that of personal morality. If we deny that it does belong to the domain of personal morality, if we refuse to allow that it does, then let us admit openly that we are neither democrat nor Christian. The democrat is the man who goes on asking awkward questions; the Christian is always in the end the man who will obey God rather than man, who acknowledges the transcendent authority of a kingdom which is not of this world. In the crucifixion as the fourth evangelist describes it we are faced with something which is supremely ironic as well as catastrophic. Caiaphas, the spokesman of ecclesiastical statesmen all down the ages, advises that one man shall die for all the people, and, continuing the spirit of his own statesmanship, the crowd whom he has bent to his will cries that it knows no king but Caesar. So today those who speak of Christian culture and Christian civilization, of our western way of life, etc., acknowledge no authority other than that of the framework which seems to them to preserve the civilization, the culture, the way of life they identify with Christian reality. Caiaphas in his supreme hour showed himself powerless to distinguish the substance of the Jewish inheritance from a particular stabilization of the situation of the Jewish state. We must, if we are Christians, be careful we do not confuse the substance and core of Christian fidelity with the forms in which we have received the same. What we believe is something which demands not that we shall cast all scruples to the wind in concern to preserve its outward embodiment; rather it is something that bids us fearlessly seek, in situations relatively novel in the demands they make upon us, new ways of fidelity to the order of Christ.

But you may well ask what this amounts to in practice. It is before all else a plea that Christians in considering these issues should be governed not by the dictates of the political tradition that they may have inherited or by the commonplaces of political analysis. They must look at what they are asked to do almost naïvely, not pretending by resource to some elaborate system of political concepts that it is other than it is. What we are being asked is in fact to say yes or no to the use of certain weapons in certain admittedly extreme situations. We pretend to ourselves that what we are being asked to discuss is whether or not a particular context for carrying on international discussion shall be maintained. We may pretend to ourselves that when we speak of thermo-nuclear weapons, we are not speaking of weapons at all but of threats which determine and compel men to converse with each other. There is, of course, a partial validity in the balance of terror as an analysis of the present state of international relations; but it is only a partial validity; for the balance of terror is maintained by weapons which in the last resort are instruments that men are prepared to use. The whole system collapses as soon as that readiness is written off.

The individual therefore has to ask himself whether he is ready, whether he believes himself morally justified in acquiescing in the use of these things. If he says no, then he must himself find his own way of making his protest effective.

One concluding note. None who have had any measure of responsibility for the pastoral care of young people can remain oblivious of the extent to which these issues press upon the minds of the most sensitive.[1] If, instead of deploring the alleged moral breakdown of the age in which we live in the field of sexual morality, our mentors would begin to comment on the psychological climate created by the suggestion that we must accept as morally justifiable the obliteration of the world we know, the climate *could* become a good deal healthier. We have to reckon with the wide dissemination of a kind of facile determinism which denounces the spirit of protest as a moral Luddism—a turning-back of the clock. But the spirit of protest is not Luddite, it is not a blind reaction to what cannot be removed from the human scene. It is the voice of those who insist that human affairs shall be humanly conducted; it is expressive of a temper at once humanist and Christian, which refuses to acquiesce in what we are told cannot be otherwise than it is, because that in which we are bidden to acquiesce is something which men have fashioned. *And what men have fashioned, men can change.* If this essay has any single integrating theme, it is a desire to bear witness to the truth, that we are not the slaves of what we have made but are able, if we have the courage, to turn what threatens us with a moral bondage corrupting the very substance of our being into something utterly different. We are so able if, individually, we refuse to be imprisoned mentally in an apparatus of abstraction, which would conceal from us our human obligations in a carefully woven texture of hardly analysable notions.

[1] This point emerged very clearly in the discussions following the presentation of this essay as a Westcott House (Cambridge) Clergy School lecture. On the lecturer, who has no such responsibility, the evident concern of those who had, made a great impression.

Part III

METAPHYSICS AND EPISTEMOLOGY

METAPHYSICAL AND RELIGIOUS LANGUAGE

PROFESSOR WISDOM has often remarked that contemporary philosophical discussions are only superficially different from those which we now call classical; that although we may often concern ourselves with the way words or sentences work, what we are really discussing are the old riddles of materialism versus idealism and the rest. The methods have greatly changed; but the questions are the same even though the new methods help us sometimes to throw light on the peculiar nature of the problems which beset us.

The phrase "metaphysical language" shows that in this paper there is an acceptance in principle of the new way of proceeding. But the problem which the phrase suggests is an old one, older even than Kant, who left us with one discussion of the issue which can properly be called classical; the discriminating reader can find the issue canvassed in the great schoolmen and their successors, and may even be led to seek its statement in Aristotle, if he has not himself already found it in Plato. If at the outset I speak of Kant, it is not because he is the earliest in time to raise these issues; it is rather because I find in his statement of them something which I would wish to call to notice before advancing further. I do this because in some of Kant's language, treated by the metaphysically curious rather than by the Kantian scholar there is much which may help to a proper definition of the problem of metaphysical language.

Kant's doctrine, of course, is in many respects *vieux jeu*; yet for all that he maintains a certain hold upon his readers, in as much as he raised problems that are with us to this present. He stated them in terms of a logical doctrine that few if any accept, and yet he brought out in an unforgettable way what I would call the metaphysical crux. Professor Wisdom has said that in the philosopher the logician melts into the poet; and although at first sight nothing less poetic than Kant's style can easily be imagined, it may be rewarding to seek hints of *vision* of men's situation revealed by the severity of his architectonic. We all know how many teachers of philosophy in expounding Kant have had occasion to speak of his judgment that it is futile for us to use "the concepts of the understanding" to scale the heights of the unconditioned. If we are self-conscious about this language, what do we notice? Are we not attributing to Kant a model of the human intellectual situation of a rather peculiar sort? We speak of concepts; we are of course thinking of Kant's doctrine of categories, perhaps recalling his suggestion that when we try to attain knowledge of the unconditioned, what we are doing is to abuse elements of our intellectual endowment. The impulse to use such language in clarifying the obscurities of Kant's meaning is almost irresistible; and perhaps if we make our own what our effort of clarification implies, we find it suggests the model of a man who has tools for one job but who somehow finds himself compelled to use those tools for a job which they simply will not do. If the impulse is inevitable, the failure is equally so. For Kant we can, in virtue of the spontaneous activity of our understanding, make the world of sense intelligible; but if we try to use (note the inevitability of that verb) the concepts of that understanding to reveal to us the reasons why there should be a world for us to understand, we abuse (again note the verb) the very character of those concepts themselves.

All this is familiar; but what I want to do is to deepen our self-consciousness about the Kantian model. Although Kant cannot be called a pragmatist, those who try to expound him find themselves speaking of concepts as tools, which will do one job and not another. Going further, the vision with which at least part of Kant's first Critique leaves us is of a man desperately trying to scale mountains with ropes which will only serve on the foothills. For when he is on the foothills, the Kantian man is dealing only with what is conditioned; but it is the summits, the unconditioned with which he is most deeply concerned. ("Most deeply?" : there again languages moves to the metaphorical.)

Perhaps others who re-read Kant in the light of Wisdom do not have this experience in respect of his doctrine. Yet increasingly it would seem one of the things which gives Kant a permanent hold on his readers is his insight into the persistence of the metaphysical pursuit and some of the obstacles that stand in the way of the completion of the chase.

Obstacles; chase. The metaphor is as plain there as when I spoke before of the scaling of mountains and the rest. Perhaps in the end the attempt to describe the impossibility of metaphysics must always involve the use of metaphor; it is not only the metaphysician who bends language to new uses, but the meta-metaphysician also. The latter sees the folly of the metaphysician's project, and he makes the definition of that folly a matter of logic. We cannot use the concepts of the understanding to scale the heights of the unconditioned, to see ourselves as we *really* are *sub specie æternitatis*. Whatever sort of "cannot" that may be, it remains a statement of the essence of Kant's critique. But what is sometimes ignored is that the sort of meta-metaphysics which Kant offers is itself a metaphysics. You may call it a psycho-metaphysics, as Professor Ryle did; but it has the curious poetic character of metaphysics all the same.[1] If you try to guess its inwardness, you have to forego your critical knowledge of his architectonic and try to see him as the scholastics who criticized him saw him. They saw that he raised a problem which by the dexterous use of Aristotelian analogy they had tried to by-pass. Being, they claimed, was an analogically participated transcendental. And therefore when one had set one's concept full-square on the scale of being, if one did not know where one was with it, at least one could use one's very ignorance as a ground of assertion. To marry the principle of the Aristotelian doctrine of categories to the exposition of the relations of man to God was an intellectual achievement of the highest order.

The analogy of the scholastics was fundamentally ontological.

---

[1] I am quite aware that in the above I have not paid the proper attention to Kant's view of the regulative use of the Ideas.

That is a commonplace of the text books. The modern reader therefore who goes to the schoolmen to find in their doctrine an answer to his peculiar problems is often rewarded and disappointed at the same time. He recognizes the strength of an experiment (note that word) which seeks to avoid the twin perils of anthropomorphism and agnosticism in respect of metaphysical speech. This does indeed seem a brilliant definition of our actual intellectual experience when we hazard speech concerning God, freedom and immortality. We know we don't mean by God a super-designer, a super-architect, a super-what-you-will; we know that by human freedom we mean something that a mere description of the difference between spontaneous and forced action will not quite catch; and again by immortality we mean a continuance that cannot be interpreted simply in terms of the prolongation of life as we know it. Just as Socrates in the *Republic* was clear that whatever else the Idea of the Good was it was not pleasure; so we know what we don't mean even if we can't catch what we do. We are agnostics before we ever dare to make any kind of positive assertion, let alone advance any positive argument. When the schoolmen insist that agnosticism comes before anthropomorphism, we are with them all the time. But, alas, their device for allowing assertion on the basis of negation demands assumptions that we cannot make. For we have to admit in knowledge a kind of intuitive awareness of analogically participated being which we do not seem to have.

The schoolmen admit a critical problem where speech concerning the ultimate is concerned. By what authority do we describe God in these terms or in those terms? It was Aquinas himself who insisted that of God we knew that he was, what he was not and what relation everything else had to him. It was a modern Thomist who spoke of the ways in which we name God as like the runways of the Clyde which issue ships on the ocean. The ways in which we speak of God issue us out on what Boethius called the ocean of his being; but whereas the runways of a Clyde contain the waters of the ocean at high tide, our names, and I suppose the thought which on a traditional view somehow corresponds with them, contain nothing of that which they name; they are runways and nothing more. No one could deny that this language, however metaphorical, states a critical problem. But suppose one has already raised a critical problem at what one may call a lower level. Suppose one has felt the sort of difficulties Hume and Kant experienced concerning such notions as substance and cause; suppose further one has given the sort of solution to those difficulties which Kant gave in terms of his theory of the co-operation of sense and understanding in objective knowledge, according to which such categories as substance and cause become concepts of the way in which a discursive understanding necessarily spells out the order of experience. It is Kant's theory of the *a priori* which contains in germ the whole of his meta-metaphysics, his whole description of the nature of metaphysical curiosity. Thus a modern theologian, Professor Paul Tillich, is right in speaking of Kant's doctrine of categories as a doctrine of human finitude. So far from being a rationalistic justification of a claim to intuitive penetration behind the veil of sense, it is rather an attempt to set out the peculiarly limited character of human knowledge. Done once for all, it naturally invites the mistrust of those who see that the philosophical clarification of a concept is not something which can ever be done finally any more than the work of the psycho-analyst is something which can be set out in a few sentences. The Analytic and the Dialectic in Kant's first Critique have to be unpacked, and the arguments set out in a different style if the modern reader is to see the continuing worth of what the author was doing, the peculiar way in which he distinguishes the metaphysical from the ordinary use of concepts, even the lessons he would teach by his very using the word "use". Suppose there is an unbridgeable chasm between ordinary everyday description and the technical language of exact science, on the one hand, and the way we speak when we try to answer questions concerning our origin, our nature and our hope, when the word "ultimate" has been inserted before the last three nouns. Kant thought there was, and he believed moreover that this difference stood whether the metaphysical question was answered in the style of Haeckel and Marx or in that of Aquinas and of Hegel. The violation in principle was the same. In the end Kant leaves us with the sort of model of the metaphysically minded which I have tried earlier in this paper to sketch. Of course in his writings his criticism of metaphysics simply prepares the way for his assertion of the primacy of the practical reason. But even those who cannot follow him here can learn something from the exhaustiveness of the way in which he delineates the plight of those who try to use the tools of ordinary empirical knowledge for opening the doors on the unconditioned. By his analysis of *a priori* knowledge he anticipated in a different style much that is commonplace to-day. Any reader of Wittgenstein's *Tractatus*, for all the difference of inspiration, receives continual reminders of the Kantian distinction of the form and matter of knowledge, from which the critique of metaphysics inevitably springs.[1]

It is, of course, the character of metaphysics as somehow satisfying the urge for seeing things as they are which makes the metaphysical claim the enemy of scientific progress. For if we claim intuitively to see things as they are, we are unwilling to give proper attention to those who bid us revise our assumptions, change our frames of reference and so on. We have an almost classical example of this sort of obscurantism in the refusal of certain realist philosophers in Britain to admit the very possibility of non-euclidean geometry. The refusal was grounded in the end in what I can only call a metaphysics of knowledge, which in the use made of it brought out, with exemplary clarity, the sort of tyranny that metaphysical conviction can exert over the proper assimilation of new insights concerning the ways of human knowing. "Concern about the ultimate" may be a perennial factor in human life. It may even sometimes be a stimulant of scientific progress; but it may easily lend its authority to canonizing as dogma some particular systematization of human knowledge. Those who gave a kind of canonical finality to Newton's view of the universe forgot the simple historical fact that such a view was once anything but self-evident! The impulse to avoid the peculiar critical experience is strong in most of us; it can easily pervert "our concern with the ultimate" into a false acceptance as final truth of that

[1] Cf. Prof. R. B. Braithwaite's Hertz Lecture.

which in its nature is inevitably impermanent and relative. No doubt Kant took Newton's physics as a last word; no doubt too he was stupid to the point of perversity in the detail of his doctrine of categories. But he saw for all that the sort of job that categories do in human thinking, and the sort of obstacles that the inescapably categorial character of human thinking put in the way of metaphysical confidence. Whether we try to use our categories as ladders to scale the heights of heaven, or deify as metaphysical finality the cosmology of a particular age, we are dodging the critical problem, turning aside from the description of our actual intellectual situation.

But what of meta-metaphysics? It has the task usually of showing the invalidity of metaphysical assertion, of revealing the type-shift involved in arguing about the transcendent, or in converting a principle of method into a description of the ultimate nature of things. Whether the style which the meta-metaphysician embraces has the psychological ring Kant's has, or whether it may be inspired by a delicate sensitivity to the workings of language, in the end the point made is the same:— the invalidity of the leap from relative to ultimate. Yet there remains the whole series of attempts which men have made to catch the sense of their world, attempts made by poets and seers as well as by metaphysicians. There remain too the efforts made by those who were certainly not scholastic in their inspiration to set out the logic of the leap, and to vindicate the peculiar way the words work by which the leap is made, even sometimes to provide criteria whereby one can sort out, even at these levels, the valid from the invalid.

I mention the poets; sometimes, as Professor Wisdom has said, and indeed borne out by his own practice, the philosopher must play the poet, and this of course not only, as I had implied, in his speculative moments, but even in the style of his criticism. Certainly the metaphysician's use of words has something of the poet's boldness, even if his justification is of a different order. For it has been a common feature in the practice of metaphysicians to claim tight logical grounds for what they say, to set out arguments in the form of syllogism, or inductive inference. Metaphysics has often simulated the style of a logical system; criticism of metaphysics has often followed revolutions in logic, in the understanding of logical truth. And this is as true in its way of Kant as of Wittgenstein.

Suppose, however, one does try to free metaphysics from enslavement to the sum of its traditional models. Take for instance the so-called causal argument for the existence of God. As we have traditionally received it, this argument depends on an intuitive grasp of the principles of being, the sort of intuition I spoke of before in this paper. Granted that we do possess the capacity of such insight, one can state the argument in the form of syllogism. But have we such capacity? Can we gain such insight, or make it our own by framing it in an intelligible sentence? But even supposing one can frame the principle on which the argument hangs, how can one justify what one says as more than the expression of a mood? That men have seen, have written of things as pointing beyond themselves (and the writing is perhaps the seeing), no one would deny; but what of the claims made for such supposed insight, for the logical powers of the expressions in which it becomes articulate? Does not metaphysics sometimes emerge as the attempt to convert poetry into the logically admissible? If one starts from a critical position, one can see the metaphysician's enterprise as almost an attempt to destroy poetry by converting it into syllogism, or into quasi-science of fact, to destroy even as the claim is extended to the point of maintaining that here we reach the ultimate.

Yet the issue of attaching the unfamiliar vision to the familiar description remains; the attachment of the strange to the usual, of the final to the relative. Few of us find it easy to accept the principle on which the doctrine of the analogy of being depends, that is the conception of being as an analogically participated transcendental; yet we may be thankful for the statement of this doctrine as revealing something of what the problem of metaphysics is. We may even in certain moods envy those who can accept analogy as men who have at their disposal a supremely effective device for reconciling the logic of the familiar with that of the unfamiliar. The close understanding of the gulf between ordinary and transcendent description which we owe to Kant and his successors prohibits our acceptance of what scholastic analogy promises, and leaves us with the problem of the relation of settleable and unsettleable questions.

But why bother about such a problem? Why not simply dismiss metaphysics as illusion, or else follow Collingwood in substituting for metaphysics the uncovering of the fundamental assumptions of our age? Why bother that people have written this sort of elusive nonsense? Lay bare the fault, the confusion that lies at the heart of the enterprise, and there is an end of the matter. Why is there a problem of the possibility of metaphysics? As soon as the meta-metaphysician has done his work, is not the impulse gone? The trouble is that it remains somehow incorrigibly active. The best meta-metaphysicians have always seen this, and have therefore written works that seem themselves to have a certain metaphysical flavour. I tried to bring this out where Kant was concerned by a deliberate choice of metaphorical language when I spoke about him. Had I gone on to deal with his ethics, which to some extent play the role of metaphysics in his developed system, I would undoubtedly have become more metaphorical still.

Perhaps to some people, it is in the domain of ethics that the impulse to continue using seemingly nonsensical language is most persistent. For after all the moralist has somehow to do justice to what he learns of human life from writers like Tolstoy and Dostoevsky, George Eliot and Joseph Conrad; his theorizing is impoverished if he ignores the dimensions of human experience to which such writers admit him. It is only if we remember these things that we can begin to understand the impulse that lies behind what the intuitionists are trying to say in their controversy with the utilitarians, a controversy which incidentally John Stuart Mill seems to have understood better than almost any one else before or after. The utilitarians are fully justified in bringing the charge they do against the intuitionists, of seeming to favour appeal in moral questions to some mysterious faculty of insight into the supra-sensible as against their own reliance on observed consequences. Certainly the utilitarians had every ground for mistrusting the intuitionists' claim to know transcendent principles of obligation; such claims to knowledge can easily be used to bolster superstition of every sort, as for instance the thesis that pain ennobles. The appeal to fact in ethics is often a liberation from bondage.

Yet others than Mill have turned aside from the construction of all principles of conduct into the utilitarian model. The attempt, as Butler had seen, inevitably distorted the actual situation of human beings, by blurring irreducible differences between various sorts of human relationships. Utilitarians can easily completely misrepresent the distinction between public and private obligations. There is a vital distinction between a diffused concern for human welfare as such and the sort of situations which arise at the more intimate levels of human existence.

It is to the intuitionists that we owe this insistence on the plurality of our obligations. Yet to set out their deep perception they have often relied on a sheerly vicious epistemology. Regularly we find them writing as if moral insight consisted in a grasp of the axioms of moral space; a model in every way intolerable, not simply by reason of the ignorance of modern geometry which it displays! But for all that the intuitionists have brought out the complexity of what we mean by morality, that it is not something which can be contained in a simple formula.

I have referred to this familiar controversy, because one can surely discern a certain parallel between what is said here about ethics, and what I have said above about metaphysics. The intuitionist is a sort of ethical metaphysician; he insists that the principles of conduct cannot be set out as if their sole sanction could be found in the observable consequences of behaviour. He does his job clumsily; the novelists really do it better. But they are not philosophers any more than the poets are; and if their insights are to be given systematic form, it must be for the philosophers to attempt the task.

It is as if there were both in the realms of understanding and of conduct a circle within which what one said and what one intended was perfectly clear and intelligible. Yet whether one thinks about being or about conduct, whether one tries to represent one's world or the conduct of individuals, to confine oneself within this circle is to omit what is only left out at the risk of a deep impoverishment. (Note the metaphorical language.) But of course when the philosopher tries to make good such impoverishment, he is always tempted to trace out schemes of pseudo-explanation or to evoke the perilous mythology of a faculty of intuition. He is also tempted to belittle, if only by the lack of time which he gives to them, the work of the physicists and the work of the psychologist. In love with the phantom of an ultimate explanation, the metaphysically minded philosopher is quite careless about scientific explanations and their logic.

But this paper bears the title of metaphysical and religious language. So far I have been concerned with some sort of examination of metaphysical language. What of religious? I hope I may be forgiven if in this second part of the paper I confine myself to Christian religious language. I can, I think, plead in extenuation the fact that the very concept of metaphysics, that besets the consciousness of those concerned with its possibility, is one that owes something to the interplay of religion and metaphysics in the Christian tradition.

The metaphysical language with which we have been concerned is one which often suggests to the modern philosopher explanation beyond explanation, insights revealing realms of relationship beyond the obvious. But characteristically religious language, the language of prayer and liturgy, does not purport to be descriptive or explanatory in the way in which some metaphysical language certainly sets out to be; it might indeed be said that liturgical language provides the philosophical student with some truly classical examples of what Professor Austin has called its performatory use. Of course religious language is often suffused by the language of metaphysics; for no religion easily survives without a theology and theology is almost inevitably drawn to the style of metaphysics (even when it is also concerned, as Christianity has been, to establish some sort of relation with history). Yet within theology itself in the Christian tradition, the relations of theological and metaphysical language provide a continuing focus of controversy; I suppose that the historian of dogma might find a classical instance of this in the controversies associated with the name of Athanasius; yet the theme is an everlastingly recurrent feature of Christian history. It was no doubt to some aspect of this story that Whitehead wished to call his readers' attention when he spoke of Christianity as a religion perennially in search of a metaphysic.

Religious and metaphysical language; the contrast is less familiar than that of metaphysical and scientific language, or of metaphysical language and the flexible universe of ordinary discourse. Yet the contrast of styles is illuminating, whether one confines one's self to theological language in the abstract, or studies that language in relation to the total symbolic expression of a great religious tradition such as Christianity. I have mentioned the language of liturgy and prayer; it remains true, however, that one of the formative literary expressions of Christianity is the four Gospels. It is a commonplace of modern New Testament scholarship to insist on the uniqueness of the Gospel form; it is also becoming a commonplace to see in the Gospel of John a crucial attempt to find a language capable of fusing that of the historian, the metaphysician and the mystic. I am aware that this is inaccurately said; perhaps I should have said the poet rather than the mystic. But if I used the latter word, it was because I wanted to bring out the essentially religious character of the author's achievement. Certainly by the peculiar interplay of factual description and metaphysical meditation, characteristic of his work, John has offered to my mind a decisive presentation of the intellectual problem at the heart of the Christian religion.[1]

There is a very important sense in which the peculiar problem of metaphysical language is a different problem from that of religious language; but the two are intimately related for us because of the actual history of our culture and the impact of theology on metaphysics in the Middle Ages.[2] Very often what gives the metaphysical problem the flavour it has for us is this background of history. The very images which

[1] All this is very baldly said; but other essays in this book together with work in preparation may go some way towards explaining my meaning. May I simply for the present insist that progress in the study of religious language can only come by the most detailed attention to its classical expressions?

[2] Compare the important writings of M. Etienne Gilson.

attend our representation of the problem to ourselves are partly religious; I mean the sort of vague pictures that attend our frustrated demand for the sense of our existence. No one would easily admit the relevance of those images to what we are asking; but none can deny their power. What is this penumbra[1] of human life and existence that we try to catch; is not this reality that we try vainly to attach to the familiar in some sense a religious reality? Sometimes too the language we use to represent the futility of our speculative efforts to scale the heights of the unconditioned recalls that of the mystics who have spoken of the dark night.

So religious are our metaphysical bewilderments that we are at first sight shocked by recognition of a possible antagonism between metaphysics and religion. In Kant ethics and religion are *almost* identified; yet that philosopher's confidence in discarding the scheme of analogy, sprang in a way from a conviction that he was liberating the essence of religion from a false entanglement with metaphysics. Those who have followed the history of theology in the nineteenth century will remember that the antispeculative influence of Kant persisted in European Protestantism as a vital counter-poise to the influence of Hegel; and that in Britain at the beginning of the twentieth century, it was Kant who enabled Peter Taylor Forsyth to shape his remarkable essays in Christology. I suspect that from the use which Forsyth made of it, we can learn much of the inwardness of Kant's criticism of metaphysics.

The criticisms levelled (however unfairly)[2] by theologians like Forsyth at Hegel are in the end criticisms of an attempt to subdue the Christian religion under the sovereignty of metaphysics. The study of the Christian protest against the Hegelian philosophy of religion, is one which throws a bright light on the claim of religious language to be something other than a mere chapter of metaphysics. The argument served men like Forsyth and Kierkegaard with their opportunity to lay bare in new

[1] I owe the impulse to use this word here to the use it has been given by Professor Wisdom; I am not suggesting that I am using it in quite the same way.

[2] Any serious student of philosophy must be deeply grateful for the work on Hegel at present being done in France by men like M. Hyppolite, and M. Jean Wahl.

ways, private to them both, that peculiar uniqueness in the language of the Christian religion which in the beginning, the Gospel form tried to catch, and in the traditions of Catholicism, the pattern of liturgy to express in the language of prayer.

Even those who reject Dr Karl Popper's interpretation of Hegel may be interested to notice the way in which in *The Open Society*[1] he quotes from Karl Barth's *Credo*.[2] He obviously finds in that most deeply anti-metaphysical of modern theologians something that appeals to him. Primarily, of course, it is Barth's unwillingness to treat historical development as if it were a kind of moral and spiritual authority which Popper enthusiastically welcomes. But Popper also makes clear that what he welcomes in Barth is not simply the latter's sense that the horizon of the future is incapable of determination by metaphysical speculation; he also seems to appreciate the grounds Barth offers for his agnosticism concerning the meaning of human history, namely his emphases on the cruciality of the particular figure of Jesus.

There is no doubt that Popper's quotation of Barth possesses a deep significance. It shows how a philosopher of strongly empirical bias can discern and welcome the element of positivism undoubtedly present in that theologian. Indeed any theologian who stresses as Barth does the ultimate particularity of Jesus and who claims to find in him and not in the gropings of speculation the ultimate sanction and direction of his thought, might have an equal attraction for someone like Popper, and for the same reason.

There is of necessity a continual shift and interplay between what we call metaphysics, and religion and theology. The laws governing the languages of religion and theology are not quite like those, if such there be, which govern impulses of metaphysical speculation. Indeed it is one of the ends of this paper, to bring out with the aid of historical allusions, how very different they are. Yet more than the mere fact of their inter-

---

[1] *The Open Society*, Vol. 2, pp. 259f.

[2] I do not forget either Barth's debt to Anselm or his eagerness to use the traditional ontology of substance, etc. in Christology. See e.g. K. D., IV, 2.

play makes the philosopher judge the problem which they both raise to be that of their validity.

The differences are crucial; it is, I think, of real importance for the philosopher to bring out those differences. Detailed description can undoubtedly rid us of some besetting confusions; it is certainly a necessary prolegomenon to an informed judgment on the claims of these sorts of language. But where description passes into justification I am not at present clear

JOHN WISDOM'S
PARADOX AND DISCOVERY[1]

I T WAS on a Sunday in November 1935, after I had
finished Greats at Oxford and was spending a fourth year
reading the Honour School of Theology, that one of my
former tutors in philosophy (Mr, now Sir, Isaiah Berlin) took
me to the Philosophical Society to hear John Wisdom give a
paper on Moore and Wittgenstein. In the intervening thirty
years, I have heard him on many occasions lecture or give
papers, and I have also enjoyed private discussion with him.
Yet, as I prepared my appraisal of this book, I found myself
recalling that first encounter, and the subject of the paper which
Wisdom gave on that occasion; for, if one has to mention the
two philosophers who have most influenced him, and to whose
ideas and teaching he most constantly refers, one has to name
the two contrasting twentieth century Cambridge giants. Yet it
would be a mistake to see in Professor Wisdom's work no more
than a continuation of the ideas of these two men; no one can
study the papers in this collection carefully, without becoming
aware that Professor Wisdom has made, and is making, his own
most important and original contribution to the development of
analytic philosophy. He is a highly original and subtle thinker,
who has experienced in different ways the impact of the work of
two men of genius; I had almost said three; for anyone familiar
at all with Moore's work, especially the writings and lectures
published posthumously, will know how much space in papers,
and time in lectures, he devoted to the discussion of Russell's ideas.

In considering this collection of papers, we may therefore
begin appropriately with the short, very perceptive study of
Moore, reprinted from *Analysis*, 1959 (pp. 82ff.). In this paper

[1] Blackwell, 1965.

Wisdom rightly stresses Moore's pervasive concern with questions of truth and falsity, his interest in what there is, and his consequent readiness to find, for example, the suggestion which he took very seriously in the form in which he found it in the writings of Russell's middle period, that material things were to be regarded as *logical* fictions, tainted with the implication of McTaggart's belief that they *were* fictions, in the sense that Gorgons and Harpies were, and as such no part of the furniture of the world. In the present volume, this paper on Moore is followed by a brief account of Wittgenstein's teaching in Cambridge between 1934 and 1937, written four years earlier, which fastens on the crucial importance of Wittgenstein's contention that we are obsessed by the habit of supposing the meaning of a word to be an object, and in consequence are impatient of the sheer hard work involved in understanding a word or expression, by mastering its role or use. Wisdom's work in this volume shows how deeply he has made his own this emancipating insight of Wittgenstein's, and how, in consequence, he is continually alert to the perilous consequences of asking questions aimed at establishing the *essential* nature, for example, of discovery concerning matters of fact, as if there were not a whole multitude of different procedures involved in factual investigation on different occasions, which we must acknowledge as valid in the appropriate context, refusing to fetter the flexibility of our understanding by acceptance of a definition endowed with sovereign authority. Yet, for all his indebtedness to Wittgenstein, Wisdom is alert, in ways in which some writers, for example Mr D. Z. Phillips in his recent, very interesting book, *The Concept of Prayer*,[1] manifestly are not, to the crucial importance for the philosopher of reckoning with what does and with what does not exist. Thus, in the valuable essay on religious belief, which is, in fact, a consideration of certain tendencies exemplified in recent writings on the philosophy of religion, including the Eddington Lecture delivered in 1955 by his colleague in Cambridge, Professor R. B. Braithwaite, Wisdom emphasizes, against the view that the function of religious statements is to persuade us towards, or to encourage

[1] Routledge and Kegan Paul, 1966.

us in, a form of action, his conviction that they are concerned with what is the case: "the words—'in my Father's house are many mansions: if it were not so I would have told you'—say something as to what is so" (p. 56). In lectures given in Cambridge in 1933–4, and recently published in a volume of his lectures on philosophy (edited by Dr Casimir Lewy), and indeed elsewhere in his writings, Moore denied that "there is any good reason for thinking that God exists".[1] Yet, to deny that God exists is to insist that a total inventory of what there is (if such could be compiled) would be complete without mention of him. The denial that God exists is expressive of the conviction that here is something to be denied, to be excluded from the totality of what there is, and this because, in saying that he does exist, a factual claim is being made, which it is of the highest importance to reject absolutely. Wisdom is too much in debt to the ruthlessly honest meticulous realism of Moore to be bamboozled by a view (encouraged by a *superficial* adoption of some of Wittgenstein's styles[2]), that religious belief has nothing to do with what is the case. If he has learnt the importance of flexibility in understanding what we think and say from Wittgenstein, he has also retained from Moore a healthy alertness to the depth of the distinction between what there is, and what there is not.

But what of Wisdom's own work? The most distinguished single essay in the volume is, in my judgment, the Howison Lecture, which gives the whole book its title. In it Wisdom discusses, with a wealth of insight and subtlety, the kind of information about the world we may win through attention to the paradoxical; for instance to Eddington's famous remark concerning the two desks in his room, or to the claim that a man may leave London Airport at 10 and reach New York at 10 to 10. It is with the enlargement of understanding and, in fact, the increase in knowledge won through such paradoxes (and Wisdom mentions also Einstein), and through the analogous paradoxes of philosophers who insist that, for example, we

---

[1] *Lectures on Philosophy*, Allen and Unwin, 1966, p. 194.

[2] But contrast the interpretation of Wittgenstein by Professor Norman Malcolm to be found in his *Knowledge and Certainty*, Prentice-Hall, 1963, pp. 96–129.

never know what is going on in the mind of another person, that he is occupied in this essay. It is with the value of "eccentric boundary breaking, or near boundary breaking statements" that he is engaged, seeing, as also in the British Academy Lecture, "Metamorphosis of Metaphysics", the philosopher as a man who first initiates violent eccentricity of statement by the proposal of what seems to violate all canons of commonsense plausibility in saying, for example, that mathematical equations say nothing, and who then goes on to lay hold of the advance in understanding which may issue from the paradox he has proposed. What does come in time is a deepened grasp of the ways in which, in different fields, one thing may be accounted ground or evidence for another. A painstaking attention to the logic of the individual case delivers the industrious from the bondage in which, for instance, the logic textbooks may bind him fast, and awaken him to a more synoptic, more detailed, more deeply civilized view of the ways in which human knowledge is advanced, and human life lived.

One of Wisdom's greatest strengths as a philosopher lies in his remarkable capacity for effective illustration, e.g. in the way in which he draws on the resources of a genuine literary culture. It is not for nothing that, in the British Academy Lecture, he asks the rhetorical question whether it is not Flaubert, Dostoevsky, Kafka, Lawrence, and Freud, much more than Aristotle, Descartes, Hume, and Kant, who "travel to the bounds of human experience" (p. 59). It is to the former, not the latter, that we owe tidings less concerned with what lies beyond human experience, than with the unnoticed, unacknowledged heights and depths of that experience in some of its most familiar, even commonplace, forms. Yet, for all this sensitivity to the limitations of the philosopher, it is clear testimony and argument of these papers that he has an indispensable role.

Wisdom often seems to identify the work of the metaphysician with an enlarged, even transformed epistemology; like Moore, to whom he owes so much, and of whom he writes so wisely, it is with knowledge and belief concerning what there is, that Wisdom sees the philosopher obsessively concerned, and this is because the philosopher wants to know what there is. A not infrequently remarked feature of contemporary philosophy is the curious echoing of idealist styles of thought among those who have become intoxicated by the insistence that in seeking to understand an expression, we should ask not for its meaning, but for its use. I do not use the term "idealist" here to indicate, for example: uncertainty as to whether or not material things are part of the ultimate furniture of the world; I use it rather to indicate an attitude which treats human experience as in some sense autonomous, as finding, sooner or later, its own justification for all its manifold forms. Wisdom may seem sometimes to encourage such tendencies; but it is not only in the excellent papers in this volume on the philosophy of religion that he also guards against them. Throughout the book we are aware of how much he has learnt from Moore of the philosopher's duty to be concerned with what is the case, and what we can properly say to be the case. To say this is not, of course, to suggest that such concern is absent from Wittgenstein's later work; it is not,[1] but a careless reading of, for example, some of the things he says concerning mathematical discovery and invention, may go some way to encourage such tendencies among lesser men. The subtlety of Wisdom's work lies in its sustained attempt to combine the insight born of alertness, to the rich diversity of human experience and the overwhelming significance of the unique, particular case, with an overall faithfulness to the importance of the distinction between what is and what is not the case. If he sometimes fails, this does not detract in the least from the importance of what he is trying to do. At the end of this discussion, I shall offer, after two fairly fundamental criticisms, a suggestion of the way the enterprise on which he is engaged might be taken further. But first I wish to make some detailed references to some of the matters discussed, and some of the issues raised in this fascinating book.

The book contains much material highly relevant, not only to the philosopher of religion, but also to the theologian. Paradox is effectively illustrated by the moral teaching of Jesus, for example, by his simultaneous affirmation and abrogation of the distinction between the lustful glance, and the act of adultery.

[1] Again cf. Malcolm, *op. cit.*

The value of the parabolic is stressed. The Howison Lecture contains a passage on Christology (p. 124). Again, he has much to say of great value on the subject of guilt and atonement; he is too well read in European literature, and too much aware of the realities of human life, to treat the sombre issues of moral guilt lightly. Freud, who is among his intellectual masters, is the pessimistic Freud, as the concluding sentence of his somewhat uncertain, yet by no means entirely ineffective, essay on tolerance bears witness (p. 147). In the paper on free will, he sheds some light on a continuing morass by suggesting that in the language, for instance, of the convinced determinist, we have to reckon with the presence of a metaphysical paradox, which compels us to deeper insight by obliterating distinctions between the action of the man who surrenders the money in his keeping because he feels the pressure of a gun at his back, the action of the girl who chooses her marriage partner or who elects to stay at home to care for her mother under pressure of conscious or unconscious emotional blackmail, and the action of the man who throws up his livelihood in the city and trains as a male nurse. He makes us see the dark underside of human motivation, the presence of unacknowledged compulsions in the nonchalance of the morally heroic as well as in the subtle, undeviated insistence on his own way of the obvious neurotic. Yet self-knowledge advanced by such comparisons does not issue in self-exculpation. We may continually revise our image of an ultimate tribunal; but we almost plead for one, and in Wisdom's view we characterize it thus: "But though we do make and need to make limited judgments, we need again and again to call to mind how different they are from the divine judgment in which both easy forgiveness and easy condemnation are impossible. This is the judgment we ask for ourselves. For we ask that at our own trial counsel and judge shall proceed with infinite patience. We ask that they shall not judge a part of the picture without seeing the whole. We ask that they shall consider, ruthlessly but with understanding, circumstances beyond circumstances, wheel within wheel" (p. 33).

One could wish that in this difficult, but searching essay, he had gone on to point out the extent to which, for instance, in the theology of the fourth Gospel, the judgment which he claims men seek is accomplished in the Passion of Christ; in the great scene of *Ecce Homo* the world is judged by the Son of Man condemned, and forced, in his supreme hour, to wear the robes of mock royalty.[1] It is Christ's objectively achieved atonement which, in the Christian vision, suffuses human actions with their truth by giving them their context in his endurance, by allowing them to find their firm foundation in his overcoming of the gulf between the claims of pity, and the claims of justice, of pity for others and justice towards others, or pity towards ourselves and justice towards ourselves. For, as Wisdom points out in his essay on tolerance, we are not ready for the school of charity and tolerance, unless there is something in ourselves and our activities, for which we deeply care.

Where religious belief is concerned, I have already stressed Wisdom's anxiety to maintain its factual import, but he has much else to say about it which is illuminating; for instance, the stress on the believer's peculiar obstinacy in the fact of what contradicts his faith, the deep significance of the invisibility, the incomprehensibility of God (a God made visible as a numinously authenticated sovereign, would by that be revealed as a non-God: is there a hint here of one of the nerves of the ontological argument?). Again, Wisdom sees that while scientists go on happily indifferent to, even a little contemptuous of, the metaphysical philosopher's comments on their procedures, religious believers are deeply engaged with the work done in critical evaluation of their commitments and assents. They are always, whether they know it or not, looking over their shoulders to hear the comments passed on their beliefs, and the justification which they invoke on their behalf: as if they knew that precariousness and vulnerability were part of the price they must pay if they are to be honest, as if the irrevocable depth of their commitment demanded, as part of itself, that they should not be at ease or neglectful of the sceptical insistence of the interrogating philosopher. Is this because to-day the philoso-

---

[1] Certainly this passage in Wisdom's essay bears impressive witness to what continues to constitute one of the profoundest grounds of the appeal of an objective as distinct from a subjective conception of the atonement.

pher mediates to the believer, at a self-conscious level at which he can understand them, the grounds of the indifference to his faith of those who regard their proved methods of enlarging knowledge of the world incompatible with the way of faith, and who, indeed, find that way a bondage rather than a liberation, confining men and women, as it seems to do, to a sterile, introspective preoccupation with the alleged eternal import of what they are? Whereas, once they see that cosmologically they matter very little, they are set free by that humility to relish their dignity as "thinking reeds", and to live in the sunlight a human life, disciplined and proportioned to actuality, not fed on the bitter nourishment of destructive, if sometimes enticing, illusion. Some such conception of the relations of philosophy to theology would seem to emerge from Wisdom's writings, and its description may serve to illustrate the kind of light he throws on philosophy, and which he believes philosophy may bring.

Certainly, these samples may serve to show the extent to which Wisdom's strength as a philosopher is found in his care for detail, the sharpness with which his eye falls on the matters which a specialist within a given field may sometimes disdain. He writes (on pp. 137–8), "The trouble is that the concepts, without which we do not connect one thing with another, are apt to become a network which confines our minds. We need to be at once like someone who has seen much and forgotten nothing, and also like one who is seeing everything for the first time." These words could be taken as the central maxim of the philosophizing which this book contains. All through it, Wisdom writes as if philosophers were only on a safe path when they recognize the paradoxical character of what they say as at once preventing themselves from taking themselves too seriously, and at the same time making them ready to see how much they have to give. If they ignore the paradoxical character, for instance, of their elaborately induced scepticism, they fail not only to understand themselves, but to be ready to learn from others, to attend as Wisdom attends to frontier-relations in their fields of discourse. Their logic will suffer from a failure to read, for instance, what pure mathematicians write, to attend to the grounds on which one theory of gravitation is judged to have displaced another, to construe the light that Newton brought in a way which neglects its analogies with, or alternatively minimizes its differences from, the Freudian revolution. One might profitably spend a long time working out what Wisdom suggests of the manners in which, for instance, Flaubert and Tolstoy, Conrad and Faulkner, Sophocles, Shakespeare, and Freud, explore the heights and depths of human existence, the light they bring, the logic by which what they offer may be justified. But enough has perhaps been said to show that this collection of essays has a seminal quality, and could bear fruit in an extension of its methods, and a further application of its insights.

There are two fundamental points to be raised, however, in criticism at the conclusion of this study.

1. If Wisdom is deficient in any respect, it is in detailed attention to the history of philosophy. I do not mean the sort of pedantic attention which a philosophical scholar may substitute for a genuine concern with answering questions; I mean the sort of attention to the great moments in the development, for instance, of the theory of knowledge, which is bound to enlarge our grasp of the subject. There is too much readiness in Wisdom's writing to impose a pattern, for instance, on the history of the problem of our knowledge of the external world, to find positions, for example, for Locke, Berkeley, Hume, and Kant, in a dialectical movement, neglecting the subtlety and complexity of their individual work, and of their relations one to another. It is as if Wisdom is not prepared to extend to individual philosophers the same eager attention to the concrete detail of their work, and the individuality of the particular case he counsels so effectively elsewhere. It is as if figures in the history of philosophy must conform to the stereotypes of the dualist, the materialist, the sceptic and so on.

2. A brief reference in passing to Kant's attitude towards examples as the "go-cart" of the understanding (p. 102) suggests that Wisdom has still to come to terms with that philosopher's very different approach to the subject of the limits of experience. For

Kant, if I understand him, the crux was that of the context, the relatively stable categorial context, including the unity of space and time, and recognizable causal continuity, into which we assimilate what is novel in our experience. His *nisus* towards effective generalization and commitment to a programme of "descriptive metaphysics" for which he would claim a certain finality, differentiates his method sharply from the looser, obstinately particularistic attitudes of Wisdom. Moreover, the programme of descriptive metaphysics to which Kant was committed was very different from Moore's concern to give an inventory of the different sorts of thing there are in the world; for his so-called "transcendental method" seems to commit him to an identification of the enumeration of the unchangeable constants of our world, with the delineation of the frontiers of the experienceable. From Kant (and I should go on here to treat at proper length the crucial question of the relation of his ethical ideas to his theory of knowledge), we may glimpse the shape of an alternative approach to one of the absolutely central questions of philosophy, namely the question of the legitimacy and nature of discourse concerning the transcendent. In one way (*but markedly not in others*) as Professor Erik Stenius has suggested,[1] this approach may be *not far from* that discernible in Wittgenstein's *Tractatus*. For the purpose of philosophy, it is most important that there should be argument between the protagonists of the two methods, argument which will be difficult because, although both are concerned with the same questions part of the time, there are also periods when they fly away from each other in different directions, to deal with different questions. But such argument could well prove creative.

[1] See the concluding chapter of his study of Wittgenstein's *Tractatus* (Blackwell, 1960).

VERIFIABILITY

T HE NOTION of verifiability in principle has been repeatedly canvassed by philosophers in recent years in discussions concerning the meaning of propositions, the limits of factual knowledge, etc. But while there has been an exhaustive discussion concerning such questions as complete and partial verification, there has been a certain unwillingness to face certain deeper questions concerning the concept of verification itself. It is with these questions that I want to concern myself here.

My paper falls into three parts:

1. Some observations on the verification principle itself. Inevitably these comments will be selective, and I cannot hope that they will satisfy all my readers, some of whom will undoubtedly judge that I have left out the most important aspects of the question.

2. A discussion of what I can only call the conditions of verification. This problem seems to me to be substantially the one Kant was concerned with in the "Analytic" of the first *Kritik*. It seems to me one of the very greatest difficulty, and I do not expect to do more than sketch its outline and perhaps convince you that there is a problem there.

3. I want to make certain observations relevant to the "principle of epistemological pluralism"; for so perhaps we should interpret the slogan "Every sort of statement has its own sort of logic", and ask how far we can accept it as embodying a final dissolution of our perplexities concerning the relation one to another of the various forms of knowledge we enjoy.

I.

The verification principle is essentially a challenge to criticism. Like most suggestions in epistemology, it does not stand by itself, but derives a considerable measure of its effectiveness from the extent to which it articulates our own already felt perplexities concerning the status of certain assertions, e.g., those which form the stock in trade of traditional metaphysics.

To take a slightly frivolous illustration. Most of you will be familiar with advertisements, it may be for a brand of chocolate not at the time obtainable or for a book of etiquette, consisting in an illustration, with a title "What is wrong with this picture?" So it seems to me the verificationist bids us face the question, "What is wrong with such and such an assertion?" Or perhaps, "How should we understand such and such an assertion in order to avoid feeling puzzled by it?" It has a vaguely "phoney" feel, and it is the claim of the verificationist that he can assist us to detect wherein that "phoneyness" resides.

The assertions with which the verificationist is concerned are, of course, in the main those commonly called metaphysical, and the challenge that he offers consists in asking us to ask ourselves what evidence we have for asserting them. The fundamental presupposition of his method might be called the evidentialist assumption, and could perhaps be formulated thus: "There is no more to the content of a statement than the total evidence which would warrant its assertion."

This identification of the meaning of a statement with its ground seems to me to constitute one aspect of Berkeley's "Esse est percipi." Every student is familiar with those moments in Berkeley's argument wherein he insists on the superfluity of the independent "material thing." It would make no difference to us whether it existed or no. For us what matters is that sensibles should continue to occur in such uniform patterns as to permit us at one level to distinguish the illusory from the real, Macbeth's dagger from a real one, and at another to plot the course of past and future events through the extrapolation of general laws with confidence.

When Berkeley faces the question of what the reality of the physical world consists in, he demands that the answer be given in terms of a distinction or of distinctions that can be drawn within our experience.

Of course in the understanding of his method, the recognition of the importance of his polemic against abstraction is fundamental. He recognizes that perception is essentially of the concrete and individual, and that consequently we must never ask a question such as, "In what does the reality of the physical world consist?", but rather seek to substitute an exhaustive study of the particular perplexities which receive generalized expression in such formulae as that. If we are to attach any sense to (let us say) our conviction of the independence of the physical world, we must find some cash value for independence in terms of our actual experiences. We must not so analyse the concept that it is robbed of all possible experiential content. The distinction between what actually exists and what is mere illusion must fall inside our experience, or be altogether without import for us.

Thus the "Esse est percipi" formula is coined to express the principle of evidentialism. If we are to say of a material object or a physical process that it exists or is real we must be able to say—Percipitur. Unless we can, its reality falls outside the by-us-observable world and is nothing for us. It is of course free to the evidentialist to point out that he must now apply his own hostility to the abstract and to the general to his understanding of that—percipitur. Clearly there is no one ostensible sort of cognitive consciousness which we can call perception. There are only the perceivings in which perception is realised, and these constitute a long series of overlapping cases. There is the case when, looking at the penny lying on the table in front of me, I say: "There's a penny". There is the case when, striving to concentrate on writing this paper, I hear an aeroplane pass overhead, or a 'bus in the distance, and say: "That's an aeroplane", or "That's a 'bus". Or, again, I may see a fire-engine rushing through the streets, and say: "Umph! A fire".

The question, "Am I really perceiving now?" is one that is much harder to answer than one at first supposed. The adverb in the question suggests the familiar fallacy in epistemology of erecting a general standard and condemning all that falls short of it, ignoring the demand that we should not be so parsimonious in our estimate of what we account justified or justifiable that we leave out much that the actual circumstances of our experience compel us to acknowledge as such. Certainly it is hard to escape altogether the opinion that we can grade our perceptions into a series more or less perfectly expressing the character of perceptual consciousness (I shall say more on this subject later); but in doing so, it is at our peril that we dispute altogether the validity of those acts of awareness that seem, as it were, to lie far out on the circumference from that norm as a centre.

I have called the attitude of the verificationist evidentialist, and I have explained what I mean by this term. We cannot so construe the content of our beliefs that what we believe is seen to be altogether alien to the evidence on which we believe it. Thus, if I attribute to Smith a sound knowledge of German, that knowledge cannot be something altogether other than, e.g., his facility in reading Kant or Thomas Mann, his valuable work as an interpreter in the examination of German prisoners, etc. Professor Price has used the term "manifestationism" to cover very largely what I have indicated by this term, but I have preferred to speak of the tendency, expressed by the verificationist, as evidentialist for reasons that will become clear later, but which I shall very briefly adumbrate now.

It seems to me that the standpoint from which the verificationist approaches his problems is, by the very term verificationist, indicated as epistemological. By that, I mean quite simply that he is offering us a "theory of knowledge", not a "theory of the nature of things", as an ontological theory might be construed as offering. He operates within the context of the subject-object relation the context sketched by Kant in his Transcendental Deduction of the Categories. Again and again he proceeds as if an answer to the question what would warrant us to say that such and such were the case is an answer to the request for an analysis of what we are saying when we say that such and such is the case. Of course, the grounds may be very,

very different. There is no such thing as *the ground* of a factual statement, and there is no such thing as *its meaning*. But still, however elastic our interpretation of ground and meaning, for better or worse, if we take a verificationist point of view, we are entangled in the necessity of intimately relating the two, and that involves us in the insistence that it is in terms of differences recognizably realized in the to-us-observable world that the content of our factual assertions must be analysed.

Consequently it seems to me that the verificationist is involved in a number of questions that are in some respects not unlike those in which Kant was involved in the *Critique of Pure Reason*. For instance—How is evidence possible? Or more clearly—Are there certain conditions which must be fulfilled if an experience is to constitute evidence for anything?

We have certainly outgrown the tendency to suppose that the end of philosophical analysis is the breaking down of complexes into their constituent simples. Certainly the verificationist is not guilty of such a mistake as that. His aim is to safeguard the authority of observation, to deliver us from the misleading supposition that, where our assertions concerning the actual world seem to outrun the limits of observation, yet actually, if we only discipline ourselves to understand what it is we are saying and what warrants us to say it, we will see that they do not. Of course, there is no once-for-all recipe in the carrying out of this discipline. Each case has to be considered on its own. The bringing of content and ground into relation is something that has to be done again and again; for linguistic usage is elastic, and governed by a less stringent conception of what may be indicated by the same symbol than the philosopher.

Yet although we have outgrown the tendency to metaphysical atomism, the character of the method sketched above leads to an atomism of another sort. We concentrate our attention on the content of individual propositions, seeking to show the identity of that content with our warrant for asserting them. And if we concede any validity at all to the empiricist point of view we will not want to quarrel with this concentration. For its goal is to assure such a readiness to wait on the observable facts as will effectively preclude the indulgence of the intemperate inclination to treat abstract thought as a substitute for observation. The end of this method of analysis is to induce in us such a sense of the elasticity of language as will prevent us supposing that we have other means of establishing matters of fact than by way of sense-observation. Yet the very subtlety of this method may prevent us from seeing that it is abstract in the sense that it concerns a part, not the whole, of the total activity in which establishing truths about the world consists.

In the long, and no doubt, to our seeing, futile, debate between defenders of the coherence, and defenders of the correspondence theories of truth, the champions of the former are continually accusing those of the latter with neglect of the relativity of the idea of truth to that of thinking. Even if the theory of objective propositions is discarded, there is still, it is urged by coherentists, a tendency to treat truth as a quality attributable to a substantival or near-substantival entity called a proposition, and to ignore in consequence the actual manner in which we arrive at what we would call the truth about a given subject-matter. Granted, of course, that coherentists always fail in the last resort to give an intelligible account of what control of thinking by fact consists in, at least they do a service in calling attention to the point that the significance of control by the facts lies in the relation of the facts to what is being controlled.

Now the verificationist is concerned to deliver us from any mistaken view of what this control must consist in. To make it more effective he is concerned, by his analytic methods, to deliver us from any temptation to suppose that somehow other methods than observation reveal to us the nature of the world. But still the question remains—What is being controlled? No account of verification can hope to be complete that does not take some account of that activity within the control of which individual acts of verification fall.

2.

The empiricist aims at letting the facts speak for themselves. He desires to free us from entanglement, whether flowing from linguistic or other sources, in the supposition that we have other means of extending our knowledge of matters of fact than that of observation and induction. He aims at increasing our self-consciousness in respect of what observation consists in. But all the while we are tempted, if we suppose him to be offering a complete theory of knowledge, to accuse him of breaking down the whole process whereby our understanding of the processes of nature is extended into a series of discrete verificatory acts.

It seems as if the verificationist is supposing a foundation laid, or a context defined, upon which, or within which, his particular enquiries have their point. Granted that we settle questions of fact by observation, we still have to remember that the posing of the questions is that which gives the observations their point.

We can only offer an intelligible account of verification, if we can include in it some account of the thinking that gives our verificatory acts their point. They may be nothing in themselves beyond the occurrence of a sensible event (we cannot take for granted the empirical truth of the act-object analysis of sensing); it is only in the context of our enquiries that they have that status.

But are there not observations establishing facts that are not verifications?

It may seem to some that to pretend there are not suggests an impossible sophistication. For what may be plausible where we are speaking of the controlled experiment of the scientist in his laboratory cannot, as it were, be carried down to the more unsophisticated levels of everyday life. We are, of course, constantly entertaining propositions, or asking ourselves questions, and verifying or settling them. We wonder whether our friend is in, or whether the cat has eaten the fish; such questions we settle by observation. But for a great deal of the time when we are learning about our world, we aren't answering questions at all. Much of our perceptual experience seems quite different, feels quite different. If I cross the floor, I am aware that the floor supports me; there's no verification about that. Of course, if I am suddenly faced by the suggestion of some writer like Sir Arthur Eddington that the floor isn't *really* solid, that crossing it is as perilous an operation as crossing the Grand Canyon on a tight-rope, I may appeal to my experience. Then, if you like, I appeal to my observation to confute him; it is as conclusive verification of the proposition that the floor is solid that I cite it.

But what actually is the nature of my earlier awareness that the floor is solid? Certainly I am aware of it in the sense that if anyone asked me—Is the floor solid?—I would have no hesitation in answering yes. But what is the nature of my awareness before the question, and how is it related to the awareness that follows? Is there a difference? Clearly there is no difference in the solidity of the floor. But can we say that what we were hitherto aware of as an *event*, we are now aware of as a *fact*?

What we have to ask ourselves is a very fundamental question —namely, how are truth and falsity related to our experience? Take a very simple factual proposition: I am holding a pen. When we say that such a proposition is true, what are we claiming? Suppose we answer that it accords with a fact. But what is the "fact" over above the event of my holding the pen? Clearly nothing; for whatever my language above may have suggested, there is not a fact-world reduplicating the event-world, merely waiting on the assertion or even entertainment of propositions to disclose itself or come near doing so. That is mere mythology. Yet we hesitate, I think, to detach our use of the word fact from all connection with thought. It seems to demand as the background of its proper use some reference to our characteristically intellectual concern with distinguishing what is true from what is false.

The very *grammar* of the word "fact", suggests it is.

It is a fact that Caesar was murdered. We use such sentences, for instance, when we are reflecting upon the crisis of the Roman republic, and wish, as it were, to control our assent to some relatively speculative hypothesis by the recollection of a bedrock certainty.

Or, again, a judge summing up may say: "It is a fact that the accused did, for some reason, on the night of the crime, bring the hatchet in from the woodshed about 12 midnight."

There the event of the accused's trip to the shed is to be used as a fact—i.e., as something related to the jury's concern with the prisoner's guilt or innocence.

Or, again, suppose we take a series of English expressions.

Go and rub your nose in the facts.

You must train yourself to wait on the facts.

The brute fact of the duck bill platypus' behaviour was most upsetting to zoologists.

We could all of us imagine ourselves using the first expression in recommending a course of study to some young dogmatist who had claimed to deduce the course of historical events at a certain period from some *a priori* established theory concerning the nature of history. Again, the second formulates the maxim of the true empiricist. The third, too, does not indicate insensibility in the duck bill platypus to the better feelings of zoologists; rather it indicates the psychological consequences of the recognition of the incompatibility of certain propositions relating to the animal's behaviour with supposedly well-established inductions.

Of course in some of the examples taken there is the hint of a certain antagonism between what is given as actual and our own constructive intellectual activity. And empirically we would agree that very many of our uses of the word "fact" more than hint at the obstinate take-it-or-leave-it character of facts. Yet this half-expressed recognition of our own unwillingness to allow our speculation to be controlled by observation does not affect the question—How is it possible for sense-experience, as it were, to speak to us in that way?

Now, of course, for the most part, when we are concerned with verification, we are trying out hypotheses of a relatively sophisticated character. Yet, as we have seen, at most elementary levels of intellectual life, the paradoxical character of verificatory acts shows itself. They are, as it were, parasitic upon interest, and upon interest of a peculiar kind—a controlled intellectual curiosity.

Our awareness of the world around us, of course, is hardly ever the expression of a merely theoretical concern. We want to know if Jones is in his room, not because we are concerned with his whereabouts for its own sake, but because we want his company on a walk or the loan of one of his books. But when we go to his room and find it empty, we have settled the question whether he is in. And his being in or out has nothing whatever to do with our inclinations.

Now it should be clear that what we are offering is not a complete theory of perception. For the example given above should have suggested that perception is a great deal more than verification. The very fact that we can pose the problem of the relation of the distinction between truth and falsity to our total experience suggests this. What we are concerned with are the conditions under which we can ask ourselves what is the case, and endeavour to answer the question, or, if you prefer the language, entertain factual propositions and seek to confirm them. Put more fundamentally, are there any necessary forms in which a concern with what is the case must articulate itself, so that in effect where that concern is present at all, such articulations must be discernible? There is an artificiality in supposing that what we are doing in daily life is verifying propositions. For instance, as I write I am conscious of the sun shining on the paper. To describe my consciousness as a verification of the proposition that the sun is shining is not merely unbearably pompous; it is to obliterate the recognizable distinction between such consciousness as I am at present enjoying and my verification of some long pondered hypothesis. There is a sense in which I can say that such consciousness is not verification. Yet in so far as I recognize the sun's shining as something objectively the case, so far is my act akin to verification.

Suppose I conceive myself at a level of sentience at which I withhold, so far as I can, any sort of submission to control by the given. Would or would not such a withholding carry me, as it were, outside consciousness of objects altogether? You notice, I say *objects*; I do not say things; and that is, I suspect, very important.

We have introduced in this paper a whole cluster of formal ideas:

Verification, fact, proposition, objectivity, true, false. We began by pointing to a frequent claim made by empiricists that there was so close a connection between meaning and ground that when we can find no traceable difference in the field of experience, corresponding to some suggested distinction in our factual assertions (cf. Berkeley's treatment of the distinction of the apparent and the real) we rule out the language purporting to represent that distinction as meaningless. Where we can collect no evidence for a belief, where we are unable to conceive what such evidence would be like, we are bound to dismiss the belief as nonsensical.

But how does acquaintance with sensibles constitute evidence? How is the object-situation constituted? Certainly the empiricist is right to insist, as he does, that, within the context of that situation, we must discipline ourselves to a more rigid control from the side of the given. We must not permit ourselves to prescribe *a priori* the structure, let alone the items, of the real. We need the critical discipline of evidentialist analysis. But such analysis does presuppose that the objective situation has been constituted, and what we must ask ourselves now is the manner of its constitution.

We have seen from the examples given above that perception is distorted if we suppose that specific activities differentiated by the formal concepts listed above were present at every level. But none the less we have seen that such activities have their place from the first in our experience of our world. There is also, of course, a very difficult question to which we will come in the last part of the paper, of their precise relation to the rest of that experience. But that investigation must wait, and we must focus on the manner of their constitution.

And this leads us to one aspect of Kant's enquiry—namely, his conception of the synthetic *a priori*. For that philosopher our synthetic *a priori* knowledge did not constitute a queer collection of structural facts about the world, revealed to thought as facts about its processes are revealed to sense. Rather we had in those truths for which he devised the name synthetic *a priori*, the articulation of the fundamental demands that our understanding makes on anything which we would render intelligible, or constitute a field of fact. Such a principle as that of the causal order of nature, analysed in terms of the conformity of events to law, is understood as the concretion of such a demand, vindicated as a condition of the possibility of factual knowledge. Our understanding is such as to demand a ground for all assertions. If we reflect on our awareness of the external world, we find our demand that it should, as it were, articulate itself in terms of such orders as will admit grounded assertions, vindicated as a necessary condition of our enjoying awareness of it as objective. We are familiar enough with the recognition that actuality is not an attributive concept. But can we stop there? When we do conceive an event as actual, what are we doing? Surely admitting some objectively determined relation to other events. Berkeley recognized this in his account of the difference between seeing the sun by day and thinking of it by night. There might be qualitative similarity between the sensuous particulars, but it was their relation or absence of relation to others that determined their admission as real or not. But Berkeley omitted to face the question of the rules whereby this objective inclusion in, or exclusion from reality was determined and consequently his theory of knowledge flops. His metaphysics compelled him to emphasize our passivity in perception. He did not face the question whether on such a view as his, sense-awareness could be the foundation of our knowledge of reality, or, if preferred, furnish the premises of our inductions.

But suppose we allow for a moment that we are impelled by the very nature of our understanding to seek connections, to trace causal lines. Suppose that mode of discursive thought, whose form we discern in hypothecation, reveals itself also where the constitution of a field of fact is concerned as an obstinate resolve to establish connections, to admit nothing as real that does not manifest some ground of its occurrence. Negatively we do display an unwillingness to admit the completely random and discontinuous as objectively real. And if we do, it is only because there is a background of relative stability, against which its randomness is recognizable.

Nothing has been said either of the synthetic unity of apperception or of the reproductive and supplementative character of perceptual synthesis as Kant's view. We have focused on his analysis of the concept of causality as the concept almost of a procedure of articulation of the given by means of tracing of laws. For many would agree that we do concede the title unintelligible to any field (say, some series of events in nature or history) where such lines have not been traced. They may, therefore, be prepared to allow some weight to Kant's contention that wherever there is any sort of objectivity or recognition of an object of which we must, as it were, take the measure, there, as a very condition of its having objective status, we must have used the generalized idea of causal order to articulate the given.

It is Kant's contention that he can reveal the indispensability of categorial principles for the constitution of the verification situation. For a series of sensible events to assume the status of a field of fact, a certain kind of articulation is necessary. To be a field of fact they must have the quality of objectivity, and that they receive only through the relation into which they are brought with a subject determined to submit himself to them, in scrutiny and investigation. The categorial principles are the articles of this submission.

But can any categories be shown to be indispensable? Clearly no one would deny that in the development of the sciences methodological postulates are of great significance. Thus the supposition that, e.g., physical laws can be represented as functions of laws governing the positional change of particles has proved very fertile. In the development of a science there is a continual invocation of and revision of such principles. But what authority have we to say that there are certain conditions so fundamental that they express the very interior structure of the understanding, so indispensable that, except in terms of the articulation of the given by means of them, factual truth is insignificant?

This question of transcendental indispensability is of absolute first-order importance. Clearly the existence of such fact-forms is not something that can be determined without reference to the nature of the given, and at this point the question of the analysis of sensation becomes important. But although their indispensability might seem more sheerly obvious on an "adverbial" view of the nature of sensation, on any view that distinguishes perception as the expression of our disinterested concern with what is the case from the higgledy-piggledy of our ordinary awareness, there must be room for principles whereby that disinterestedness is to become effective.

The empiricist is concerned to let the given speak. Yet this speaking of the given is not something of worth except we know the syntax of the language. Certainly the given can only speak to one whose attention is directed towards it, and whose receptivity is conditioned by his acknowledgment of its objective structure. The categories, if they are to be validated, must be validated as involved in objectivity.

3.

This last part of my paper is concerned with rather a different question, and I want to introduce it by a summary of what has gone before. We have concerned ourselves so far with a discussion of the conditions under which alone the establishment of factual propositions is possible. We have agreed with the empiricist that the given must have the last word, but it has been suggested that this does not alter the fact that the given can only so speak in a context defined by the character of our interest.

But at once the question arises—How is this related to the total field of our experience? For one thing, we are deeply conscious here that we are concentrating on a relatively sophisticated moment in our transaction with the world around us.

If we ask how it is related to that which underlies and contains it, we find two views:

1. The agnostic,
2. The idealistic:
    (α) transcendent,
    (β) immanent.

(1) Kant's view is agnostic. He is convinced that we must conform anything about which we could make intelligible, objectively valid statements, to the forms of our understanding. We can't say anything about it save in those terms. But to

relate this process of description to anything outside itself is clearly alien to Kant. He knows that it leaves a whole lot out, and his ultimate answer is a question mark.

(2α) *Per contra* the idealist.

It is no accident that Berkeley advances to idealism by way of phenomenalism. For the phenomenalist the physical world has always a quasi-panoramic character. Here Berkeley is no exception. For him the world is a panorama, and our relation to it is ultimately that of spectators.

We must not caricature either phenomenalist or idealist. Yet for both the significant thing about the world is its existence for consciousness. It is allowed to be nothing in itself. For Berkeley it is willed by a transcendent God as the object of finite consciousnesses. It is, in order to be known by them. Thus the purpose of the world is in its self-disclosure to human consciousness. It is hard not to feel that on this view the actuality of man's relation to the world around him and the being of the latter are subtly distorted.

(2β) In the later immanentist idealism the rest of our experience is, as it were, teleologically orientated towards the emergence of the conscious distinction of the true from the false. But of this there is no need to speak at length.

Now although there are very grave objections to idealism, we have to allow that once in our experience the recognition of an objectively valid distinction of the true from the false has emerged, there is no going back on it. Although we would not allow as a true ontological statement that all facts are facts for consciousness, it still does remain true of what we discover, that once we have made it our own by an act of discovery, we cannot detach it from the whole context of our understanding of our world and our relation to it, in which we have necessarily set it.

Thus in our reflection on verification we were in effect deepening our understanding of the fundamental nature of our knowledge of objects. We were asking ourselves what it is like to investigate objective fact, and we were compelled to recognize as present at all levels in the investigation two inseparable moments.

We are familiar with the distinction between induction and deduction. We recognize that such forms of cognition as perception and memory have their own interior criteria. But the distinctions we draw between these types of cognition, and especially, perhaps, that between the whole field of the empirical and that of the *a priori*, must not be such as to atomise the fundamental activity of knowledge. We do not know a given aggregate of truths, some *a priori* and some empirical. It is surely bad grammar to speak of having established eighteen *a priori* and twelve empirical proportions to-day. The distinction of the two is functional. We can hardly, moreover, concede any ultimate validity to a view that reduces, e.g., mathematical reasoning to the mere manipulation of symbols, from whose sense we have averted, according to rules, or to one that endeavours to show our knowledge of the world as somehow built up out of atomic acts of acquaintance.

Rather we have to see the differentiation between empirical and *a priori* as one that seeks to articulate and develop the fundamental character of objective knowledge through the more adequate and exhaustive specification of the moments involved in it. Empirical and *a priori* are complementary factors, and though within the compass of each other we must discipline our tendency to dogmatism, through ceaseless reaffirmation of the peculiarities characteristic of its movement, we must not ignore the unitary character of the act in which they both have a part—the development of the world as an intelligible object of consciousness.

It may seem as if such a view as this turns its back on the recognition, *e.g.*, of the formal character of mathematics, and its freedom from concern with and control by the actual. That is not so. Nothing said constitutes a repudiation of the doctrine that the logic of factual statement is one and geometrical demonstration another. But the orientation of knowledge upon the actual is fundamental and inescapable and though we must submit its moments to analysis and differentiation, this must not be done in such a way as to conceal their ultimate complementarity, when we resolutely set ourselves the task of compelling the actual to disclose itself.

Thus there are in the development of human knowledge some elements to which no natural process affords any precise parallel. It possesses at once a tendency to recognize its structural differentiation and an insistence on the unity of the end by which it is controlled. Moreover it possesses a continuous self-critical readiness to recognize its own limitations and to contrast its essentially abstract and discursive activity with a more comprehensive, "intussusceptive" grasp of the actual. Though this last conception may have for us no more than the "donkey's carrot" validity of a Kantian "Idea", at least it serves as a continual protection against the tendency to topple into idealism. And if to end thus seems to end on a somewhat metaphysical note, it might be said in extenuation that the more one reflects upon human cognitive consciousness, the harder it is to admit that its peculiar activities are entirely patient of explanation as naturalistic phenomena. To go farther would lead us into very deep waters indeed, but perhaps these concluding remarks on a possible redintegration of the *disjecta membra* of human intellectual activity, provoked by our reflection on the conditions under which phenomena are constituted for us as objective, may not be entirely without point.

P. F. STRAWSON'S *THE BOUNDS OF SENSE* [1]

I F WHITEHEAD is right in speaking of all Western philosophy as a series of footnotes to Plato, one is tempted to say that a great deal of post-Kantian philosophy, if much more than a footnote to Kant, shows somewhere or other the need of coming to terms with what he did.

Mr Strawson's essay on the *Critique of Pure Reason* is not a commentary in the strict sense; but it does comprise a very clear and philosophically very exciting study of the central argument, in both its positive and its critical aspects.

The heart of Kant's achievement is to be found in his metaphysics of experience, where for instance, he establishes by arguments that sometimes assume a more decisive shape as he develops and alters them in the course of his work—the sort of world that ours must be, if it is to be the field of our experience, if moreover we are to be able to distinguish effectively the order and point of view of our own individual experience from the order of that common, public system of things around us with which we contrast our private, subjective lives. Mr Strawson's treatment of this central section of Kant's argument does abundant justice to its extreme intricacy. He shows how in fact Kant does succeed in establishing that the fundamental assumptions we make about the shape and order of our world are capable of vindication as the condition without which nothing worthy to be called objective awareness could occur. He rightly recognizes the cruciality of Kant's treatment of self-consciousness for his whole argument, and it is no accident that one of the very best sections in the whole book is that in which he discusses Kant's appendix to the central argument of the Analytic of Principles—the so-called paralogisms of Pure

[1] Methuen, 1966.

Reason, where Kant submits to a most searching criticism arguments seeking to establish the immortality of the substantial soul from a radical misconstruction of the unique role we rightly recognize to belong to self-consciousness in knowledge of the world around us.

If it is Kant's view that only e.g. if our several experiences constitute temporally extended experiences of a single objective world can they belong to a single consciousness, and that in consequence the unity of consciousness is the foundation on which his whole vindication of our convictions concerning the structural order of the world turns, we must be on guard against the confusion of the "unity of experience with the experience of unity"—as if recognition of the special role of the subject in establishing a metaphysics of experience enabled us to infer from that role a status and dignity to belong to that subject which we must find in the last resort unintelligible.

I know of few other writers who bring out more clearly and in a more exciting way the detail of Kant's exhibition of the conditions under which alone an individual's experiences are revealed as a single, subjective, experiential route through the world, effectively distinguished from that world, through which it is one route among many such. But the question with which he sees Kant as concerned is in the end one that must sooner or later occur to any reflective person. Are there limits (positive and negative) of our experience? Can we assign frontiers to what we can imagine as conceivable on the plane of matter of fact? Can we—and this is the positive counterpart of our seemingly negative request to know the limits of the conceivable—claim to know, apart from the unfolding of the detail of our experience, features that it must manifest in all circumstances? In other words, can we know what a characteristically human experience must be like?

The sheer ingenuity Kant displays in attempting to answer in the most general terms this last question enables him both gravely to criticize the recurrent classical empiricist conviction that human knowledge is built up from the fragmentary, individual data of essentially private sense-awareness, and the claim of the speculative metaphysician to offer theoretical answers to questions concerning transcendent reality, concerning the origin of the world, and the ultimate destiny of man. Mr Strawson effectively brings out the extent to which Kant's criticism of transcendent metaphysics, especially perhaps his arguments against the treatment of the soul by such philosophers as Descartes, and against certain styles of speculative cosmology, issue directly out of his exhaustive analysis of the conditions of experience.

At the centre, then, of Kant's achievement, according to Mr Strawson, lies this metaphysic of experience and its corollaries; the delineation of the conditions of a characteristically human experience, especially on its objective side, establishing thereby the illusions both of a dogmatic empiricism and of a confident claim to offer theoretical answers concerning a supposedly transcendent origin and destiny of the world, and its nature, which ignore the duty of assigning sense to our concepts within and not without the framework of experience. But he recognizes that this central achievement, focused in the section of the *Critique* called the Analytic of Principles; is not the only strand in Kant's thought. As he presents it, we find it woven tight with two other theses, all comprised under the rubric of the book's central preoccupation with the limits of experience, with the bounds of sense and thought.

The first of these I may call the preoccupation with the subjective conditions of experience. I have already mentioned the cruciality in Kant's whole argument of self-consciousness; and I have not begun to do justice to the skill with which Mr Strawson brings out the depth of Kant's achievement here. But the self-consciousness which he stresses is that which we came to recognize as possible only if the structural order of the world conforms to those general assumptions Kant seeks to vindicate. The stress is laid on the objective. There is another side to Kant's work in the Analytic, which Mr Strawson indeed often mentions and sometimes calls a "story", and elsewhere suggests might provide valuable material for a critical essay in the philosophy of mind. Mr Strawson's Kant is in his own language elsewhere a "descriptive metaphysician", offering a superbly systematic account of the pervasive features of our world, and vindicating our conviction of their constancy. But there is another Kant, the Kant of the "Copernican Revolution", the Kant who is almost the descriptive historian of the *arcana* of perception, who has much to say of what he calls *synthesis* of imagination, of the distinction between sensibility and understanding, and of the latter's endowment of the pure categories. His language is frequently metaphorical, and oscillates uneasily between that of traditional logic, and of highly speculative psychological generalization. Yet it is to this side of Kant's *Critique* that, for instance, his reflection on the significance for the theory of knowledge, of the experimental method, belongs; to this side also his amplification and modification of Hume's important insights concerning the fragmentary and interrupted character of the sense-awareness through which alone we have commerce with the world around us. It is almost as if Kant is comprising under the same cover two treatises on the limits of human experience, on the bounds of sense and thought; one, the extraordinarily powerful set of arguments that Mr Strawson traces and evaluates, and side by side, related in his own mind, but separable by the critic, something much less rigorous, I had almost said more meditative, assuming its outline in the *Critique* almost before the nerve centre of the Transcendental Deduction of the Categories is reached, and in that section, finding itself more at home in the so-called subjective than in the objective deduction, in the narrative of the "threefold synthesis" rather than in the arguments establishing the conditions of an object in general.

Mr Strawson *does* have a good deal to say on Kant's insistence on the complementary roles of sensibility and understanding in human knowledge. But he does not, I think, quite bring out the extent to which Kant's insistence, for instance, on human understanding as discursive, as needing a matter to work on, to sort out, carries with it, almost by itself, a doctrine reflected in the procedures of the laboratory, which Kant recognized as inventive and artificial, yet as never dictating the results obtained by their means. As Mr Strawson continually insists, there is a good deal of the idealist in Kant, in spite of his searching criticism of Descartes' assumptions; and there is alongside, and by no means fully integrated with the central argument Mr Strawson emphasizes, another exposition of the limits of human knowledge, rooted in a scrutiny of its conditions, that is fundamentally an essay in a very special sort of self-knowledge. Kant writes part of the time as if fulfilment of the Socratic imperative—know thyself—would by itself preserve men from the pretension to penetrate the secrets of the unconditioned. Where such emphasis predominates, Kant certainly emerges innocent of the charge sometimes brought against him: that of supposing that we could ferret out the fundamental laws of nature by a kind of specialized introspection; he appears rather as an agnostic, whose delineation of the most pervasive features of the objective world is but a propaedeutic study to the definitive recognition of our ineradicable intellectual limitation.

There is, of course, for Mr Strawson a third facet to Kant's doctrine of the *Critique*: and that he calls the "metaphysics of transcendental idealism". Its prominence and influence he recognizes throughout, showing with particular effect the way it shaped Kant's discussion of such topics as the question whether the universe was finite or infinite, and the extraordinary tangles in which the careful student is involved in working out its implication for Kant's doctrine of self-knowledge. It is, of course, Kant's notorious insistence that knowledge is of appearances, not of things in themselves, that space and time, forms of outer and inner sense respectively, belong to the ways in which things affect our consciousness and, although in his phrase empirically real are transcendentally ideal. No praise can be too high for the pains with which Mr Strawson seeks to make sense of ideas that he finds deeply unsympathetic and which he sees as continually vitiating or obscuring the central sanity of Kant's metaphysics of experience. There is much indeed of Kant's language that no defence can excuse; passages in which he disregards altogether his principle of conceptual significance, and uses the notion of causality not within the framework of experience, but to attach that framework to its alleged transcendent ground. Moreover to the modern reader the whole of this section of Kant's work must often seem otiose and pointless, contrasting with the extraordinarily strenuous argumentation whereby he exhibits, e.g. the indispensability of the principles of permanence and causality as enabling us to separate off the sequence of our own biography from the course of events in the world on which our biography is a single point of view. Yet conceivably, if one attaches this element in Kant's doctrine closer to the subjective concentration, subordinated by Mr Strawson to his "descriptive metaphysics", one may make something more of it. What I would suggest (I repeat) is that in Kant's *Critique* we have to reckon with two doctrines of the limitations of experience: one that would seek to establish the pervasive features of an experiencable world, and another that would, for instance, use to the full the resources of Kant's distinction between an intuitive and a discursive understanding, between a supposed awareness to which all objects are transparent because they are its own creation and one that proceeds piecemeal, as ours does. God, if he exists, doesn't have to ask and answer questions; but we do, and if in the *Critique of Pure Reason*, Kant, while writing illuminatingly on the differentiae of scientific explanation, has little to say directly on the subject of induction, he is on the contrary regarded as something of a prophet by those modern logicians who belittle the role of the colligation of instances and generalization therefrom in scientific discovery. None the less it could be claimed that he has very much made his own the openness of inductive procedure, the element of rational hazard in the suggestion of hypotheses, and has extracted from his reflection important insights concerning the limitations of characteristically human experience, indeed of the world as we experience it. There are conditions which objects of experience must fulfil, or the world as the system of objects falls outside our experience. But these conditions reflect before all else, the characteristic limitations of our own experiencing, and if we could think those limitations away, we could conceive a world of objects quite other than our own. What we are to say of such a conception is obscure; certainly there is no suggestion that we can argue here from bare concept to actuality any more than we can elsewhere; but even as an *Als ob*, the viability of the act of conceiving involved, remains obscure. Yet it would seem to be integral to a sort of self-knowledge which for Kant would at once liberate men from the fantasies of the speculative metaphysician and admit them to a proper appraisal of the methods of theoretical, experimental and natural science—and by way of recognition of the limitations of theoretical penetration, provide that context in which it becomes at last possible to admit the reconciliation of a strict methodological determinism in physical and psychological theory with the sort of creativity on the part of the individual Kant believed implied by consciousness of categorical moral obligation.

The frankly agnostic tone of his essay on self-knowledge prepared the way for the claims he wished to make of the transcendent import of the individual's response to the demand made upon him e.g. to treat human nature in himself and his neighbour as an end, and not simply as a tool to be used to further his own private and collective purposes. If the precise relation of the realm of freedom to that of nature, the latter being the system of observable objects whose status as such was inconceivable apart from the operation of causal laws, remains an insoluble, even an inexpressible, mystery, at least the agnosticism of Kant's theory of knowledge disciplines the man who has mastered it against forgetting that any argument he may invoke to discredit the possibility of the order of freedom has ignored some aspect of the principles governing the use of theoretical concepts in significant descriptive discourse concerning matters of fact.

To write in these terms is to offer (to use Mr Strawson's language concerning the *a priori* status of e.g. the principles of permanence and causality) an "austere" interpretation of Kant's unbalanced metaphysical language concerning phenomena and things in themselves. But at least it relates this language to that undeniable strand of thought in the *Critique* which is less exclusively preoccupied with the characteristics of objects in general, with the central elements necessarily present in any field of our awareness that we are prepared to acknowledge part of our common world, and is orientated more generally upon the question of the limitations of characteristically human knowledge. It was part of Kant's genius that he attempted to attack the two problems at once: providing, as he believed, and as I think Mr Strawson believes, the most nearly successful account offered by any philosopher of the framework we take for granted in assimilating the most novel physical, biological or cosmological discoveries and arguing the case for its indispensability, and at the same time attempting to relate this framework to the characteristic limitations of the human experience in such a way that its effective delineation might at the same time prove a significant advance in human self-knowledge.

Mr Strawson's book (and I have said nothing of his very interesting concluding chapter, defending a part of Kant's treatment of geometry against positivist criticism) is the most valuable and exciting study of the *Critique* we have had in this country for a long time. If I have suggested that there may perhaps be more unity between the three dominant trends in the argument that he has disentangled than he allows, it remains true that no other recent work has more effectively brought out the supreme relevance to absolutely central philosophical issues of Kant's delineation of the fundamental constants of the world of our experience.

$5.95

Living and working at the heart of the theological, philosophical and scientific ferment in the University of Cambridge, England, Professor Donald MacKinnon occupies a key position in the intellectual life of the modern world. An Anglican layman, Dr. MacKinnon was Fellow and Tutor in Philosophy at Keble College, Oxford, and for thirteen years was Regius Professor of Moral Philosophy at Aberdeen. Since 1960 he has been Norris-Hulse Professor of Divinity at Cambridge and Fellow of Corpus Christi College.

This collection of Professor MacKinnon's writings shows his three related preoccupations, philosophical, theological and ethical. As a philosopher and theologian working in one of the world's great scientific centres, Professor MacKinnon is aware